Lebanon's Jewish Community

"...an important contribution to the literature on the tragic and forgotten fate of the Jewish communities expelled from Arab lands after the creation of the State of Israel. Highly recommended for both academic and general readers who are interested in the old Lebanon."
—Meir Zamir, *Ben-Gurion University of the Negev, Israel, and Author of The Formation of Modern Lebanon and Lebanon's Quest*

"A deeply researched, solid piece of scholarship, in an area that very few dare explore; history that reads like a thriller."
—Nassim Nicholas Taleb, *New York University, USA, Author of The Black Swan, Antifragile, and Skin in the Game*

"Franck Salameh has artfully woven the story of the Jewish community in Lebanon, and in effect the story of Lebanon *and* its Jews...a must read for whoever wishes to know more about an important chapter in Lebanon's history and the history of the Jews in the Middle East."
—Eyal Zisser, *Tel Aviv University, Israel, and Author of Lebanon; The Challenge of Independence, and Commanding Syria*

"...a long overdue contribution that sheds light onto one of the many taboo topics that still haunt Lebanese society."
—Mahmoud Rasmi, *American University of Beirut, Lebanon*

"A fascinating and deeply moving book, recalling the precious Lebanese dream of the early twentieth century: making Lebanon a free democracy, a refuge for the persecuted."
—Bat Ye'or, *Author of The Dhimmi and The Decline of Eastern Christianity*

Franck Salameh

Lebanon's Jewish Community

Fragments of Lives Arrested

Franck Salameh
Boston College
Chestnut Hill, MA, USA

ISBN 978-3-319-99666-0   ISBN 978-3-319-99667-7   (eBook)
https://doi.org/10.1007/978-3-319-99667-7

Library of Congress Control Number: 2018953105

Cover image: jinjo0222988/iStock/Getty Images; patat/iStock/Getty Images
Cover design: © Tjaša Krivec

This Palgrave Macmillan imprint is published by the registered company Springer Nature Switzerland AG
The registered company address is: Gewerbestrasse 11, 6330 Cham, Switzerland

Rien n'est vrai, rien n'est faux,
Tout est songe et mensonge;
Illusion du cœur,
Qu'un vain espoir prolonge.
Nos seules verités, hommes,
Sont nos douleurs.
Alphonse de Lamartine (1790–1869)

To the Jews of my life;
To humanity's first literate people;
To the teachers of the teachers of our human race;
To my teachers;
To Avigdor, Noam, Gisèle
אמת
אומץ
תקווה

ACKNOWLEDGEMENTS

This book could not have been written without the contribution and generosity of a great number of friends, colleagues, teachers, and acquaintances, all of whom deserve recognition, all of whom are owed a debt of gratitude.

For advice, time, guidance, and moral and intellectual support, I am privileged to have had very near to me Avigdor Levy, Noam Stillman, Nadim Shehadi, Robert Rabil, Asher Kaufman, Roger Makhlouf, Uzi Rabi, Maxim Shrayer, Michael Connolly, David Corm, Scott Abramson, David Silverstein, and Suzanne Kurtz Sloan. Owed thanks are also Hagop Toghramadjian, Rana al-Aggad, Jean-Claude Kuperminc, Rose Levyne, Mordechai Nisan, Jean Laloum, Mary-Jane Deeb, Marius Deeb, Jacques Stambouli, David Daoud, Haim Saadoun, Joël Kotek, Joshua Landis, Gabe Scheinmann, Helen Kedourie, and the late Sylvia Haim Kedourie ל״ז.

Financial support for the bulk of this project was provided through a variety of Boston College research grants—namely Research Incentive and Research Expense Grants. Likewise, generous awards from the Association for the Study of the Middle East and Africa in Washington DC, and the Ben Zvi Institute in Jerusalem, were crucial in supporting research in Beirut, Tel Aviv, Jerusalem, Washington DC, Paris, and New York.

A particular debt of gratitude is owed the staff of the Boston College Libraries, the archives of the Alliance Israélite Universelle in Paris, the archives of the National Institute for Holocaust Documentation (the

Jacob Rader Center of the American Jewish Archives) in Washington DC, the Charles Corm Archives in Beirut, the archives of the Ministry of Foreign Affairs (MAE, Quai d'Orsay) in Paris, the Ben Zvi Institute Archives in Jerusalem, and the *Patrimoine et Cultures des Juifs du Liban* in Paris.

Most importantly, I would like to thank those Lebanese Jews who generously shared advice, direction, hints, names, research trails, personal stories, and sumptuous tables laden with Lebanese foods and flowing libations. My heartfelt thanks go also to those who opened their homes and the vaults of their memories sharing snippets of their lives with me eagerly, devotedly, like they knew me all their lives and were simply "catching me up" on the last forty years of their lives. Many respondents in Lebanon proper will remain anonymous; others in the "diaspora" have opted to give their testimonials under borrowed names. They all know who they are. They all deserve my gratitude and respect. Those who have given me their stories, who have hinted to stories of others, or who have directed me to trails after additional stories (most still untold) and whom I can mention by name include Alain Abadie, Shirley Grego, Yitshak Levanon, Isick Kamhin, Ya'ir Ravid, Dany Liniado, Fady Gadeh, Lucy Galante, Davide Galante, Batia Sasson, Moïse Chems, Zahava Ganor, Edy Cohen, Gina Diwan, Ishac Diwan, Ben Battat, David Bukai, and Hilda Peled. I wish to single out the Lebanese Jews of Israel in particular, *les beaux enfants de ma race,* who took my heart and took me in like a returning relative, and who from Haifa, Jaffa, Bat-Yam, Tel-Aviv, and Jerusalem, still yearn for Lebanon, from a distance they still can't bridge.

At Palgrave Macmillan, I am indebted to Farideh Koohi-Kamali who took a genuine interest very early on in this project's live, at its inception more than three years ago and made sure I signed on the dotted line. I am also grateful to Alina Yurova, Editor for Regional Politics and Development Studies, and Editorial Assistant Mary Fata for seeing this book through, and for the generosity and advice that they offered throughout. Most of all, I must thank Alina for her elegance and patience granting me one extension after the next, *years* past the manuscript's original "delivery date."

Finally, without Pascale, my partner in crime, without the love, poise, counsel, and Cartesian perspicacity that she gives, and likewise without her patient reading, proofreading, re-reading, and then her deliberate relentless questioning of people, record, and text (both at the archives and during the writing and proofing process), this book would not have seen the light of day. And of course, the "gems" of this book—should I be fortunate enough to have brought any—are all owed to all those I have mentioned above. The failings are all my own.

Andover, MA, USA   Franck Salameh
March 2018

CONTENTS

1 Prolegomenon: When Lebanon Loved the Jews   1

2 Lebanon of the Jews: An Introduction   23

3 Lebanese Jewry: Memory Fragments   45

4 Rootedness and Exile: Holocaust and Aftermath   77

5 Lebanese Jewish Memory and Memorial: Personal
  Recollections   101

6 Through the Eyes of Others: History's Reckoning   181

7 On Lebanese Jewish History and Memory: A Conclusion   197

Bibliography   201

Index   205

About the Author

Franck Salameh is Associate Professor of Near Eastern Studies and Chair of the Department of Slavic and Eastern languages and Literatures at Boston College. His academic work focuses on the intellectual and cultural history of the states of the Levant, comparative Middle Eastern languages and literatures, and the history of ideas and political thought in the Modern Middle East. He is founding editor-in-chief of *The Levantine Review*, and author of *Language Memory and Identity in the Middle East* (Lexington, 2010), *Charles Corm: An Intellectual Biography of a Twentieth-Century Lebanese "Young Phoenician"* (Lexington, 2015), and *The Other Middle East* (Yale, 2017).

CHAPTER 1

Prolegomenon:
When Lebanon Loved the Jews

A Greek-Orthodox friend of mine from Byblos-Lebanon
used to say that he could not possibly be a Christian-Lebanese
without first being a Jewish-Lebanese.

Fady Gadeh (July 2017)

While on a furtive visit to Lebanon in the summer of 1986, I made
pilgrimage to the celebrated biblical "Cedars of the Lord," in Bsharré. At
that time, Lebanon was still in the throes of "civil war," its government
a "puppet regime" beholden to the Syrian occupation army controlling
large swaths of Lebanese territory, ruling them in classic colonial fashion.
The cruelty visited on the Syrian people in our time, in these sad decades of twenty-first century, had their first dress rehearsals and dry runs
in Syrian-occupied Lebanon of the late twentieth century. The Syrian
Arab-Baath regime, that has been beating the Syrian people to a pulp in
our times, is the same one that had pummelled Lebanon and battered the
Lebanese into submission during the 1970s, 1980s, and 1990s, mur-
dering thousands of civilians, wiping out entire neighborhoods, raining
destruction on schools, hospitals, churches, and other sanctuaries where
the powerless ordinarily sought shelter. Much like the French under
Nazi occupation, Syrian-occupied Lebanon was rendered a "slave state"
wrapped inside a "police state" apparatus. Syria maintained a strangle-
hold not only on the government, policy, political loyalties, school curricula, the media, and the military, but indeed on the smallest minutiae

© The Author(s) 2019
F. Salameh, *Lebanon's Jewish Community*,
https://doi.org/10.1007/978-3-319-99667-7_1

of Lebanese public and private life. Merely, speaking of a "Syrian occupation" as such was met with the cruelest of punishments. Likewise toeing a political line or trotting out an idea, innocuous as they might have been in any different context but deviating from what is normatively "Arab," "Arab nationalist," and therefore "rejectionist" was also viewed as conspiratorial, subversive, disloyal, treasonous, and indeed "Zionist" and punishable by kidnapping, disappearance, death, or worse.[1] "Lebanon's erstwhile democratic foundations and its once diverse political landscape have all but crumbled as a result of Syrian tampering," wrote the *Middle East Quarterly* in September 2000, a brutal occupation bringing about a "systematic alteration of Lebanon's character," atrophying what had in effect become "the world's only satellite state" by the late 1980s.[2]

That was the Lebanon that I was visiting in 1986, a grotesque deformation of the model of diversity and tolerance and freedom that I had left five years earlier. Even in its war-torn state, Lebanon still held on to its image as the "Switzerland of the Middle East". And I still held on to that old snapshot of the Lebanon of old remembrances, even as I could see its degradation, in real time, before my eyes...

Bsharré, or "the Cedars"—(*L-arez*), as the region is referred to colloquially—is a village of northern Mount Lebanon, perched at a five-thousand-foot altitude over an abyss astride the edge of the biblical cedar forests and the mouth of the Maronite's Valley of the Sainted, *Wadi Qodishe*. Bsharré was also the native village of Kahlil Gibran (1883–1931), the doyen of modern Lebanese literature, a national icon and an author and mystic who wrote the bulk of his work in English; a beloved household name in America of the early twentieth century as much he is a "revered prophet" in Lebanon proper today. Although he lived most of his life between Boston, New York, and Paris, Gibran's wish had been to be buried in his native village, in the Maronite monastery of his youth, where he received his early education. His surviving sister answered her brother's deathbed wish, and in 1931 purchased that seventh-century

---

[1] I realize this may be read as hyperbole. What can possibly be worse than death in the crescendo of cruelty? But I'll leave the reader to his/her imagination poring over the behavior of the Syrian regime today, inside Syria proper. Cruelty may indeed be a "creative art" in the universe of totalitarian regimes, and death may not necessarily be the end of an ordeal. Indeed death may in fact be the least of the worries of those subjected to Syrian "state cruelty."

[2] *The Middle East Quarterly*, "All Syrian Forces Must Leave Lebanon," Volume 7, Number 3, September 2000, 91–92.

hermitage of his yearnings, which was to become his final resting place. My visit to Bsharré in 1986 was mainly to "make pilgrimage"—a national ritual of sorts for Lebanese expatriates and residents alike—to cast a gaze over at Lebanon's national symbol, the "Cedars of the Lord," and call on the Saint-Sergius Monastery of Gibran's youth and eternal life, which in 1975 had become the Kahlil Gibran Museum.

Housing some 450 originals of the poet's paintings and charcoal drawings, the museum also contained a good number of his personal effects, including items of clothing, painting, and writing tools (easels, brushes, notebooks, palettes, empty canvas, etc.,) and the original furnishings of his New York and Boston work studios and apartments. While walking through a biographical memorial swarming with "pilgrims" meandering quietly, pensively, wandering through the exhibits, muted, as if in a spiritual trance or on some religious quest, I stopped at a replica of what looked like Gibran's "living room," intrigued by an ornate menorah that had caught my eye sitting atop a reddish-brown mahogany cabinet. As I began remarking to a companion on "how interesting," and indeed "how distinctly characteristic" of "Gibran the ecumenical mystic" it was to have among his personal (American) possessions one of the most distinctively Jewish of symbols, we were intruded upon by a curt corrective from an uninvited "tour-guide": "That's a simple candelabrum, sir," he told me rather abruptly, in a loud reproachful tone. "Gibran hated the Jews, and could not have possibly owned a menorah," he barked. "Gibran hated?" I inquired softly, with the somewhat condescending smirk of an opinionated twenty-three-year-old fresh-out-of-college know-it-all. "What happened to Gibran the mystic, the humanist, the universalist 'lover of mankind' trotted out by your museum, sir?" I asked. "Yes," retorted the unsolicited expert, "Gibran was all of that, you're right, but he hated the Jews too; and what you have wrongly identified as a 'menorah' is in fact a seven-branched candlestick, that's all!" Unable to contain my contempt for this poor man's towering intellect, I burst out in laughter, disturbing the serenity of the monastery museum where visitors had surely come for meditation, not to be dealt my crazy laughter. With tears in my eyes, I reached into my pocket, took my wallet out, and started handing my uninvited guide a 5 Lebanese Liras bill—the equivalent of a single shiny US dime at that time—as my mind went racing for some sassy comeback. But before I could open my mouth, before I could tell that village-idiot what to do with his dime (mind you my intent was noble; I simply wanted him to buy himself a dictionary and look up the word "Menorah"), my Lebanese friend had yanked me by my arm, almost dislocating my shoulder, whisking me out of the museum and into his car, driving off, his wheels screeching in a cloud of burnt rubber as if fleeing a bank robbery scene straight out of a Starsky and Hutch episode.

As the car went off careening down Mount Lebanon, in the direction of the coast below—out of Syrian-controlled Lebanon and into the safety of Christian-held East Beirut—Ziad, the childhood friend, who had driven me to Gibran's hermitage, went off the handle screaming his head off, tearing my ears out with insult and invective, wishing I had never come to Lebanon that summer. "What are you insane?" he kept howling; "you think this is America, eh?" "You think you can speak your mind here like it's the Boston tea party? You think you can tell a two-bit Syrian thug off and live to tell about it here? You think you can advertise your righteous indignation with our anti-Semites and get away with it here? Shut up, man! Just shut up, okay?! This is not America here, okay? Look around you! Please, for the love of God just look around you and keep your big fucking mouth shut over here!!" I was dumbfounded. I couldn't squeak out a single solitary peep.

Then, taking a deep breath, clearing out a throat audibly strained by the sustained screaming of earlier, Ziad picked up where he had just left off and began yelling again, his voice now skipping, slipping like the tires of his Citroën hugging the narrow turns of the mountain terrain, sounding more like a little girl's little shrieks, than the authoritative angry priest of earlier, preachifying. But he also sounded a bit worn out, all the energy drained out of him, and so he switched down to his calmer, more reasoned sermonizing; a friend offering friendly advice. "If someone here tells you Gibran hated Jews," he said, "then the right answer is 'yes, sir, he sure did; and a fine anti-Semite he was; like you; like me; like all of us righteous victims of them rapacious Jews!' Understood?" I shook my head approvingly. Reluctantly. "The Lebanon of your memories is finished, my friend," said my priest friend; "it's kaput; yesterday's news; this is a new era now; and don't you dare try countering the inverted realities of this new age; *our* new age! Re-read *1984* perhaps, before your next visit to Lebanon, okay?!"

Those words seared me to the depths of my being back then, in the summer of 1986. Yet they never rang more true than they do today, at this writing more than thirty years since they were first uttered, since they ripped to shreds all my smug assumptions about an idealized Lebanon. Ziad passed on in the Fall of that same year, and I never got the chance to tell him how right he was; how sorry I was, to have put his life and the lives of his family and his parishioners in danger practicing my silly "freedom of expression" and "freedom to dissent"; in a place that had just committed collective suicide; and a country that had lost all its bearings and all its reasons for being as a "federation of minorities." By 1986, the Lebanon of my younger years, the Lebanon of Ziad's childhood and mine, liberal, unorthodox, irreverent, libertine, iconoclastic, open to its own diversity and to a world beyond nationalist prison walls, had become a "slave-republic" beholden to the phobias of its neighborhood, the hang-ups of xenophobes and pan-nationalists and champions of motley fronts "of rejection and steadfastness and confrontation."[3]

But there were better days for Lebanon once. One needed not be overly old or nostalgic noted the late Fouad Ajami, to recall with affection a multi-cultural Lebanon where eighteen different communities jostled and feuded for power and influence and relevance; where Lebanese beholden to the creed of Arab nationalism met their match in "Lebanese who thought of their country as a piece of Europe at the foot of a splendid mountain [... and who] savored the language of France" as if it were their own.[4] This was the Lebanon of the Jews; a Lebanon with Jews; and a Lebanon where Jewish life was also a Lebanese mode of being. There are many cultural, literary, and political snippets from a Lebanon of a mere century ago that bear this out. Many of them populate the text of this volume. Others are revealed here as prefatory testimony, as "primary sources" revealing a Lebanese political culture and social ethos unrecognizable in today's obscurantist climes.

The first passage reproduced herewith, revealing a Lebanon at odds with its "tarnished" early twenty-first century image, is the text of a letter from the Maronite Archbishopric of Beirut, addressed to the Chairman of the United Nations Special Committee on Palestine. In 1947, under a United Nations charter demanding recommendations be made on the future of British Mandate Palestine—sovereignty over which was then being disputed by both Muslims and Jews, under very difficult, violent

---

[3]This "Front of rejection and steadfastness and confrontation" was an alliance—of histrionics and hectoring and sloganeering more than anything else—founded in 1977. Composed of Libya, Syria, Iraq, the Palestine Liberation Organization, the People's Democratic Republic of Yemen, and other "standard bearers" of the Arab nationalist "cause," this rejectionist front took upon itself the task of keeping Arabs in check, preventing them from considering "normalization" with Israel, on the heels of Egyptian President Sadat's visit to Jerusalem in 1977.

[4]Marius Deeb, *Syria, Iran, and Hezbollah: The Unholy Alliance and Its War on Lebanon* (Stanford, CA: The Hoover Institution Press, 2013), xiv–xv.

circumstances—UNSCOP, made up of representatives of eleven UN member nations, was tasked with investigating the cause of the conflict in Palestine and if possible, devising a solution. In June 1947, the Committee arrived in Palestine with the objective of collecting testimony from representatives of Jewish and Muslim (Arab) Palestinians. The Arab Higher Committee, the representative body of then the Arabs of British Mandate Palestine, refused to meet with UNSCOP on the pretext that the Committee was pro-Zionist, and the Arabs' "natural rights" to Palestine did not need validation from the United Nations body. On July 21, UNSCOP members traveled to Lebanon where they met with Lebanese Prime Minister Riad al-Solh, a committed Arab nationalist whose testimony was in line with the anti-Zionist version of events and in solidarity with the Muslims of British Mandate Palestine. On July 23, UNSCOP got an earful from representatives of the Arab League then gathered in the Lebanese mountain resort town of Sofar, where they also met with pro-Zionist Lebanese Christian politicians and organizations, among them representatives of the Maronite Church. The letter of the Archbishop of Beirut, who was traveling outside of Lebanon during UNSCOP's visit, encapsulates the Maronite's early twentieth-century position vis-à-vis the events in British Mandate Palestine, the conflict between Muslims and Jews, and overall the status of Christians and Jews in the Middle East.

Archbishopric of Beirut
August 5, 1947

To: Judge Alfred Emil Fredrik Sandström
President,
United Nations Special Committee on Palestine (UNSCOP)
Geneva, Switzerland.

Dear Mr. President,
I regret that my current absence [traveling] in Europe has coincided with the Commission of Enquiry on Palestine's visit to Lebanon. Otherwise I would have been given the opportunity to make my voice heard on the matter, providing my opinion, which is also the opinion of the majority of the Lebanese people.

Please know that this is not the first time that I shall be expressing my sentiments on this matter; indeed much ink has already been spilt over it, and following each of my past declarations the world press has been quick to seize upon them, scrutinizing them, interpreting them, analyzing them.

Allow me to set the record straight once and for all, noting that in this majority-Muslim Middle East, where the current Lebanese Government is alleged to be speaking officially on behalf of the Lebanese Nation in its entirety, the reality is otherwise. Indeed, today's Lebanese officials are representatives only of themselves, and their so-called "official statements" are decreed by ephemeral expediencies, imposed by an enforced sense of solidarity forcibly tying this majority-Christian country to the Muslim nations surrounding it on all sides, compelling it willy nilly into their political-economic orbit.

Given its distinct geographical location, its history, its cultures, its traditions, the character of its inhabitants and their attachment to their faith and their principles, Lebanon has always been immune to the influences of neighboring nations—even when under the grip of the Ottoman yoke—always managing to maintain its traditions intact, untouched.

Palestine, on the other hand, the ideological hearth and center of both the Old and New Testaments, has been subjected to all manner of vexations and persecutions. For a very long time now, anything remotely reminiscent of historical memories preceding Islam has been sacked, pillaged, mutilated. Temples and churches were turned into mosques, and the role that this eastern part of the Mediterranean has traditionally played in Judeo-Christian traditions has been reduced to naught, and for good reason. Historically speaking, it is undeniable that Palestine was for all times and at all times the homeland of Jews and early Christians, none of whom were of Arab origin. Yet the brute force of the Muslim conquest has reduced their numbers and forced their conversion to the Muslim religion. This is the origin of the Arabs in Palestine. Can one then seriously deduce from the preceding that Palestine is Arab, or that it had always been Arab [as is claimed by some? ...][5]

The historical remains, the monuments, the sacred memories of the two religions [Judaism and Christianity] are alive to this day, attesting to the fact that this land has always lived apart from the inter-Arab wars waged by the princes and monarchs of Iraq and Arabia. The Holy Places, the Temples, the Wailing Wall, the Churches and the Tombs of the Prophets

---

[5] See for instance the Summary Records of the Meetings 25 September–25 November 1947 (New York) of the *United Nations Assembly Ad Hoc Committee on the Palestinian Question*, specifically Mr. Husseini's testimony (on behalf of the Arab Higher Committee) noting that "Palestine was Arab by virtue of centuries of permanent occupation and possession and that the Arabs were entitled to the right of shaping the government and forming the constitution of their own country..." https://unispal.un.org/DPA/DPR/unispal. nsf/0/FCFDBC89E49CB80A852573520053605D.

and Saints in themselves negate all the false assertions of those who are intent on turning Palestine into an Arab country. In short all the memories of Judaism and Christianity are living symbols that dismiss the claims of those insisting on making Palestine an Arab country. To include Palestine and Lebanon in the framework of Arab countries is an affront to history, an absurd kind of denialism aimed at destroying the social order of the Near East.

These two countries, these two [national] homes, are today's living proof of their utility, indeed the crucial necessity of their continued existence as distinct independent entities.

Lebanon has always been, and remains, the sole singular refuge of all the persecuted Christians of the Middle East. It was here, in Lebanon, that the Armenians, decimated in Turkey, found refuge. It is here that the Chaldeans of Iraq, hunted down from their homeland, have found asylum. It was here also that the Poles, hunted down in a Europe in flames, have found safe haven. It is here, likewise, that the French chased out of Syria found shelter. And finally it was right here, on this very spot in the world, that the English families escaping terrorism in Palestine were given respite and sanctuary.

Lebanon and Palestine alike must remain the permanent homes of the minorities of the Near East.

What was the role played by the Jews in Palestine? Studied from this vantage point, the Palestine of 1918 was nothing more than an arid, poor, desiccated land devoid of all manner of resources; indeed it was the least evolved of all the neighboring Turkish vilayets. The Arab Muslim colonies living there were on the edges of abject misery. But as soon as Jewish immigration began, settlements started sprouting and forming, and in less than twenty years' time the country was transformed, ushering in a flowering of cultural life, the establishment of advanced industries, and the creation of new wealth throughout the land. The presence, next to Lebanon, of an industrious people, so evolved and so hard-working can only contribute to the well being of us all in this region. The Jews are doers; the Lebanese are masters of adaptability; that is why a neighborhood such as ours, with both our peoples, can only serve to improve all the living conditions of all of us.

From a cultural standpoint, these two peoples, the Lebanese and the Jews, can boast having among the two of them alone the highest numbers of educated individuals than all of the countries of the Middle East combined. It is not right that a law be imposed by an ignorant majority intent on having its will at all costs. It is unacceptable that a million educated, evolved human beings be made to toe the line of a few opportunists leading a few million backward or retrograde making law as they wish. There is something called "world order" in this world. It is this order that gives equilibrium to our world. If the United Nations is truly committed to maintaining this world order, then it has the responsibility to cement and consolidate it.

Major social, human, and religious reasons require that there be in these two lands, Lebanon and Palestine, two national homes for minorities: a Christian home in Lebanon as has always been the case; a Jewish home in Palestine. These two focal points of minorities, geographically connected to each other, economically supporting and assisting one another, will form the indispensable bridge between East and West, on both the cultural and civilizational planes. The good neighborly relations between our two peoples [in Lebanon and Palestine] will help maintain peace in the Middle East, a region so riven by divisions, and will reduce the persecution of minorities who will always find an asylum in one of these two countries.

This is in sum the opinion of the Lebanese people that I represent; this is the opinion of this people whom your Commission of Enquiry was prevented from hearing.

Behind the shuttered windows and closed doors of the Sofar Hotel, you could only hear the words dictated to our so-called legal representatives, dictated by their foreign masters and overlords from neighboring Muslim Arab countries. The real Lebanese voice was stifled by a horde of charlatans, defrauders of the May 25 elections.[6]

Lebanon demands freedom for the Jews in Palestine—just as it insists on its own freedom and independence.

With my highest consideration,

---

[6]The May 25, 1947 Lebanese elections are acknowledged to have been mired in voter fraud, institutional corruption, and procedural irregularities that should have rendered them invalid. Bechara al-Khoury and his Constitutional Bloc then, currying favor with Arab nationalist groups, "maneuvered the parliamentary elections to assure" his ascension to the presidency. "His opponents were furious, and even his own brother-in-law, Michel Chiha, something of Lebanon's ideological conscience, was appalled." Khoury's second term as President, an Arabist or a pragmatist depending on the analysts' biases, "began in an atmosphere of tension, and [...] corruption. [...] The architect [...] of the National Covenant had provided the state with an inauspicious beginning." See David Gordon, Lebanon; *The Fragmented Nation* (Stanford, California: The Hoover Institution Press, 1980), 49.

(Signed) Ignatius Mobarak
Maronite Archbishop of Beirut[7]

Read from the purview of twenty-first century assumptions, this impassioned assessment of a Maronite Christian prelate beholden to minority narratives and minority rights, may seem somewhat unsettling. But in the context of a post-Ottoman political map still "under construction," where the rights of Near Eastern Christians and Jews were on the verge of being surrendered to the will of a dominant ethnos with a complicated history vis-à-vis its minority peoples, Archbishop Mobarak's memorandum deserves a nuanced treatment. Whatever the case may be, it is representative of Lebanese attitudes with regards to Lebanese Jews and Middle Eastern Jewry in more general terms. But there are more texts representative of this early twentieth-century Lebanese cultural iconoclasm. Sixteen years after the publication of the first issue of *Al-Aalam al-Isra'iili*, Lebanon's Arabic language Jewish periodical, and on the occasion of its rebirth as a weekly newsmagazine in February 1938, Georges Nicolas Baz, a renowned Beiruti Christian journalist and women's rights activist, penned the following essay, titled *O Daughters of Israel*, for the inaugural issue of the resurrected Jewish periodical:

> I was delighted to learn of the republication of *Al-Aalam al-Isra'iili* as a weekly magazine. And at the risk of sounding somewhat indecent, I must mention that I had been a regular contributor to the weekly newspaper in the past, publishing in it mainly on the topic of women's rights. And so it brings me great pleasure today to address the female readers of this magazine, on the occasion of the publication of its first issue as a newsmagazine.
>
> For sixteen years prior, I had been watching the dynamic activities of Lebanese Jewish women in spheres ranging from the sciences, to patriotic national work, to human rights activism and benevolent service. Things have not changed. I must say that the nucleus of all of your admirable

---

[7] © Abbé Alain René Arbez pour Dreuz.info. Excerpts from a letter dated August 5, 1947, by Ignatius Mobarak, Maronite Archbishop of Beirut, addressed to Judge Emil Sandström, the Swedish Chairman of the UN Committee of Enquiry, UNSCOP, Geneva, Switzerland. See *Official Records of the Second Session of the United Nations Assembly Ad Hoc Committee on the Palestinian Question*; Summary Records of the Meetings 25 September–25 November 1947 (New York), https://unispal.un.org/DPA/DPR/unispal.nsf/0/FCFDBC89E49CB80A852573520053605D.

work issues from the same headspring: Indeed, among you are women lawyers, physicians, authors, and directors of leading organizations. You are not bereft of initiative, native intelligence, and brilliance. Indeed, Ms. Esther Azhari Moyal, this fine daughter of Beirut, once filled the lecture halls and the free tribunes of venerable publications [of this country] with her advocacy on behalf of women; but ever since France's commitment on our behalf began waning, so has Esther's voice gotten muffled.[8]

It should be mentioned parenthetically at this point that Esther Azhari Moyal (1873–1948) was the child of a renowned Beiruti Jewish family, and a famous—one might even say a feisty—journalist, feminist, and translator. Georges Nicholas Baz published much of Moyal's work, specially in his periodical *Al-Hasnaa'* (Ar. *Belle*); articles that even by today's standards would be considered refractory, subversive, not to say incendiary, specially so in traditional male-dominated Muslim societies. To wit, in an article published by Moyal in the January 1911 issue of Baz's *Al-Hasnaa'*, she cautions Muslim men "who think it's permissible to demean women and disrespect them." Beware, she wrote:

Mind your own business, and do not get yourself entangled in questions that are beyond your mental capacities. In fact, you would do well channeling your energies into doing something useful for a change [instead of oppressing women] and try learning a thing or two from the fine lessons given you freely by your foreign neighbors. Those foreigners who have come to you only a few years ago, penniless, owning very little save the clothes on their backs and their drive and energy and enterprise. Why don't you try to learn something from their lust for work, their curiosity for learning, and their resolve to perfect every task assigned to them! On their wits alone, they collaborated with one another, they created new industries, they gathered sizeable capital, and set they up industrial and agricultural projects of the most advanced kinds... They bought your arid lands where only weeds and thorns once grew, and transformed them into

---

[8] Esther Azhari Moyal issues from a well-known Beiruti (Sephardic) family. Her maiden name (Azhari) means "Azharite" in Arabic, but it is in fact a corruption of "Lazari." She was educated in Arabic, French, and English, and accosted a veritable who is who of Arabic literati of her times, among them the Lebanese Arab Nationalist Christian author Amin Rihani. See Lital Levy, "Moyal, Esther Azhari," in *Brill Encyclopedia of Jews in the Islamic World*, Executive Editor Norman A. Stillman. Consulted online on March 8, 2018, http://referenceworks.brillonline.com/entries/encyclopedia-of-jews-in-the-islamic-world/moyal-esther-azhari-SIM_0015860.

lush gardens with rivers running underneath. And yet, you go on wallowing in your stagnant seas of ignorance and inertia and indolence.[9]

Read from the context of a twenty-first-century Western world blasé with the Zionist project of a hundred years ago, this snippet may be dismissed as "Zionist propaganda" at best, an anti-Arab screed at worst. Its importance, however, dwells in the fact that it was written in Arabic, penned by a female author who may be referred to as an "Arab Jew" in today's terminology—even though such taxonomy was non-extant and meaningless in the early twentieth century—and more importantly perhaps, it was published in an Arabic-language Lebanese "women's magazine," *Al-Hasnaa'*, edited by Georges Nicholas Baz, an ecumenical free-thinking public intellectual, who also published at that time vociferous advocates of Arabism, among them the renowned Lebanese-American Amin Rihani (1876–1940).

It is worth noting in this regard that even committed Arab nationalists, at the height of Arab nationalist fervor during the 1950s and 1960s, wrote in terms similar to Moyal's calling Arabs to task, castigating them for their indolence, and excoriating their societies and political cultures condoning patriarchy, misogyny, and retrograde traditional ethos. Nizar Qabbani (1923–1998) was one such critic. Writing in 1968, on the heels of the Six-Day War, he noted that, as Arabs,

> We have donned the veneer of culture, while our very souls have remained primitive… / Our obsession with virility and manly spontaneity has cost us fifty-thousand brand new tents. / Do not curse the heavens for having forsaken you… / Do not curse the circumstances. / For, Allah grants victory to those who desire it… / And you haven't even got a single native blacksmith chiseling your swords for you… / The Jews did not breach our borders. Rather, the crept in like ants through the cracks of our flaws…[10]

But going back to Georges Baz's essay in *Al-Aalam al-Isra'iili*, after mentioning Esther Azhari Moyal and her sudden silence, he went on exhorting Lebanese Jewish women to re-engage their activism of times past, to honor Azhari Moyal's memory and tradition of "dynamism

---

[9] Esther Azhari Moya, "Women of Palestine," *Al-Hasnaa'* (Beirut: January 1911), npn.

[10] Franck Salameh, *The Other Middle East: An Anthology of Modern Levantine Literature* (New Haven and London: Yale University Press, 2017), 82–83.

and enterprise"; "O proud daughters of Prophetesses and Queens," he wrote:

> The pages of the Holy Bible are replete, adorned with the memory of the righteous Prophetesses. Among them are Miriam the sister of Moses, Deborah the Judge, Hulda the trusted Prophetess of the King of Judah, Athalia the daughter of King Ahab, and finally Esther, the savior of her people from Babylonian captivity. O Arab women, and Arabized Jews, we wait for you and await your critical work, your contributions in the service of humanity, in the service of political and economic life, in the service of educating our children and sharing the duties of men. Indeed, acquiescing to doing only household chores is no longer enough for a Humanity that is now owed much more; a Humanity owed wider and more comprehensive Human Rights. Onward we go for the sake of Humanity, you the finest from among God's Chosen People.[11]

These Lebanese attitudes vis-à-vis Jews—*Lebanese* Jews in particular— have many analogues in various other sources. In a confidential 1964 "profile" of the World Jewish Congress, an anonymous correspondent writing based on the testimony of Lebanese Jews and non-Jews alike, traced the origins of Lebanon's Jewish community "back to antiquity," and "well before the Christian era."[12] The writer noted that

> relations between the Jewish community and the authorities have been good, even considering the political upheaval which the region as a whole has experienced in recent years. The community has its roots in the Lebanon going back to immemorial times, and there has been a traditional recognition of the Council of the Community through the Grand Rabbin[ate,] as well as attendance by high State dignitaries representing the political and civil authorities in the principal temple of the community on important Jewish holidays. In fact, Yom Kippur and the first day of Passover figured in the official list of [Lebanese] public holidays.[13]

[11] Georges Nicholas Baz, "O Daughters of Israel," *Al-Aalam al-Isra'iili* (Beirut: February 1937), 8.

[12] Anonymous, *Profile of the Lebanese Jewish Community* (Beirut, Confidential, June 1964), Jacob Rader Marcus Center of the American Jewish Archives, The World Jewish Congress Collection, Series H: Alphabetical Files, 1919–1981, Box: H235, File 3, Lebanon, 1960–1969, 04.031.

[13] Anonymous, *Profile of the Lebanese Jewish Community* (Beirut, Confidential, June 1964), Jacob Rader Marcus Center of the American Jewish Archives, The World Jewish

Even as the 1960s and 1970s were exerting increasing pressure on the Lebanese government and Lebanese society as a whole to pay increasing lip service to Arab nationalist hang-ups vis-à-vis the Jewish state—and by association increasing hostility toward a by now more vulnerable and apprehensive Lebanese Jewry—Lebanon would still attempt to cling to its reputation as a safe space for a liberal, even unorthodox, ethos of openness. This was generally the attitude among expatriate Lebanese communities in the Americas and elsewhere. Relative to this, in a February 1958 article in the Detroit-based Lebanese Gazette, Checri Kanaan, who wrote in a similar vein into the late 1960s, urged his fellow Lebanese at home to "Make peace with Israel now!"[14] "How long will the world remain blind to the realities of the Middle East?" he began his exhortation;

> A couple of dictators have formed a partnership aimed to destroy several nations, and we seem to be fooled. Wake up America. Wake up, leaders of the democracies of the world. First Nasser and Kuwatly would like to destroy Israel. Then they will seek the destruction of Lebanon. Iraq and Jordan will follow... Wake up, Lebanon. You are in greater danger than even Israel. [... Lebanon] is a Christian country, but the Moslem dictators of Syria and Egypt would like to swallow her up. Then, woe unto our fellow Christians. Their lives will be worthless. [...] What action is to be taken in this dangerous time for the Middle East and the world? We urge an immediate peace between Israel and Lebanon. Then the two democracies can work together, they can act jointly in protecting their common borders and they can appeal to the world against aggression [...] How long will the world remain silent? How long will the Lebanese remain blind to the dangers that face them? We appeal to our kinsmen and coreligionists in Lebanon, especially to the Christians in our former homeland, to act now, to make peace with Israel, to prevent the damage that is sure to come from the "federated union" of Syria and Egypt. [...] Let us have peace with Israel first, then blessing will be poured upon the entire areas

Congress Collection, Series H: Alphabetical Files, 1919–1981, Box: H235, File 3, Lebanon, 1960–1969, 04.042.

[14]Checri Kanaan, "Now Is the Time for Lebanon to Make Peace with Israel," *The Lebanon Gazette* (Detroit, February 20, 1958), npn. Jacob Rader Marcus Center of the American Jewish Archives, The World Jewish Congress Collection, Series H: Alphabetical Files, 1919–1981, Box: H235, File 9, Lebanon, Hyman, Abrahan S., 1954, 1958, 10.005.

and there will be greater security for Lebanon. Fellow Lebanese, make peace with Israel now.[15]

To conclude where this prologomenon had begun, it ought to be said that not only was there a period in time when "Lebanon loved the Jews," but also a time when Lebanese Jews themselves committed—and the few of them that remain today continue to commit—to Lebanon, even a flawed Lebanon of the twenty-first century that is in many ways unrecognizable compared to the Republic's early iterations of a hundred years ago. And so, not only did Gibran *not* hate Jews as that adamant "tour guide" had insisted in 1986, but indeed the Jewish Bible and those whose stories it told populated Gibran's life and his life's work. And so Lebanese Jewry loved Gibran back.

In the summer of 1931, Gibran's remains were exhumed from the Mount-Benedict Cemetery of Boston's flagship Maronite Church (Our Lady of the Cedars of Lebanon), to be returned—as had been his final wish—to their final resting place in Bsharré. On August 21, Gibran was received with great reverence by his countrymen at the Beirut Harbor, from where he was carried over to Bsharré on foot, in a cortège stretching over a fifty-mile distance.[16] Along the way, his remains were blessed by the Beirut Maronite Archbishop, Ignatius Mobarak, before beginning a trek to "the Valley of the Sainted," interrupted by some twenty "stations" along the way, in twenty different Lebanese villages, as if in a twenty-step devotional commemorating a "Prophet's" life. Lebanese Jews took center stage in these processions. The Jewish Scouts troupe, the Maccabis, in full official uniform, festooned in their flags and regalia, "earning the admiration of all those present," proudly walked alongside the casket, accompanying other participating Christian, Muslim, and Druze youth organizations.[17] Likewise, members of Lebanon's *Chesed Shel Emet* burial organization, whose charity work included readying the deceased for burial according to Jewish tradition, had an active role and visible a presence in the procession; this, along with representatives of Beirut's *Hachnasat Orchim* shelter (in keeping with the traditional

[15] Checri Kanaan, "Now Is the Time for Lebanon to Make Peace with Israel."

[16] Jean Gibran and Kahlil Gibran, *Kahlil Gibran; His Life and Work* (New York: Interlink, 1998), 407–8.

[17] *Al-Aalam al-Isra'iili*, "A Glimpse of the Life of Kahlil Gibran" (Beirut: August 28, 1931), 1.

mitzvah, or Jewish duty, of hospitality), and other local Jewish institutions.[18] This is indicative not only of the great esteem that Lebanese Jews—like others of their compatriots—heldfor Gibran, who was by then a "national icon" of universal renown claimed by all Lebanese as one of their own, but this also hinted to the special place that the Jewish ethos and experience held in Gibran's own life. Mariana, Gibran's youngest sister, the last surviving member of his nuclear family and executor of his will, was present at the Beirut-Bsharré processions celebrating her brother's life. Mournful as she might have been, there must have also been a tinge of tranquility in her heart, content that her brother's last wishes were fulfilled, bringing together all of Lebanon's communal groups—chief among them Lebanon's Jewish community—in a single "national family".

"The Levant is an area, a dialogue, and a quest," wrote Philip Mansel in his monumental 2010 social and cultural history of the port cities of the Eastern Mediterranean.[19] A geographic conflation of interests, cultures, civilizations, and times, where East and West—Jewishness, Christendom, and Islam—meet, duel, and sometimes "drop in on one another [... and] salute each other in solemn veneration," the Levant is indeed at once a place of intercourse and exchange and conflict; a challenge for understanding; a summons to compromise; and an entreaty for treaty.[20] Looking askance at prevalent comfortable orthodoxies, stereotypes, and assumptions, the Levant is also a confluence of cosmopolitanism and nationalism bundled together, flourishing in unison and generating both affection to diversity and longing for oneness, attraction for the ways and languages of outsiders—from across the Mediterranean—*and* repulsion and rage against them.

"Smyrna, Alexandria, and Beirut were at the heart of [this] Levantine dialogue," noted Philip Mansel.[21] They were at once worldly and provincial, sophisticated, and parochial, "Mediterranean and Middle Eastern, Ottoman and European, nationalist and international. [And] they were mixed cities where mosques, churches and synagogues were built side by

---

[18] *Al-Aalam al-Isra'iili*, "A Glimpse of the Life of Kahlil Gibran," 1.

[19] Philip Mansel, *Levant: Splendor and Catastrophe on the Mediterranean* (London, UK: John Murray Publisher, 2010), 1.

[20] Michel Chiha, *Visage et Présence du Liban*, 2ème edition (Beirut: Le Cénacle Libanais, 1984), 49.

[21] Mansel, 1.

side," often sharing the same ancient stonewalls and common frayed roof tiles, the same fragrant courtyards and private gardens.[22] Even in their names, these Levantine ports-of-call radiated their ancient multi-cultural, polyglot lineages, redolent in age-old patrimonies. To wit, the ancient toponym Beirut is *not* Arab, as modern observers may assume, but Canaanite-Phoenician for "water springs"; likewise, Smyrna, the modern Turkish Izmir, is of Classical Greek provenance, and Alexandria, in modern-day Egypt, betrays origins as an ancient Greek settlement and namesake of Alexander the Great (ca. 331 BC). It is best one stayed away from the "can of worms" that may be delving into the non-Arab etymologies and cultural accretions of Sidon, Tyre, Acre, Haifa, Jaffa, Jerusalem, Israel, and, yes, Palestine. But it's a topic that requires an honest conversation beyond the scope of this volume.

Going back to the congenital diversity and colorful selfhoods of the Levant, it is important to note that there was liberty and libertinism in the world of Levantine port cities, Lebanon's port cities chief among them, standing sentry in the face of the more insular traditional metropolises of the Middle East's hinterlands—what Lebanese Druze politician Kamal Jumblat dubbed "the realms of sands and slumbers and mosques and sun" that remain to this day narrowly Muslim in dogma, jealously Arab in their ways, etymologies, histories, intellectual space, and outlook.[23] Staid, rigid, traditional, ordered, the Middle East of the interior rises (or rather slumps) in stark contrast to the dynamism, the irreverence, the fluidity, the intellectual bustle, *even* the happy disorder of the Eastern Mediterranean. And so, contends Philip Mansel, just as Europe may be unthinkable without Paris, so the diversity, flexibility, spaciousness, and moral elegance of the Eastern Mediterranean would have been unthinkable without the port cities of Lebanon.[24]

There, in Lebanon, a small sliver of land straddling multiple worlds, peoples switched identities and traditions and assumptions just as seamlessly and intuitively as they wielded multiple languages.[25] They were prisoners of neither religion nor nationality, nor linguistic norms or social expectations. How can anyone not heed the reality that a country such

[22] Mansel, 1–2.

[23] See Camille Abousouan's "Présentation," *Cahiers de l'Est* (Beirut, Lebanon: July 1945), 3.

[24] Mansel, 2.

[25] Mansel, 2.

as Lebanon, wrote Michel Chiha, "would be literally decapitated if prevented from being bilingual (or even trilingual if possible)?"[26]

Early twentieth-century Francophone Lebanese poet, Charles Corm (1894–1963) stressed diversity—specifically Lebanese diversity—as being a form of Humanism; indeed the most exquisite incarnation of Humanism; a "supreme blessing of Mankind's, bestowed upon Mankind above and beyond all other riches," he claimed.[27] Humanism, noted Corm, is a notion "so enamored of the truth, so impassioned by justice, so acutely sensitive to love [...] to the point that nothing of that which is human may be deemed alien."[28] And Lebanon, in Corm's telling, was the birthplace of that form of Humanism,

> A Humanism in its most exquisite unvarnished incarnation [... issuing from Beirut's] own Ulpian, this Magistrate from Lebanon, who would marshal dauntless audacity, inconceivable for his time, announcing from atop his pulpit as advisor to the [Roman] throne, the equality of all men down below, and Man's inalienable natural right to liberty. At a time when emperors and their empires, officially still avid practitioners of slavery, relishing the sight of tortured men women and children being devoured alive by wild beasts in the State's sports arenas, our very own Ulpian would face down mighty Rome, shouting out his cry for moral justice, a cry which would soon become the collective cry of all of humanity for virtue and justice.[29]

In this sense, one may argue that Lebanon—at least in the voice of its own children—might have been humanist before Humanism, global before Globalization, and urbane, worldly, cosmopolitan, ecumenical, universal, "New Yorker," before the Universal Declaration of Human Rights, before the United Nations, and long before there had been a New York City crucible of cultures. And although the Lebanese of today may be a sad emaciated image of their former glorious past, and although our times' Beirut may be a far cry from the Roman *Nutris Legum* (Mother of Laws) where diversity was *the* mode of being, that Beirut does endure and survive as a Levantine archetype of sorts; a

---

[26] Chiha, *Visage et Présence*, 49–52 and 164.

[27] Charles Corm, "Déclaration de M. Ch. Corm," *Les Principes d'un Humanisme Méditerranéen* (Monaco, November 1935), 25.

[28] Corm, "Déclaration," 25.

[29] Charles Corm, *6000 Ans de Génie Pacifique au Service de l'Humanité* (Beirut: Editions de la Revue Phénicienne, 1988), 113–14.

"dialogue and a quest,"[30] where no single resentful jingoist hegemon dominates; where Christians, Jews, and Muslims can still meet, embrace, bicker, and assimilate; "where varied civilizations [can still] drop in on one another, and where bevies of beliefs, languages, and cultural rituals [can still] salute each other in solemn veneration."[31]

Redolent in these imageries and passions of the Levant, Amin Maalouf's 1996 novel, *Les Échelles du Levant*, tells a particularly Lebanese life in a particularly gripping story.[32] This history's events take place in the early twentieth century, in an era of "reconstruction," and a time period where, in the midst of war and despair, there was still much stability and rootedness in fluidity, and perhaps even optimism for the future of diversity and cosmopolitanism and multiple identities.

Reflecting a millennial, congenital Levantine jumble of cultures, Maalouf's was a fantastic deeply moving story, told by a Franco-Lebanese narrator rendering in his own words the oral testimony of one Turco-Armenian prince, "Ossyane." "Ossyane" in both its etymology and its anthropomorphic temperament was an "insurrection" in the face of "orthodoxy"'; a name with attitude, as it were, redolent of class and pedigree and elegance and meaning; a "rebellion" pure and simple—in Arabic "Ossyane" connotes "defiance," "dissent," "insurrection"—in the face of stale stereotypes and prevalent assumptions about people's origins, memories, and identities.

And so, the Ossyane presented us by Maalouf was a lovechild, the outcome of an Armenian-Turkish love story, born from a princely line on

---

[30] Mansel, 1.

[31] Chiha, *Visage et Présence*, 49.

[32] "There are few greater pleasures than to extricate oneself from the caulked circumference of a ship and step forth upon the quay of a Levantine city." Those words belong to Eyre Evans Crowe, taken from his *The Greek and the Turk; Or, Power and Prospects in the Levant* (1853). They speak to the alacrity and fancy with which outsiders "ascended" to the Levant, but they also provide an accurate description to what the French referred to as "les échelles du Levant," the literal translation of which is "ladders" or "stairways to the Levant," suggesting the "movable connectors" or "boarding bridges" attaching boats to their ports of call. Yet the French term itself refers to the port-cities of the Eastern Mediterranean holdings of the former Ottoman Empire, where the Sultan had renounced some of his authority, namely with regards to non-Muslim minority populations, in favor European—and namely French—protection. Thus, Levantine non-Muslims would, juridically speaking, become "protégés" of the "kings of France," who would in turn favor them and grant them certain privileges not afforded Muslim subjects of the Ottoman Empire.

the banks of the Bosphorus, in the dying days of the Ottoman Empire, at a time when, in Maalouf's telling, an Armenian and a Turk could still hold hands and mix languages and traditions in the midst of tragedy and cruelty and despair; "a sepia-colored universe" where men of varied origins could still be brothers to one another.[33] After 1923, Ossyane's family takes up residence in Beirut, and Ossyane himself, answering to his Turkish father's (now a Beiruti) Francophile sympathies goes on to pursue studies in medicine in France. But soon World War II breaks out, and Ossyane is compelled to abandon his future in the medical field to join the frontlines of the Maquis and the French Resistance. There, in the ranks of the French resistance to Nazi domination, Ossyane meets his future wife, Clara Emdem, the daughter of a Jewish family with origins in Austria, Odessa, and in Maalouf's telling "other places of residence and migration" along paths where people spilled the blood of their millennial identities and went on defying oblivion.

After the war and the defeat of Nazism and resentful pan-nationalisms, Ossyane and Clara moved back to their ancestral Levant, commuting between two homes in Beirut and Haifa, with the Sunni Ossyane making the case for the Jews of British Mandate Palestine, and the Jewish Clara advocating on behalf of Arabs, and with both doing so with clarity and alacrity, and moral elegance and empathy for peoples and ideas different from their own.

Ossyane's and Clara's travels along the coastal road, between their two homes in Lebanon and Israel, would continue long into the Winter of 1948. But soon Beirut and Haifa, once twined twin port cities, children of the same *Stella Maris*, would become, as if, two separate planets in two distant disparate solar systems—a drama with real-life analogues in the stories of Lebanese Jews, post-1948, no longer able to travel along that same coastal highway, visiting family and friends in Haifa, Jaffa, and Jerusalem.

Pregnant Clara would thus remain stuck in Haifa, and Ossyane is forcibly committed to a Beirut insane asylum, in vain awaiting news of the birth of his daughter, Nadia. And so, in his anguish and despair, Ossyane would begin imagining his awaited offspring a splendid Levantine archetype, a beautiful girl who is "perfectly Muslim and perfectly Jewish at once," because "the more our 'tomorrows' proved themselves bleak and

---

[33] Amin Maalouf, *Les Échelles du Levant* (Paris: Grasset, 1996), 49.

somber, the more our 'days after' shone brighter..." And with "Islam being patrilineal, and Judaism matrilineal" noted Ossyane, "Nadia would be fully Jewish from a Jewish perspective, and fully Muslim from a Muslim one... proud of all of the lineages strewn on her path, conduits and passageways of conquests and escapes and births, stretching from Central Asia, to Anatolia, to the Ukraine, Armenia, Bavaria, and back to the Levant... Nadia would never feel the need to sort out the droplets of her blood, nor unravel the intricate patchworks of her soul..."[34]

But the story of Ossyane, his ancestors, and his offspring is indeed a familiar one. It is the story of the Levant to be sure, but the story of Lebanon and of Jewish lives and trials and tribulations and peregrinations; the stories of others still, non-Jews uninterested in Arab resentments and phobias, invested in an ecumenical fluid conception of their Eastern Mediterranean.

There are, of course, historical affirmations of this sort of spaciousness—which some may relegate to poetic flourish or romantic literary musings. But as will become clear through the pages of this volume, this is a story quite familiar to Lebanese Jewry. Passersby may stop for a glimpse of this Lebanon of the Jews, intrigued, puzzled, endeared, or moved by their stories as if by snapshots, relics from a past frozen in time. I myself cannot look at these stories with the detachment of an outsider's cold eyes, because I am myself *not* an outsider, *nor* a passerby. Albeit an academic expected to present a life's snippet in an academic light, I remain a Levantine, born, socialized, and lulled in the melodies of Levantine mountains and seashores. And so, I do identify with, and take possession of characters and stories revealed in this book as building blocks of Lebanon and the Levant, as essence of my own being, and foundation of my profession.

And so, what I have hoped to transmit in this book remains an incomplete unfinished bit dealing with a particular history, the actors in which lived in a limited time period during which Lebanon and its Levantine neighborhood were under another "reconstruction" in the early decades of the twentieth century—not very much unlike the *other* "sorting out" that the Middle East is undergoing in these turbulent first decades of the twenty-first century; a period where there was still much fluidity and

---

[34] Maalouf, *Les Échelles du Levant*, 217.

perhaps optimism (or at least, a period where there were still some people who still clung to some semblance of fluidity and optimism).

But, ultimately, this will remain a modest installment in a monumental story whose actors, narrators, heroes, victims, and authors are only beginning to emerge from the shadows of mutism—some gingerly, others eagerly—wishing to contribute their versions of events past, present, and some still to come…

CHAPTER 2

Lebanon of the Jews: An Introduction

There are records of exchanges, both cultural
and trade, between [the Phoenician]
King Hiram of Tyre and King Solomon.
An Old Testament Hebrew prophet is buried
on Lebanese territory in Sujod [...]
a place of pilgrimage [for Lebanese Jews and others.]
Jewish communities of merchants and artisans
flourished at Deir al-Kamar, Saïda and Tripoli,
and in Beirut [...] ancient synagogues bear
witness to an active Jewish life in those times...[1]

(World Jewish Congress, 1964)

Researchers doing work in the Middle East, those with intimate Lebanese connections among them—present company included—may be cursed with too much confidence, convinced that upon showing up at the doorsteps of, say, Beirut's Jewish community, they would be

---

An earlier version of this chapter was an essay published in the *Journal of the Middle East and Africa*, Volume 6, 2015. I would like to thank the JMEA editors for granting permissions to reuse in this volume.

[1]Anonymous, Profile of the Lebanese Jewish Community (Beirut, Confidential, June 1964), Jacob Rader Marcus Center of the American Jewish Archives, The World Jewish Congress Collection, Series H: Alphabetical Files, 1919–1981, Box: H235, File 3, Lebanon, 1960–1969, 04.031.

© The Author(s) 2019
F. Salameh, *Lebanon's Jewish Community*,
https://doi.org/10.1007/978-3-319-99667-7_2

greeted like the returning prodigal son, doted on by eager hosts trip-
ping over themselves to lay long-hidden archives and lives bare before
the outsiders' prying eyes. Yet Lebanese "old hands" know all too well
that Lebanese Jews today, remnants of an ancient and venerable community that has been bruised and degraded in a modern Lebanon that
has lost its bearings, are more likely to remain circumspect and reticent
in the presence of "outsiders" asking too many questions. For good reasons, Lebanon's tiny Jewish community of the early twenty-first century,
unlike the children of its diaspora who may be warm, ebullient, loqua-
cious, and eager to tell their stories outside of Lebanon, remains small,
insecure, cagey, almost invisible in Lebanon proper, and politically mar-
ginalized in the crowded turbulent Lebanese ethno-religious landscape.
But this situation might have been otherwise in times past.

As the smallest of Lebanon's twenty legally recognized ethno-religious
groups, the Lebanese Jewish community has received very little attention
in the study of states and minorities in the Middle East, and in the study
of modern Lebanon in particular. This neglect, writes Kirsten Schulze, is
no doubt due primarily to the community's size, which was some 14,000
strong at its height by the most ambitious estimates and is much smaller
in the Lebanon of today.[2] But this neglect can also be attributed to other
factors, most notably perhaps the community's identification with political Maronitism in the years leading up to Lebanese independence in
1943, and later its (feigned) position of nonalignment in the Christian–
Muslim rivalries that have riven and dominated Lebanon's political life
since the country's inception in 1920.

Still, the Jews of Lebanon are the oldest and arguably *the most* "indigenous" of the country's communal groups, "the ones who were there
first," as it were. Accordingly, it is reasonable to suggest that they might
have participated more fully and explicitly than other groups in the formation of modern Lebanon's political life. In fact, since the establishment of the Lebanese state as a "federation of minorities" under French
Mandate rule in 1920, through the young republic's years of trial in
the heyday of pan-Arabism and the vagaries of the Arab–Israeli conflict,
and into the "civil war" years of 1975–1990, the Jews of Lebanon—or
Lebanese Jews as they prefer to be referred to—*did* exercise their full
"national prerogatives" as Lebanese citizens: They *did* have a stake in

---

[2] Kirsten Schulze, *The Jews of Lebanon: Between Coexistence and Conflict* (Brighton, UK:
Sussex Academic Press, 2001), 4–8.

the country's "identity politics"; they *did* choose allies and make enemies in the political process; and they *did* have active representation in the Lebanon's political parties, parliamentary system, armed forces, and during the "civil war" years, joined various, albeit exclusively Christian, militia groups.

Unlike non-Israeli Jews elsewhere in the Middle East, the Jews of Lebanon from the very beginnings of Islam were not *dhimmis*, were not subject to the legal restrictions imposed by traditional Islam, and did not experience the degrading treatment or discriminatory policies inflicted on minorities—Jews and Christians alike—elsewhere in the world of Islam. In that sense, Lebanon's Jews from early on in the life of the Lebanese republic committed themselves to maintaining Lebanon as an independent, sovereign, multicultural "haven of minorities"; a neutral "Levantine" intermediary and cultural conduit, weary of—even if not unconcerned with—the squabbles between Arabs and Israelis, and accordingly more in tune with the ideas and politics advocated by Lebanon's Maronite community.

There had clearly been a cultural and historical "romance" of sorts between the Jews and the Maronites of Lebanon, and this seemed clearly *not* a one-sided affair. Maronite Patriarch Antony Peter Arida, who headed his community between 1932 and 1955, and who was commonly known in Lebanon as the "Patriarch of the Jews," took special interest in the well-being of Lebanese Jewry, standing firmly behind the valorization of Lebanese Jews at home, in Lebanon proper, *and* advocating for the creation of a Jewish national home in Palestine corresponding with what he considered the neighboring "Christian national home" in Lebanon.[3]

As a result of the privileged and secure position that Lebanon's native Jewish population enjoyed in the country at large, its size actually grew and flourished after the establishment of the State of Israel in 1948, rather than shrinking as had been the case elsewhere in the Middle East. This was no doubt a reflection of a general sentiment toward the community among Lebanese Christians who well-nigh dominated Lebanon's

---

[3] See, for instance, Laura Zittrain Eisenberg, *My Enemy's Enemy: Lebanon in the Early Zionist Imagination, 1900–1948* (Detroit: Wayne University Press, 1994), 79; Kirsten E. Schulze, *The Jews of Lebanon: Between Coexistence and Conflict* (Brighton: Sussex Academic Press, 2001), 39. See also Ministère des Affaires Étrangères Archives (MAE), Série E-Levant, Sous-Série Syrie-Liban, Presse Syrienne et Libanaise, 1930–1931, Vol. 527 (Paris: Quai d'Orsay).

political culture into the early 1960s. But this was also due in no small part to the Maronites' own positive attitude toward the Jews in general, and the Jews of their own country in particular.

Conversely, the Jews of Lebanon were—and what remains of them today remain—committed to the Maronite vision of Lebanon as a multi-ethnic, not specifically Arab, Mediterranean federation of minorities.

JEWISH BEIRUT; JEWISH LEBANON

As a cultural and ethnic crucible of millennial existence, the Beirut of the late nineteenth century differed little from the bustling metropolis that is this Mediterranean port city of today. During the 1890s, the Ottoman *vilayet* (province/state) of Beirut and its capital city of the same name were shaking off the grime and dust of the miseries wrought by the Druze-Maronite conflagrations thirty years earlier. And while attempting to leave its bloody nineteenth-century past behind it, the Beirut of the early twentieth century still marched on to the drumbeat of a looming World War I that was soon to consume a brittle ailing Ottoman Empire, and with it, the Beirut *vilayet* and the autonomous *Sanjak* of Mount Lebanon contiguous to it.

Likewise, our times' city of Beirut, while attempting to suppress the memories of Lebanon's devastating 1975 "civil war," maintains an intuitive foolish optimism, even as it teeters at the edge of the raging wildfires engulfing a Middle East trying to quench a searing "Arab Spring" gone awry. Nevertheless, Beirut has remained the "spiritual beacon of the Eastern Mediterranean," practicing one of the region's most exquisite forms of humanism and cultural, ethnic, religious, and linguistic diversity.[4] Like the Beirut of today, the Beirut of Ottoman times and the early twentieth century can be characterized as feisty, resilient, modern, old, irreverent, conservative, libertine, seductive, warm, addictive, enchanting, and unforgiving all at once. In it cavorted, jostled for relevance, and feuded for influence twenty different ethno-religious groups, each with their own distinct identity, each with their own special conceptions of their *vilayet*, its capital city, and what may arise in their place as a tattered Ottoman Empire breathed its last and fell apart in 1918.

---

[4] Maurice Barrès, *Une Enquête aux pays du Levant* (Paris: Librairie Plon, 1924), 33.

Paraphrasing a Lebanese poet from the early decades of the twentieth century, in this Lebanon and Beirut of the Jews, the enigmatic Druzes rubbed shoulders with the Maronite Catholics, the Melkites bickered with the Armenians, and all in turn trafficked, feuded, and reconciled with Syriacs, Gregorians, Latins, Jacobites, Sunnis, Shi'ites, and Israelites (the community's legal name then).[5] Yet each of these groups were at once Beiruti, Levantine, and Lebanese in their own way—each different and distinct from the other, yet all so much alike.

From the hills of this Beirut, one could hear the voice of Ezekiel lamenting the fall of Tyre, a Phoenician port city standing sentry at the gates of the Mediterranean, trading with every other nation of classical antiquity, defining the very notion of humanity and the very history of mankind.[6] In Beirut, one could feel the roar of a river racing down the Lebanon ranges, heavy with the blood of Adonis, mingling with the sobs of a bereaved Venus. From Beirut, one can behold the stone of Abel, stained with his martyr's blood, or hear the sobs of Phoenician maidens weeping at the gravesite of King Ahirom, builder of Solomon's Temple. From Beirut, one can cast a gaze over at the snowcapped summits of Mount Lebanon, throwing the crushing shadow of their fragrant cedar forests over a Mediterranean below, swarming with Phoenician triremes setting sail on to some new voyage, itching for some new horizon. Indeed, in this, the Beirut of Lebanon, the Lebanon of the Jews, one can be everywhere, in a thousand places and a thousand times all at once, setting out on a thousand journeys at one time, reading the history of mankind lain open over the span of seven thousand years, yet never leave the docks of a quaint Mediterranean harbor, slumbering in the shadow of a hoary mountain.

It was in this enchanting vista of millennial memory and promise and regrets, at once compassionate and cruel, that Lebanon's ancient Jewish community came into the twentieth century. And it is no coincidence that Lebanon itself, or what became Lebanon in the early twentieth century, had been a natural home and a safe harbor to a vibrant millennial

[5] See Charles Corm's *La Terre Assassinée ou les Ciliciennes* [*The Slain Homeland or the Cilicians*] (Beirut: Éditions de la Revue Phénicienne, 2014), 131–32 and *La Montagne Inspirée* [*The Hallowed Mountain*] (Beirut: Éditions de la Revue Phénicienne, 1987), 53–54.

[6] Paul Morand, *Méditerranée, Mer des Surprises* (Paris: Éditions du Rocher, 1990), 206.

Jewish community for a very long time. A reality attested to by Lebanese Jews and others. A reality that still seeps out of the recollections, regrets, and yearnings of Lebanese Jews and others, some of whose personal testimonies are featured in this volume.

During a 1937 visit by judeophile Maronite Patriarch Arida to a Jewish community center in Beirut, community president Joseph Farhi bragged about the age-old Jewish connection to Lebanon. "For us Jews," noted Farhi, "our attachment to Lebanon is not a modern phenomenon";

> It has existed for thousands of years. Already Moses solicited God's favor to see the promised land—the enchanting Lebanon. Later our biblical poets celebrated the marvelous sites, the majestic cedars which Solomon preferred for building the Eternal Temple. Time has not diminished our attachment to the land which we inhabit; [it] has nothing but fortified our feelings of loyalty and devotion to Lebanon, which in our days, following the example of its glorious ally France, is maintaining rights and a regime of liberty and justice for all its citizens without distinction of race or confession.[7]

Jewish connection to Lebanon was therefore seen in a biblical light; a theme trotted out in literary and political motifs emanating from early twentieth-century Maronite intellectual circles, but also in journalistic renditions of Lebanese Jewish history as featured in the community's early twentieth-century mouthpiece *Al-Aalam al-Isra'iili* (the Lebanese Arabic-language rendition of *L'Univers Israélite*).[8] But in its modern incarnation, the Jewish Lebanese kinship was also the outcome of a number of ideological, political, and cultural circumstances specific to the complex communal makeup of Lebanon itself, and in that context, the Lebanese Jews' conceptions of themselves, their country, and their countrymen were not very much unlike those of other Lebanese communities.

---

[7] Kirsten E. Schulze, *The Jews of Lebanon: Between Coexistence and Conflict* (Brighton, UK: Sussex Academic Press, 2001), 39.

[8] *L'Univers Israélite* was a monthly—later a weekly—Jewish magazine, established in Paris, 1844, by Simon Bloch, a French writer and future secretary of the *Alliance Israélite Universelle*. The Lebanese version of the journal simply borrowed the publication's French name, otherwise remaining independently owned by Lebanese Jews, and acting as the community's main Arabic language newspaper.

Even in the Zionist vision of future inter-state relations—following the anticipated establishment of a Jewish home in Palestine—perceived the Jews of Lebanon differently, seeing in them a community that enjoyed a particularly secure position in its home country that was at odds with the tenuous conditions of Jews elsewhere in a Muslim-dominated Middle East.

LEBANON'S POLITICAL JEW

Likewise, enthusiasm for Zionism varied within Lebanon's Jewish community, and evidence suggests that the country's Jews were by and large more invested in local politics than in what was going on further south in British Mandatory Palestine. And just as they enjoyed cultural and commercial representation incommensurate with their small numbers—being among the most successful of Lebanon's merchant classes—the Jews of Lebanon also exerted significant influence in local political affairs. This, however, is not to suggest that Lebanese Jews were disinterested or unconcerned with the goings on in British Mandate Palestine of the early twentieth century, or in the calamities lurking in their coreligionists' future in Europe and the Middle East.

Still, like other Lebanese communities, the Jews of Lebanon enjoyed a high level of independence and freedom in the practice of their cultural, educational, and religious rituals. And although they often remained restrained and aloof from Lebanon's sectarian politics and tried to maintain a low political profile, they did participate in the country's electoral squabbles, and both Christian and Muslim Lebanese political parties did actively court and receive their support. In those instances, the community often leaned more sympathetically toward the Christian—especially the Maronite—political camp, with many well-to-do Jewish families sending their children to Christian and Maronite schools, even though the bulk of the community frequented the *Alliance Israélite Universelle* schools—a system that was by and large uninterested in Zionist activities in Palestine.[9] More importantly perhaps, Jewish surnames were practically indistinguishable from Lebanese Christian (sometimes even Muslim) names, abounding in Stamboulis, Malehs, Mallahs, Chahines, Hassouns, Attiés, Salamés, and Srours.

[9] Norman Stillman, *The Jews of Arab Lands in Modern Times* (Philadelphia and New York: The Jewish Publication Society of American, 1991), 89–90.

Still, even though Lebanon's Jews did not feel particularly vulnerable—many of them, for instance, traveling extensively along the Beirut-Jaffa coastal corridor exchanging regular visits with family members in British Mandate Palestine—they *did* "play it safe," straddling both the Maronite and the Muslim worldviews. The overwhelming majority of the Lebanese Jewish leadership, even those with Zionist sympathies, maintained a somewhat fuzzy stance vis-à-vis the Zionist enterprise, seldom adopting active pro-Zionist positions. Still, under Maronite cover, the Jews of Lebanon raised money for the *Yishuv*, fought anti-Jewish hostility in the local Muslim press, committed to a distinctly Maronite vision of Lebanon, and during the 1940s and 1950s, namely after the establishment of the State of Israel, hid Jewish refugees within the community, and worked with segments of Lebanese authorities to facilitate safe-passage of Jewish refugees to British Mandate Palestine, and later Israel.[10]

Yet Lebanese Jews themselves had little desire—and indeed expressed rare inclinations—to immigrate to Palestine.[11] And although the *Yishuv's* Jewish Agency did maintain relations with Lebanon, its strongest contacts were mainly Christian, not Jewish Lebanese. The rationale of this approach might have been to avoid endangering the Lebanese Jewish community's standing with Lebanese Muslims, who were already overwhelmingly hostile to a distinctly "Lebanese" national project, let alone a Zionist one in Palestine. More importantly perhaps, the Zionists of the *Yishuv* did not need the assistance of the Lebanese Jewish community, given the intimate relations that they already had with the country's Maronites.

Modern Lebanon is arguably the Middle East's only mountainous haven for minority populations where, until very recently, Muslims and Arabs have been numerically inferior to and culturally less dominant than non-Muslim communities.[12] Meir Zamir has noted that by the time Lebanon was established in 1920, it had become for all intents and purposes a national homeland to the Middle East's largest non-Muslim population—particularly, Christian populations. "Maronite political, economic, social and numerical dominance," Zamir has observed, was foundational to Lebanon's very existence, and "the Maronites were the

---

[10] *L'Orient*, "La chaine des attentas continue" (Beirut: November 3, 1957).

[11] Kesrouan Labaki, "De bons libanais," *Le Soir* (Beirut: February 29, 1952).

[12] Meir Zamir, *The Formation of Modern Lebanon* (Ithaca and London: Cornell University Press, 1985), 5–6.

driving force behind the Lebanese national movement; it was thanks to their efforts that the Lebanese state was established in 1920."[13]

Other "Lebanese" on the other hand, in the main Sunni Muslims, but also some Greek Orthodox Christians, remained for some time reluctant to join into a "Lebanese" entity as it was then defined. Some, especially among the Sunnis, resented their incorporation into the nascent Lebanese state, which they had deemed not only "Christian," but *also* artificial—as opposed to a larger, ostensibly more "natural" Syria, which, with its over-whelmingly Sunni population, had been their lodestar. For the Sunnis,

> Their incorporation in Lebanon involved [...] a grave religious, cultural, polit-ical, and economic crisis and a powerful emotional blow. For the first time in their history they were a minority in a Christian state. [...] For Muslims, the role of the state is to implement and defend the shari'a (religious law.) The Sunnis in Lebanon could therefore never fully identify with the Lebanese Christian state set up and guaranteed by a foreign Christian power.[14]

It follows from the above, that geographically and demographically speaking, Lebanon is strikingly different from the countries of its neigh-borhood, including Syria, Israel, and Egypt. Aside from the country's Sunni population, Lebanon's minority communities were never particu-larly enthralled with the idea of Arab nationalism and the notion that the Lebanese people were somehow, organically or emotively, beholden to their neighbors by bonds of Arabness, Arab culture, Arabic lan-guage, and Arab history. Indeed, among Beirut's and Mount Lebanon's minority populations—especially the Christians among them—rare were those who viewed themselves or were viewed by others as Arab. In fact, the Maronite Catholic community, although indigenous to the region and hailing from an ancient stock of Syriac-Aramaeans, considered itself a sanctuary of Christendom—and Western Christendom at that—in a Muslim-dominated East where Muslims themselves were exogenous interlopers. To the Maronites, Lebanon was a "little piece of France," as it were, on the seawalls of the Levant, guarding Christendom. Confirming this prevalent attitude of the times, a nineteenth-century French traveler depicted the proud Maronites, in the midst of "Ottoman barbarity," as "the sons of the elders of the masters of the universe";

[13] Zamir, 5.
[14] Zamir, 126.

children of ancient Phoenicia.[15] Other travelers wrote in a similar vein
noting that elsewhere in the Ottoman Empire the highlands and hillsides
were like deserts:

> dreary and silent; [their] rocks bare, [their] soil almost barren. But here on
> the other hand, on this [Maronite] spot of Mount-Lebanon, life seems to
> pulsate more vigorously. And as one gazes over the crops covering the diz-
> zying slopes of this mountain, it is almost unavoidable to not take note of
> the robust, fearless breed of little children swarming about, growing up in
> these happy villages, eager to take on the toils and crafts of their forefathers.
> Here on this mountain, the Lazarist fathers had established in the midst
> of these villages a number of schools where young Maronites were taught
> the rudiments of Classical Arabic, Syriac, French, and Italian. These fine
> institutes of learning are of particular importance to the Maronites. In these
> provinces [of the Ottoman Empire,] where despotism often wallows and
> drowns in ignorance, these colleges are a powerful and progressive harbor
> of civilization and learning. I can still recall with great emotion the thrills
> of a day I spent at the Antoura monastery. As I entered the grounds, I was
> overwhelmed by the beautiful courtyard of this place, shaded as it was by
> giant lush orange trees, giving way to an open-space terrace commanding a
> breathtaking view of the Mediterranean Sea below. There, some seventy to
> eighty young boys frolicked noisily, playing ball in the shade of those trees,
> their beautiful intelligent eyes animated, sparkling with passion. I could
> hear them quarreling and shouting in French—a scene that gave me pause,
> leaving me in awe, crouched behind a doorway, seized with profound emo-
> tion. This "little France," hidden in the confines of the Lebanese moun-
> tains, in the midst of a barbaric empire, touched me to the very depths of
> my soul, filling me with bewilderment and admiration. I had just crossed
> the Dog River below, having spent some time prior in the midst of mot-
> ley Arab villages. Yet, here, at Antoura, I was suddenly back in the depths
> of my own childhood, engrossed in the games and pursuits of my youth,
> thousands of miles from Paris. Yes, here, I could hear my own school-bells
> ringing, calling students back to work. Here I could savor the sounds of my
> own language, in the shade of Lebanon's orange-trees, at a stone's throw
> from the Cedars of Solomon. [...] The times of the Crusades have long
> since gone away; but it seems to me that it is a question of national honor
> for us Frenchmen to never abandon these Christians of the Near East, chil-
> dren of an ancient race, reaching out to us, wishing to embrace us.[16]

---

[16]Charles Reynaud, "Catholiques et Français, Toujours!" in *Le Voyage en Orient*, 771–72.

[15]Vicomte de Vogüe, "Voyage au Pays du Passé," in *Le Voyage en Orient; Anthologie des
Voyageurs Français dans le Levant au XIXème Siècle* (Paris: Robert Laffont, 1985), 778.

In a sense, this was a description of Lebanon and the Lebanese as a challenge to their neighborhood; as a geographic, topological, cultural, and sociological oddity in an otherwise oppressive Ottoman dominion deemed homogenous and uniform. In Lebanon, wrote French politician and historian Comte de Volney in 1784, it was easy to forget that one was in the midst of the Ottoman Empire, because people in Lebanon were quite different from others in the region.[17] As one of the most renowned early Western travelers to the East, Volney provides an important anthropological portrait of the Lebanon of his times. Nothing was trivial and nothing was unworthy of being recorded in Volney's travelogue. From people's habits, to peculiarities of language, food, and drink, to geographic details and agricultural methods, and from architectural features to local industries and weather patterns, nothing escaped Volney's flattering paintbrush when it came to Lebanon. It was "un pays délicieux" (a delicious country), he wrote, and a "charming little province."[18] Within his recollections, Maronites and Druzes seem to have been the only groups that mattered and merited mention, and Volney's admiration of both communities was hardly concealed. He specifically referred to the Maronites as a distinct, majestic, and enterprising nation and compared their attachment to their ancestral soil and their manifest *esprit de corps* to those of European nations. Conversely, Volney described the Ottomans as "pernicious and marauding," trying to stifle the autonomy and spiritedness of the Maronites. "The Maronite peasants," he wrote, indeed,

> the [Maronite] nation in its entirety is agrarian; everyone of its members tills in his own hands the little domain that he possesses and holds dear. Even the [feudal lords] themselves live in that same manner. They all live in frugality, bereft of many comforts, but they do not live in penury. Needless to say, they lack many of modern life's luxury items. In general, the [Maronite] nation is modest, but none of its members are needy. And if one happens to come across paupers, chances are they originate in the coastal towns, not in the country [of Mount-Lebanon] itself. Private property [in Mount-Lebanon] is as sacrosanct as it is in Europe. Here [in Lebanon] the

[17] Jean Raymond, "Le Liban: Terre Traditionnelle de Liberté; Textes Commentés, Tirés des Récits des Voyageurs Occidentaux du 16ème au 18ème Siècles," *Cahiers de l'Oronte*, Number 7 (Beirut: 1967), 16.

[18] Jean Raymond, 14.

looting and injustice, so commonplace in the lands of the Turks, are nonex-
istent. One can travel through Lebanon by day and by night, in a safety and
confidence unknown in the remainder of the empire.[19]

In Volney's eyes, not only was physical Lebanon a geographical mar-
vel to behold and a challenge to its neighborhood, it was more importantly a refreshing cultural, sociological, ethno-religious, and political
oddity in the Ottoman dominions of the East. In that sense, Volney's
narrative often referred to "Syrians," "Lebanese," and "Maronites" as if
interchangeably, distinguishing them from the dominant "Turkish" and
"Arab" ethnos of his times.

In a similar vein, early twentieth-century Maronite Catholic jurist and
political thinker Jacques Tabet used such terms as "Lebanese," "Syrian,"
and "Phoenician" interchangeably, but never in apposition to "Arab,"
and never to mean "Arab." Syria and Lebanon, he wrote in 1915, are
no more Arab than they are Ottoman; indeed, they are nothing if not
Phoenician, he claimed, and their

history and geography attest to that undeniable reality. Today, their aspi-
ration is to become once again their true selves and to live their own
independence and specificity. [... Alas,] the Muslim element in Syria will
only reluctantly consent its separation from Arabia. [...] This reluctance is
born less out of feelings of Arab kinship than fears of sharing power with
non-Muslims [...] Yet this is by no means a feeling shared by all Muslims,
across the board.[20]

Similarly, early twentieth-century Lebanese intellectual and author of
Lebanon's first constitution, Michel Chiha, wrote that,

The Lebanese Mountain is a spiritual sanctuary. All of the ethno-religious
minorities who live there [...] have found in these high mountains a refuge
from oppression, and a haven for freedom. [...] The mystique of Lebanon
is in the fact that its Mountain was gradually populated by restless people,
by hunted people. [... The Lebanese] are a breed of mountaineer-naviga-
tors, markedly different form those nations that surround [them.][21]

[19] Jean Raymond, 16.

[20] Jacques Tabet, *La Syrie; Historique, Ethnographique, Religieuse, Geographique,
Economique, Politique et Sociale* (Paris: Alphonse Lemerre, 1920), 29.

[21] Chiha, *Visage et Présence*, 147 and 166.

Likewise, in a 1919 letter from the Buenos Aires chapter of the *Union Libanaise* addressed to then French Foreign Minister, Aristide Briand and soliciting his support for the establishment of an independent Lebanese entity, one could read what amounts to a history lesson, beginning with the following sweeping introduction:

> On the shores of the Mediterranean Sea, at the gates of this distant Orient, which has for so long transfixed the Superpowers' attentions, one can find in the midst of disparate peoples a small and steadfast nation, vigorous and determined, distinct form those who surround it: this nation is the Lebanese Nation. Its origins are quite removed in time. The Lebanese are in fact descended form the ancient Phoenicians; the latter, having extended their highly evolved civilization throughout their then known world, at a time long before today's great nations had ever come into being. Assembled in the framework of autonomous communities, the Phoenicians lived according to their own laws and their own customs, under the governance of their own local princes. Through their long history, they were subjected to the suzerainty of Rome and Byzantium, as well as to that of the Arabs, the Crusaders, the Sultans of Egypt, and the Ottoman Turks. Yet, they were able to preserve their own distinct customs and national attributes.[22]

[handwritten: Similarities to Israel come to mind here, for me.]

Thus, the ancient Phoenicians were depicted as the forefathers and progenitors of the modern Lebanese, whose ethnic and cultural authenticity was never diluted or altered by the series of conquerors, whether Romans, Arabs, Turks, or others, who remained outsiders to the nation. Lebanese-American historian Philip Hitti noted that modern presidents of the Lebanese Republic may legitimately recognize as ancestors and equals such counterparts as French High Commissioners, Ottoman Governors, Arab Administrators, Crusader Princes, Byzantine Envoys, Roman Potentates, as well as Assyrian, Babylonian, Egyptian, and Phoenician rulers.[23]

[handwritten: Again, this seems similar to the story of the Jews, in a sense.]

[22] A 1919 Memorandum from the Buenos Aires chapter of the Union Libanaise, MAE, Levant 1918–1940, Syrie-Liban, Volume 17, Série E. Carton 313, Dossier 27.

[23] Philip Hitti, *Taarikh Lubnan* [*The History of Lebanon*] (Beirut, Lebanon: Dar al-Thaqafa, 1985), 4–5. Note this is the Arabic translation of Hitti's English language *Lebanon in History* and will be referred to herewith under that title, not *The History of Lebanon*.

Along those same lines, a letter by another Lebanese diaspora lobby, addressed to the same French Foreign Minister argued that "the Lebanese do not belong to the same ethnicity as the Arabs," and that there was never any kind of ethnic fusion between them and the Arab conquerors; "as successors of the Phoenician Civilization, and as heirs to Greco-Roman culture, the Lebanese betrayed greater affinities to the [Mediterranean] West than to the peoples of the hinterland whom they have outpaced in culture and civilization by many centuries."[24]

Such were the realities and nomenclatures of the early twentieth century, when Arab consciousness and Arab nationalism were still inchoate concepts utterly divorced from the Middle East's, and more specifically Lebanon's prevalent parameters of selfhood. Consequently, Middle Eastern events, peoples, and concepts of that period, which today are often anachronistically referred to as "Arab," meant something entirely different in the late nineteenth and early twentieth centuries. What some might have prematurely deemed and labeled "Arab movements" in 1914, wrote André Duboscq, "were no more than the expressions of local parochial visions that are hardly in concord with the varied identities of the Levant [...]; Yemen, Najd, Baghdad, and Syria are not about to march under a single banner, for the sake of Arab dominance and sovereignty," he stressed.[25] Duboscq's comments echo Lawrence of Arabia's characterization of the notions of an "Arab nation" or an "Arab people" as spurious constructs imposed on a part of the world where identities are millennial, varied, elastic, and diverse.[26]

Lebanon's distinction in the past hundred years of its modern political history has dwelt in the fact that it viewed itself—and was recognized by others—as a mosaic of ethno-religious groups and a federation of minorities. Within this context, the native Maronite Catholics, armed with a long historical association with Europe, and particularly with Catholic France—the Elder Daughter of the Church—have benefitted since the times of the Crusades from official French protection. And so, in addition to their clear sense of a distinct identity, it had been this strong association with France that differentiated Lebanon's Christian communities—at least in terms of their political behavior—from the rest of

---

[24] A 1921 Memorandum from the *League for the Defense of Greater Lebanon's Rights.* MAE, Levant 1918–1940, Syrie-Liban, Volume 17, Série E. Carton 313, Dossier 27.

[25] André Duboscq, *Syrie, Tripolitaine, Albanie* (Paris: Librairie F. Alcan, 1914), 5.

[26] T. E. Lawrence, *Seven Pillars of Wisdom*, 33.

their coreligionists in other parts of the Middle East and the Ottoman Empire before the emergence of the modern 1918 state system. Even post-revolutionary, anti-clerical, secular France had remained committed to Lebanon's Catholics and supportive of their autonomist streaks.

It is within this context that the Jewish community of Lebanon developed into modern times. Scholars working on the Jews of Lebanon have generally attributed the community's "privileged" status in modern Lebanon to a combination of factors, the most important of which were the Ottoman *Tanzimat* reforms of the late nineteenth century, and the *Imtiyazat* privileges accorded by European powers—namely France—to non-Muslim minority communities in the Levant, Lebanon in particular. These changes, especially the rapid urbanization of large swaths of Lebanese communal groups toward the end of the nineteenth and the beginning of the twentieth centuries, played an important role in the revitalization of Levantine port cities, and by association non-Muslim minority communities already attuned to the cultural and linguistic conflations of the Mediterranean basin. These changes certainly affected and transformed the Jews of Lebanon, throwing them in the cauldron of diversity, cosmopolitanism, and hybridity that were the port cities of the Mediterranean.

This was the universe of Lebanese Jewry. Within it, there seems to have been a "natural bond" between Jews and Maronites. The Jewish community contributed to Maronite charities, attended Maronite functions, sent its children to Maronite parochial schools, maintained close relationships with the Maronite political and clerical leaderships, and most importantly perhaps, were conspicuously present and active in distinctly Maronite political parties.[27]

And so, the Jews of Lebanon found their closest allies among Lebanon's *Young Phoenicians*, a group of mainly Maronite intellectuals and political activists who saw Lebanon and Lebanese identity as

---

[27] As will become clear in the personal testimonies in later chapters, Lebanese Jews were active members of the Christian Social Democratic (Kataëb) party. Likewise Jewish graduates of the *Alliance* schools—whose curricula did not go beyond sixth grade—regularly attended the *Lycée Franco-Libanais* (which was part of the French *Mission Laïque* in Lebanon) or more commonly the *École de la Sagesse* (a flagship of the Beirut Maronite Catholic Archbishopric) and the *Collège Saint-Joseph Antoura* (the Near East's first Jesuit mission, first established in 1651, later ceded to the local Maronite Lazarists in 1773, after the Jesuit Suppression).

the progeny *not* of "the recently arrived Arab conquerors," but of the Canaanite-Phoenicians of classical antiquity, friends and allies of the Biblical Israelites, builders of the Temple of Solomon in Jerusalem.[28] During the 1930s, a Maronite political party called the Social Democratic Party, known colloquially as the *Kataëb* or *Phalanges libanaises*, became the leading Lebanese political organization advancing a "Phoenicianist" vision, and attracting an openly Jewish membership. As the end of the British Mandate in nearby Palestine loomed near, and as trouble seemed imminent, radicalizing Lebanese Muslims and imbuing them with a new "zeal" for Jew-hatred, Lebanese Jewish youth began enlisting in the ranks of the *Phalanges*, in droves, to receive rudimentary military and self-defense training. Indeed, during the 1948 war over Palestine, both Jewish and Maronite members of the *Phalanges* party took on the responsibility of protecting Lebanon's Jewish quarters from Arabist and Muslim reprisals. This would remain the case through the 1950s and 1970s, when Arab nationalist and anti-Jewish demonstrations became a staple of Muslim Lebanese political life.[29]

It was in the main Maronite Lebanese nationalism, and its vocal rejection of Lebanon's putative Arab identity, that drew the Maronites and Jews closer to each other. Maronites believed in a Western-oriented, politically sovereign and militarily strong and self-reliant Lebanon, dominated by a Christian worldview, and separate from the rigid nationalist models emanating from the Arab Muslims of the neighborhood. But the Maronites were divided among themselves over the future of Lebanon: Some factions believed in total divorce from the Arab world; others pushed for an *entente cordiale* with Lebanon's Muslims and advocated for a power-sharing arrangement that would recognize Lebanon's inevitable "coming to terms" with the neighborhood's changing demographics and an imminent "triumph" of an Arabist "narrative" of modern Middle Eastern history.

Still, the Maronite advocates of "Phoenician"—as opposed to later "Arab" or "Arabized" Lebanon—were the ones who were to maintain and nurture a commitment to the Jewish cause, both in Lebanon proper and within the confines of British Mandate Palestine. Albert Naccache, a

---

[28] Charles Corm, *6000 ans de genie pacifique au service de l'humanité* (Beirut: Éditions de la Revue Phénicienne, 1988), 31–32.

[29] *L'Orient*, "Le Cas des Libanais Israëlites" (Beirut: February 29, 1952).

Beiruti engineer who belonged to the *Young Phoenicians* circle, was one representative of that group of Maronites. An ardent Zionist sympathizer who grew up in the hybrid cosmopolitan circles of aristocratic Beirut, Naccache fell in love and ended up marrying a young Zionist activist while studying in Europe. Upon returning to Lebanon, he held important positions in the Lebanese government under French Mandate, and as he mingled with the times' Phoenicianist crowd, he ended up meeting Eliyahu Epstein (the Jewish Agency's representative in Lebanon) subsequently introducing him to the poet Charles Corm, a close friend of Naccache's and the guiding spirit behind the *Young Phoenicians* movement. Corm and Epstein would remain friends for many years to come, maintaining an active correspondence schedule, frequently visiting each other, traveling regularly along the Beirut-Haifa-Jerusalem highway, and taking special interest in each other's national projects—the Zionist and the Lebanese.[30]

As mentioned earlier, the *Young Phoenicians* argued that the Lebanese, and specifically the Maronites, were the rightful heirs of the ancient Phoenician mariners of classical antiquity, and therefore, that the Phoenician civilization—one indigenous to Lebanon—preceded and superseded that of the seventh century Arab invaders. Therefore, the *Young Phoenicians* sought to restore this Lebanon of their yearnings to its ancient Canaanite heritage and establish a state with cultural foundations based on a millennial history tied to the Mediterranean rather than to the "realms of sands and mosques" in the East.[31] Charles Corm and his group even advocated for the revival of the Phoenician language as the indigenous ancestral tongue of the Lebanese, to replace the motley languages that "troubled and tormented" Lebanon's saturated linguistic repertoire; "Grief, O grief, O unspeakable grief" began one of Corm's poems on the topic,

> Once upon a time, our grand-parents spoke, Syriac at Ghazir, / Syriac, where the Phoenician's flair, / Their vigor and finesse, / Are still extant today; / Alas, no one today, / Can fancy finding shades / Of our grandparents' footsteps, / In the shadow of old vines; / The bygone language

---

[30] See, for instance, Charles Corm Archives; letters between Corm and Eliahu Epstein dated January 25, 1938; February 22, 1938; March 3, 1938; April 26, 1938; Beirut, Lebanon: Charles Corm Archives.

[31] Camille Abousouan, "Présentation," in *Les Cahiers de l'Est* (Beirut, Lebanon: July 1945), 3.

of yore, / Is choked for evermore, / In our muzzled scrawny throats. / And now our Mountain, / Ever kind to her sons, / Beholds its splintered skies / Riven by the sounds, / Of foreign Western tongues; / It is a bitter clash / That ails and torments her / With quarrels and heartaches. / For, languages like Italian, / Like English and like Greek, / Like Turkish and Armenian / Clutter and jam her voice, / While she willingly yields / To the sweet Tyranny / Of the language of France...[32]

And so, reviving the Lebanese' national and linguistic consciousness, and directing them toward the Phoenicians' heritage and away from the Arabism that was in the early twentieth-century beginning to take hold of some Lebanese Maronite elites became the *Young Phoenicians'* mission. Some dubbed their ideology "Lebanese Zionism,"[33] and their Jewish sympathies and close ties to both the *Yishuv* and the Lebanese Jewish community certainly contributed to validating that comparison.

Many Zionist figures from the *Yishuv* made frequent trips to Beirut in the early twentieth century, and quite a few of them became fixtures at Charles Corm's weekly *Amitiés Libanaises* cultural gatherings, to which the "who is who" of Lebanon's intellectual elite, many of whom hailed from the country's Jewish community, came to partake of the opulent cultural scene on display. These trendy and much-coveted weekly gatherings featured a number of eminent local and international political and intellectual figures—among them Pierre Benoît, Paul Valéry, Eliahu Epstein, Charles Plisnier, Paul Morand, and F. Scott Fitzgerald to name only those.

Among the scholars and intellectuals of the *Yishuv* who took part in these gatherings were the Hebrew poet Haim Nahman Bialik and author Rachel Ben-Zvi—both of whom were personal friends of Lebanese Jewish community leader Joseph Farhi. Other names included those of Semitist and archaeologist Nahum Sloucshz, and sculptor Chana Orloff, the latter a mutual friend of Charles Corm and Marc Chagall.[34]

---

[32] Charles Corm, *La Montagne Inspirée* [*The Hallowed Mountain*] (Beirut: Éditions de la Revue Phénicienne, 1987), 101.

[33] Zittrain Eisenberg, *My Enemy's Enemy*, 65.

[34] Charles Corm Archives; letters from Eliahu Epstein dated May 6, 1935 and January 25, 1938. In the 1938 letter, Epstein informs Corm that Nahum Slousch was currently "out of Jerusalem but is expected back next week. On his arrival I shall discuss with him the matter [of giving a lecture in Beirut] in a more definite fashion and will let you have details."

During a 1933 talk at the *Amitiés Libanaises*, Zionist leader and diplomat Victor Jacobson, who had business interests in Beirut (and possibly with Charles Corm himself, who at the time owned and operated Ford Motors dealerships in Haifa and Jerusalem), spoke of the Biblical relationship between King Solomon and the Phoenician King of Tyre, Hiram, the builder of Temple of Jerusalem. This talk drew enthusiastic applause from the Lebanese audience, a reception that was indeed a reflection of the affection that many in Charles Corm's Phoenicianist circle exhibited toward the Jews of classical antiquity and their modern descendants in both the *Yishuv* and Lebanon proper. Indeed, Charles Corm himself, a few years later, would name his own two newborn sons David and Hiram—the former after Corm's own father *and* King David, and the latter a namesake of aforementioned King Hiram of Phoenicia.

Many Lebanese Maronites and Jews furnished great efforts during the early twentieth century to give concrete political expression to their cultural affinities. Indeed, one of the early Presidents of Mandatory Lebanon, Emile Éddé, a close friend of Charles Corm, who feared Arab irredentism, advocated for a positive alliance with Jewish Palestine, so as both Maronites and Jews would be able to protect their political interests and their shared coastal regions from impending "Arab expansionism." In this context, in 1935, Patriarch Arida, along with senior Maronite clerics, met with Zionist leaders to discuss the creation of a "Lebanon-Palestine Society"—a *bon voisinage* or "good neighborly relations" idea proposed by Charles Corm— in order to serve as the basis of future formal diplomatic ties.[35] These talks went on into the late 1930s, and Charles Corm himself is claimed to have drawn up the "legal governing document" of the society in question.[36]

However, the aims of that group never came to pass. By 1939, the world was already in the throes of a new global conflagration, and other immediate concerns stood in the way of local Maronites and Jews and their mutual relations. The Lebanon Mandate had by 1941 fallen under British control—so as to prevent Vichy France from gaining a foothold in the Levant. This threw the Maronite community in turmoil, splitting it between Britain's "Arabist" sympathies and the weakened French "minorities" policies that had initially privileged the Maronite narrative. And so the Lebanon of Charles Corm and the *Young Phoenicians* would

---

[35] Eisenberg, *My Enemy's Enemy*, 73 and 89–90.
[36] Eisenberg, *My Enemy's Enemy*, 73 and 89–90.

be dealt a devastating blow—and with them "Jewish Lebanon" whose gambit had been the Maronites' own would fall into disarray.

CONCLUSION

The instinct of both the Maronites and the Jews in Lebanon to identify and nurture a concordance of interests was neither misplaced nor faulty. That this commonality of interests was never consummated in a Lebanese entity reflecting both groups' visions remains an unfinished chapter in their communal and national chronicles of regrets.

In a 1946 Letter addressed to Chaim Weizmann, Maronite Patriarch Antoine Pierre Arida wrote that,

> the Maronites have always looked affectionately and with great sympathy to the Jewish Nation and are very sensitive to the interest that the Jews have taken in Lebanon's own national struggles. It goes without saying that the Maronites' relations with the Jewish Nation have always been founded in the spirit of justice and humanism. [...] It is from this premise that we shall always pursue friendship and cooperation with the Jewish community.[37]

Those feelings were echoed within the Lebanese Jewish community; one Lebanese resident of Jerusalem, who had "left" Lebanon *only* because she had met her future husband while on an earlier trip to British Mandate Palestine, noted that when she headed south, from Beirut to Jerusalem, she had no idea a Jewish state would be born, and that the borders between the nascent Jewish state and Lebanon would be sealed off in an overnight:

> [When I left Lebanon] I did not take anything with me besides my wedding gifts. I thought I would go back on weekends to visit my family. [But this was never to be.] Yet, I always longed to go back to Beirut. Then [1967 happened, and] my mom came to live with us. But she too regretted leaving Beirut. All of us still remember Lebanon with love.[38]

This sentiment is echoed in more, similar personal recollections and ruminations revealed in this volume of "memoirs" and "fragments

---

[37] Eisenberg, 163, Letter from Antoine Pierre Arida to Chaim Weizman, May 24, 1946.

[38] Schultze' interview with Vicky Angel (1995), in *The Jews of Lebanon*, 69.

of lives arrested." Among those are the memories of an exiled septuagenarian Lebanese Jew who currently lives in Montreal: Remembering his childhood, Moïse fondly evokes images of his physician father making regular visits from Beirut to Haifa, where he kept a local clinic and regular consultation hours. The trips were as commonplace as they had been charming for a young boy walking in his father's footsteps, eying the "family business," riveted by the ebbs and flows of a Mediterranean along which he had trekked back and forth throughout his childhood. "It was our way of life" recalled Moïse, "and we hadn't the faintest idea that my father would one day be prevented from keeping his office hours in Haifa, and that our trips would cease."[39] This was 1948. Yet, in spite of having left Lebanon in 1967, some twenty years after the trips to Haifa had stopped, that image of fluidity and movement along the coastal highway of the eastern Mediterranean never left the grown-up doctor that Moïse, the child of 1948, had become: "This Lebanon is always with me; I still dream of this Lebanon; I still remember my house; our street, the temple, my girlfriends, our travels along the coastal road…"[40]

These yearnings remain as commonplace among Lebanon's Maronites and Jews today as they might have been during the formative years of the nascent Lebanese and Israeli states. And so, this tale is not ended in this count of odd events and peoples and ideas Middle East. Even though this halcyon Jewish-Maronite vision may deform our modern perspectives, even as it may seem to be the stuff of fairy tales, there were real affinities between Jews and non-Jews in the Middle East of the modern era, and Lebanon did offer a template for meaningful Jewish life *outside* of Israel and *outside* of the devalued existence that is the norm for non-Muslims in "Muslim lands."

It is the aim of these *Fragments of Lives Arrested* to bring to life a Jewish experience in the Middle East that, for a fleeting moment in time, provided an alternative to narrow conceptions of the region as volatile, dogmatic, monochromatic, and parochial. Yet, this book is also a summons to Lebanon and the Lebanese, on the centennial anniversary of the establishment of modern Lebanon, to "redeem" themselves, bring back from oblivion and restitute a suppressed and forgotten facet of their history.

---

[39] Franck Salameh, Interview with Moïse S. [last name omitted at the request of respondent] (Boston, MA, 2014).

[40] Salameh's interview with Moïse S.

CHAPTER 3

Lebanese Jewry: Memory Fragments

Le souvenir d'une certaine image
n'est que le regret d'un certain instant;
et les maisons, les routes, les avenues,
sont fugitives, hélas, comme les années

Marcel Proust (1871–1922)

A great deal was written in the late twentieth century about Maronite–Jewish and Israeli–Lebanese relations. Namely, there is much in the literature on the furtive fitful "alliance" that tied Lebanese Christians to their southern Jewish neighbors during the days of the Lebanese wars of 1975–1990 and even earlier flirtations going back to the pre-state period during the 1920s and 1930s.

But beyond passing references, often in the context of Zionist–Christian or Israeli–Maronite relations, during and immediately following the French Mandate period (1918–1946), the literature strictly speaking on the Jews of Lebanon remains scant, fragmentary, and restricted in scope. Two major, seminal works come to mind in this respect: Kirsten Schulze's excellent *The Jews of Lebanon*, which was researched some two decades ago and may be in want of some updating; and Tomer Levi's *The Jews of Beirut*, published more recently in 2012, but as its subtitle suggests, a work limited to "*The Rise*" of the Beirut Jewish community during late Ottoman times and the early French Mandate period. More importantly, Levi's work focuses primarily on four major themes in the development of Beiruti Jewish life, which he describes as "migration,

© The Author(s) 2019
F. Salameh, *Lebanon's Jewish Community*,
https://doi.org/10.1007/978-3-319-99667-7_3

commerce, cultural diversity, and philanthropy."[1] By contrast, the present volume focuses on both "the rise" *and* "fall" of Lebanese Jewry, and primarily so in the context Lebanese Jewish–Christian—and to some extent Jewish–Muslim—relations. And so, the inquiry into the lives and times of the contemporary Jews of Lebanon *does* indeed reveal some lacunae and consequently *does* merit—even requires—wider expansion, further development, and deeper analysis.

Therefore, this chapter mines an early history of modern Lebanon by placing a special focus on the country's Jewish community and examining inter-Lebanese relations where Lebanese Jews took center stage. This is done in the wider context of this volume primarily by giving voice to personal testimonies, family archives, private papers, recollections of expatriate and resident Lebanese Jewish communities, as well as rarely tapped archival sources: namely the relevant Lebanese press of the early twentieth century, the archives of the Maronite Patriarchate in Mount-Lebanon, personal papers in the diaspora, archives of the World Jewish Congress, and private collections (and recollections) in Lebanon proper *and* the Lebanese Jewish diaspora whose testimonies might have been previously thought not distinctly germane to conventional historical inquiry.

From the outset, I must make clear that I am not a specialist of the Jews of Lebanon. Historian by formation, my area of concentration is modern Middle Eastern intellectual history and history of ideas, and the bulk of my work has dealt primarily with Lebanon and the role that Lebanese Christians might have played in the establishment of the modern Lebanese Republic (*Grand Liban*, 1920). And so, I have worked extensively on early twentieth-century Lebanese nationalism—namely the Phoenicianist and Lebanonist intellectual currents—where Jewish history and Biblical references have loomed large in the national imagination and political writings of Lebanon's "Young Phoenicians" circles—i.e., the Lebanese nationalists of those times.

While recently working on an intellectual biography of an early twentieth-century Lebanese nationalist and "Young Phoenician" luminary, Charles Corm (Lexington Books 2015), I came across a rich collection of unpublished materials within Corm's private papers, where multiple references were made to a Biblical Jewish-Phoenician alliance, and by

---

[1] Tomer Levi, *Jews of Beirut: The Rise of a Levantine Community, 1860s–1930s* (New York: Peter Lang Publishing, 2012), xii.

association modern Maronite–Jewish affinities during the formative years of the modern Lebanese republic. These fragmentary hints became my main goad to begin investigating matters further.

Charles Corm himself, in his private memoirs and correspondence, spoke with much affection and with a great deal of nostalgia and enthusiasm about Lebanon's millennial Jewish community. Upon further dredging of the sources, other archival evidence began showing that, not unlike Lebanon's Christians, the Jews of Lebanon were heavily invested in the idea of the nascent Lebanese Republic as a "confederation of minorities" rather than as an "Arab state" in the making.

Lebanon's Jews, therefore, revealed themselves to have played an important role—albeit perhaps a discreet and low-pitched one alongside the country's more vocal Christians—in the establishment of modern Lebanon as it came into being socially, culturally, and politically during the first half of the twentieth century. However, this all too important "Jewish story," and its "Jewish voices" seem to have been left out of traditional history books.

What might have contributed to this "muting," or "suppression" of Lebanese Jewish voices can be attributed to the rise of Arab nationalism during the 1940s and 1950s, the establishment of the state of Israel in 1948, the residency that Hajj Amin al-Hussayni—one of the most strident anti-Semitic Arabist bullhorns—took up in Lebanon during that time, and the subsequent resurgence of anti-Semitic sentiment throughout the Middle East—even though Lebanon's Jewish community itself had grown markedly in size and influence, and even in stability prosperity and security, after 1948.

But changing fortunes regionally, the pressures that the Arab League was beginning to exert on a militarily weak Christian-dominated Lebanese entity that wasn't wholeheartedly committed to Arab causes, and the intimidation and hectoring of local Arab nationalist operatives active in Lebanon beginning in the early 1950s (engaging in activities often veering into violence and physical attacks on Lebanese Jewish interests and persons) all these led to the onset of the "quiet muffling" of Lebanese Jewish voices, culminating in the "silent exodus" of the community's members, the suppression and erasure of their history, and ultimately the dwindling of their numbers into a handful of families by 1967. After all, the liquidation of Middle Eastern cosmopolitan societies had been a generational feature of an Arab nationalism dedicated to cultural homogeneity. In Egypt, this meant the destruction of old venerable Italian, Greek,

French, and Christian Syro-Lebanese communities—in addition to a millennial Jewish society—that had once constituted the core of Egyptian culture and its urbane ecumenical way of life. In the second half of the twentieth century, Arab nationalism's assault turned to Lebanese cosmopolitanism: Lebanon's non-Arab heritage had to be extirpated; its most immediate targets were the Jews; their expulsion was a natural order of things; a given of Arab nationalism; and by 1967 the near-destruction of Lebanese Jewry was all but complete. Most of those Lebanese Jews remaining today are at best "museum curiosities," living in dissimulation and seclusion, often marrying into Christian families, and slowly committing their Jewish heritage and identity and contributions to oblivion.

A VISION OF MODERN LEBANON WITH THE JEWS IN IT

But things have not always been so. The Jews of Lebanon had their pride of place within the Lebanese mosaic and its body politic. Unlike non-Israeli Jews elsewhere in the Middle East, Lebanese Jews did not fall under the *dhimmi* status; they were not subject to the legal restrictions imposed by Islam; they did not experience the degrading treatment or discriminatory policies suffered by minorities elsewhere under Muslim rule. And so the wager of Lebanese Jews had been on maintaining Lebanon as an independent, sovereign, multicultural "haven of minorities"—a neutral "Levantine" intermediary and cultural conduit unencumbered by the Arabs' identity politics and the resentments of an Arab–Israeli conflict in the making, and accordingly, a Jewish identity more in tune with the ideas, cultural accretions, and politics advocated by Lebanon's dominant Maronite community.

This Lebanon, noted in 1936 Pierre Gemayel, leader of the country's largely Maronite Social Democratic party (known colloquially as the *Phalanges*),

> our Lebanon, the Lebanon of the Phalanges, is neither Greater Lebanon, nor is it merely Mount-Lebanon. Our Lebanon is the Lebanon of an illustrious history, a Lebanon 6000 years young. It is the Lebanon of the early Lebanese who came to this land in order to till it into the homeland of liberty and freedom, the homeland of humanism, the homeland of all of those ancestors of ours who were smitten by a lust for sovereignty and freedom. Lebanon is not a Christian country; nor is it a Muslim or a Jewish country for that matter. Lebanon is not merely a piece of territory;

nor is it only a constitution. Lebanon is the stuff of dreams, it is the stuff of human conscience and spiritedness and kindness. And it is in this spirit of Lebanon's that we have conceived our own principles of being Lebanese.[2]

The significance of this quote stems of course from its allusions to the Phalanges' valorization of Lebanon's multiplicity and diversity and hybrid pedigree, placing the Jews as a chief ingredient in this varied cultural melting-pot. In a sense, Gemayel was upholding an otherwise numerically miniscule community as "first among equals" within the constitutive elements of Lebanese society and its ethno-religious makeup. But this quote of Gemayel's is likewise important because the Phalanges, an otherwise predominantly Maronite political group, proudly counted within its ranks (and boasted) a large number of Jewish members: Lebanese Jews, in communion with Lebanese Christians, who advocated for a distinct "Lebanonism"; an essentially secular multiethnic multi-confessional, and in Gemayel's telling a "humanist" interpretation of Lebanese identity, that could not be defined as exclusively "Arab" without misleading and distorting.

Within this context of humanism and multiplicity and cultural diversity, and paraphrasing Charles Corm himself, the country's leading "Phoenicianist" intellectual at the time, in *this* Lebanon of the Jews, the enigmatic Druzes rubbed shoulders with the Maronite Catholics, the Melkites bickered with the Armenians, and all in turn trafficked, feuded, and reconciled with Syriacs, Gregorians, Latins, Jacobites, Sunnis, Shi'ites, and Israelites (the Jewish community's legal name under the Lebanese constitution then). Yet each of these groups remained at once Lebanese in its own way—each different and distinct from the other, yet all so much alike.

It was within this setting that Lebanon's ancient Jewish community came into the twentieth century. And it is no coincidence that *this* Lebanon itself had been a natural home and a safe harbor to this vibrant ancient Lebanese group, with even the Lebanese state in later times of trouble, both actively and legally protecting Lebanese Jews from Arab nationalist and Arab Palestinian reprisals. During a 1937 visit by judeophile Maronite Patriarch Antony Peter Arida to a Jewish community center in Beirut, community president Joseph Farhi bragged about the

---

[2] Jacques Nantet, *Pierre Gemayel* (Paris: Éditions Jean-Claude Lattès, 1986), 173.

age-old Jewish connection to Lebanon. "For us Jews," he said, "our attachment to Lebanon is not a modern phenomenon";

> It has existed for thousands of years. Already Moses solicited God's favor to see the promised land—the enchanting Lebanon. Later our biblical poets celebrated the marvelous sites, the majestic cedars which Solomon preferred for building the Eternal Temple. Time has not diminished our attachment to the land which we inhabit; [it] has nothing but fortified our feelings of loyalty and devotion to Lebanon [as a land] of liberty and justice for all its citizens without distinction of race or confession.[3]

Arida himself reciprocated these sentiments on multiple occasions, privileging the Jews of Lebanon. As will become clear in this narrative, it is not without reason that Arida was referred to fondly in Lebanese Jewish quarters as "the Patriarch of the Jews." "The Maronites have always looked affectionately and with great sympathy to the Jewish nation," famously noted Arida, "and [we] are very sensitive to the interest that the Jews have taken in Lebanon's own national struggles... [our] relations [...] have always been founded in the spirit of justice and humanism [... and it is] from this premise that we shall always pursue friendship and cooperation with the Jewish community."[4]

In more concrete terms, Lebanese Jews—their small numbers notwithstanding—were invariably, civil servants, school teachers, university professors, physicians, and leading members of the liberal professions and merchant classes. They were also soldiers in the Lebanese Armed Forces, active members in Lebanese political parties, and all around full participants in the country's bustling cultural, social, intellectual, and political life. Their representation in the Lebanese Parliament, or in the leadership of local political parties, not as salient or discernible as one might expect, may be attributable to their importance in the country's commercial and economic sectors, their position in the main as merchants (and therefore as intermediaries), and consequently their reluctance to be in the political limelight and in the midst of partisan bickering, which in Lebanon often involved Christians opposed to

---

[3] Kirsten E. Schulze, *The Jews of Lebanon; Between Coexistence and Conflict* (Brighton: Sussex Academic Press, 2001), 39.

[4] Charles Corm Archives, *Letter from Antoine Pierre Arida to Chaim Weizmann* (Lebanon: Bkérké, May 24, 1946). See also Eisenberg, 163.

Muslims.[5] And so, Lebanese Jews were content with their representation in Parliament being in conjunction with the country's Protestants—another numerically small community—with their seat traditionally held by a Protestant representing both "Israelites" and "Other Minorities." Yet there were at times impulses within the community to take on a more active political role. In 1937, community leader Joseph Farhi pressed then Lebanese President Émile Éddé for a distinctly Jewish seat in Parliament. Éddé, a known Zionist sympathizer, jokingly told Farhi at the time that "the Jews were already very well represented in Lebanon; 'I am (said to be) a Jew',," quipped Éddé, as were Jewish his Minister of Interior Habib Abi-Chahla and Prime Minister Kheireddine el-Ahdab—both of whom were reportedly present at that meeting, and neither of whom were Jewish.[6] Yet, five years earlier, Lebanese Jews were already clamoring for fair and fitting representation in government. The community's periodical *Al-Aalam al-Isra'iili* noted in an early 1932 editorial that recent censuses revealed the numbers of Jews to exceed 6000 in Lebanon, "the largest among the country's smallest communities."[7] "It is our right to be represented by an Israelite deputy," stressed the article, "as six years have already elapsed since the Lebanese Republic and its new Constitution came into being, and the representative of the Israelite community is still someone chosen from another community [traditionally a Protestant...] The least we ought to expect from our government is an Israelite representative in the Lebanese House of Representatives to speak in our names, protect our interests, and safeguard our rights. [...] But we shall revisit this crucial question," concluded *Al-Aalam al-Isra'iili*, "and we do hope that this lapse in judgment on the government's side is only temporary, and unintentional."[8] A few weeks later, *Al-Aalam al-Isra'iili* published

---

[5] The leader of the Phalanges Party, Pierre Gemayel, a traditional protector of Lebanon's Jews, feared that their departure would lead to the collapse of the Lebanese economy. His fears were of course exaggerated. Nevertheless, his sentiment was reflective of both the importance of the community—at least among certain sectors of Lebanese society—and the emotive attachment that some Lebanese politicians had vis-à-vis the Jews. See, for instance, Fred Anzarouth's, *Les Juifs du Liban*, http://www.farhi.org/Documents/JuifsduLiban.htm.

[6] Schulze, *The Jews*, 56. Incidentally, Habib Abi-Chahla was a Greek Orthodox, and Kheireddine el-Ahdab a Sunni Muslim.

[7] *Al-Aalam al-Isra'iili*, "Jews in Lebanon Are the Largest Minority" (Beirut, Lebanon: February 19, 1932), 1.

[8] *Al-Aalam al-Isra'iili*, "Jews in Lebanon Are the Largest Minority" (Beirut, Lebanon: February 19, 1932), 1.

another article on this topic, reassuring readers that the Lebanese Council of Ministers is "dealing with this matter with utmost responsibility, determined to designate a Jewish 'guardian angel' for the Jewish community."[9]

Regardless, Lebanese Jews were part and parcel of, and indeed leading figures in, Lebanon's cultural, social, and intellectual life. Some of their more recognizable names included Yfrah Neaman (1924–2003) a gifted musician and world-renowned violinist who was a native of Sidon, and Guy Béart (b. 1930), singer-songwriter and father of French actress Emmanuelle Béart, whose passion for music was nurtured in the Lebanon of his childhood where his parents had taken refuge after their expulsion from Egypt. Worth mentioning also is Dr. Nessim Chams (1900–1969), known locally as "the healer of the poor"—a compassionate physician who lived true to his Hippocratic oath, operating a series of health clinics along the Beirut–Haifa coastal road, tending to the ill often free of charge, and treating Christian, Muslim, and Jewish patients in equal measure.[10] Other figures of note also included Eliyahu Salim Mann (1872–1969) and Toufic Mizrahi (1898–1974) who were leading Lebanese Jewish journalists of the twentieth century. Mann founded and edited the Lebanese Jewish community's first Arabic language periodical to be published in Greater Lebanon beginning in 1921. *Al-Aalam al-Isra'iili*, the newspaper's name, an Arabized title of the older prestigious French *L'Univers Israélite*, would remain the voice and conscience of an assertive ascendant Lebanese Jewish community until 1948. But the establishment of the State of Israel would signal the beginnings of the changes of fortunes of Lebanese Jewry—circumstances which will be elaborated in subsequent sections of this volume.[11] Mizrahi

---

[9] *Al-Aalam al-Isra'iili*, "An Israelite Deputy in Lebanon's Chamber of Deputies" (Beirut, Lebanon: March 4, 1932), 1.

[10] Magda Abu-Fadil, "Lebanon's Jews: Loyalty to Whom? BBC Documentary Tracks Vanished Community," *The Huffington Post* (September 26, 2010), http://www.huffingtonpost.com/magda-abufadil/lebanons-jews-loyalty-to_b_739583.html.
This is also confirmed in the personal testimony of Nessim Chams's own son, Dr. Moïse Chams, shared with the author in November 2014.

[11] To wit, the Arabic title *Al-Aalam al-Isra'iili*, an otherwise innocuous apolitical translation of the French *L'Univers Israélite* (or the "Israelite Universe") became problematic, in Arabic, with the establishment of a Jewish state christened "Israel." Suddenly the "Israelite Universe" came to connote the "Universe of the Israeli State" in Arabic imaginations and in bruised Arab nationalist self-worth, even though for centuries prior, the Arabic term "*Isra'iili*" meant "Israelite" and caused no more problems than the term "Yahuudi" (Jewish) might have. But given the lack of an Arabic designation differentiating "Israelite"

on the other hand would become founding editor of the prestigious *Le Commerce du Levant* in 1929, which remains to this day the preeminent French-language economic magazine of the Middle East.

Lebanon's cultural life was also graced by Jewish activity and prominent Jewish names. To wit, Edouard Sasson was General Manager of the Metro Goldwyn Mayer Studios Middle East Branch, and served in that position for twenty-five years, until his assassination at the hands of Palestinian terrorists in 1970.[12] Sasson helped transmit the golden age and glamour of Hollywood to the Beirut cultural scene, contributing to turning Lebanon into a world-class destination for the jet-setting glitterati of the 1960s and 1970s. Actors like Peter O'Toole, Omar Sharif, Ginger Rogers, David Niven, Françoise Dorléac (the elder sister of Catherine Deneuve), Kim Novak, Brigitte Bardot, and Ann-Margaret, among others, were Lebanese fixtures, and the Sasson Beirut home often played host to them and local dignitaries. Lebanon reaped great benefit as a prime cultural and tourist attraction in the process, thanks in no small part to Sasson's prestige, connections, energy, and urbane savvy.

Likewise, Lebanese Jews were at the heart of Lebanon's urban bourgeoisie, bringing vitality and energy into the country's commercial lifeblood—most notably with the Safra and Zilkha banking families who, for all intents and purposes, helped turn Lebanon of the early twentieth century into one of the world's leading financial and banking hubs.[13] Indeed, Lebanon's reputation as the "Switzerland of the Middle

---

from "Israeli," and given the etiolation of Lebanon's presumptive role as a Middle Eastern "federation of minorities" and the rise of the tides of Arab nationalist fervor, one can only imagine the anxieties that the term "*Isra'iili*" might have elicited for Lebanese Jews, and the animus—even violent backlash—that it spurred in anti-Zionist Lebanese and their foreign Arab nationalist co-conspirators and enablers.

[12] *The Spokesman-Review*, "Top Lebanon MGM Man Found Shot" (Beirut, Lebanon: The Associated Press, March 1, 1970), https://news.google.com/newspapers?nid=1314&dat=19700301&id=1rMyAAAAIBAJ&sjid=YOsDAAAAIBAJ&pg=211 9,307840&hl=en.

[13] Schulze, *The Jews*, 5–6.

East"—owing no doubt the sobriquet at least in part to its climate and snowcapped mountains and the multiplicity of its languages and ethno-religious groups all crammed in a geographically constrained space—was surely also due to the country's banking system and its laissez-faire economy, sectors in which Lebanese Jews commanded a role incommensurate with their relatively small numbers.

Equally importantly perhaps, the Jews of Lebanon, who in modern times were almost in their majority the product of the *Alliance Israélite Universelle* schools (with main campuses in Beirut and Sidon), were instilled with a strong sense of civic duty and loyalty to country; they were "overtly tepid and covertly hostile to Zionism," remarked a prominent historian of Oriental and Sephardic Jewry.[14] Indeed, the *Alliance*'s philosophy had been one of "integration," inculcating into its charges French republican values and love of country, and the adoption of local cultures in addition to the valorization of French culture, language, and history—as in fact had been the case with all of France's other secular and religious educational missions, in Lebanon and elsewhere.[15] In a 1920 address to General Henri Gouraud, High Commissioner and representative of the French Mandate in Lebanon, the director of the *Alliance* school of Beirut, M. Danon, made this "republican mission" of his institution evidently clear. He noted that in places and countries where Jews were traditionally ostracized and severed from the benefits of civilization, the *Alliance Israélite Universelle* "was always at the forefront of bringing Jews, but *not only* Jews, children of other communities as well [Christians and Muslims in the case of Lebanon,] the benefits of French knowledge and French learning."[16] In so doing, stressed Danon, the *Alliance*'s instrument had been discernably French, "an instrument that had proven its worth; a French language that is an incomparable vehicle of generous ideas and noble sentiments. [In that sense,] the *Alliance* is a missionary of civilization as elaborated by way of the French language, French methods, and the French spirit."[17] The pastoral mission of the *Alliance* concluded Danon,

[14] Norman Stillman, *The Jews of Arab Lands in Modern Times* (Philadelphia and New York: The Jewish Publication Society of American, 1991), 89.

[15] Stillman, *The Jews*, 89–90.

[16] *L'Univers Israélite*, "Le Général Gouraud aux Écoles de l'Alliance Israélite à Beyrouth," Paris, Volume 75, Number 30, 469.

[17] *L'Univers Israélite*, "Le Général Gouraud," 469.

is to form and train free human beings, conscious of their duties vis-à-vis others, never discriminating against others, and never distinguishing themselves from others except in their moral qualities; [the mission of the Alliance is] fighting evil by way of an army of good people, whose only aim remains achieving the greatest amount of good in this world and to the benefit of all mankind.[18]

This certainly contributed to the respect and place of honor that Lebanese Jews had earned within the Lebanese family. But their privileged status, living a *primus inter pares* kind of Lebanese existence, also had historical justification stemming from the history of the Maronites. Indeed, modern Lebanon under the Maronites, unlike neighboring state formations outside of Israel, was a non-Muslim republic, ruled by a self-reliant intractable non-Muslim majority that never thought of itself as a minority in the "world of Islam," and that was never treated as a chattel of the *Umma*. In point of fact, during times past, rather than paying tribute to the Umayyads of Damascus, Lebanon's Christians—Maronites in particular—boasted having exacted tribute from Muslim rulers in return for keeping their turbulent recalcitrant Mountain population tame. The Maronites' independent tenacious nature, wrote one observer, and "their military achievements were upsetting (even destabilizing) to the Umayyad rulers [...] Their goal was [not merely to defend their mountain citadel from Muslim encroachments, but indeed] to reverse the New Order of the region by obliging the Arabs to withdraw [back] to the[ir] Peninsula."[19]

It is upon these biases of diversity, openness, national hubris, and a—real or imagined—history of sovereignty and vitality and vigor, that the Maronites enshrined a modern Lebanese republic—a bulwark, as it were, preserving their own specificity, and an instrument of their dreams and aspirations from which *other* minorities could also draw solace and security. And so, unbeholden to Arab obsessions and their *causes célèbres*, and dedicated to a distinct Lebanese identity, they opted for a "communion of fates" among minorities, *with* the Jewish

---

[18] *L'Univers Israélite*, "Le Général Gouraud," 469.

[19] Walid Phares, *Lebanese Christian Nationalism: The Rise and Fall of an Ethnic Resistance* (Boulder-London: Lynne Rienner Publishers, 1995), 33.

community in tow—*and* alongside other like-minded components of their nascent republic.

CHANGING TIMES, CHANGING FORTUNES

But the cultural and political honeymoon that had been Lebanon—not only for Lebanese Jews, but also for the Lebanese in general who had opted to remain outside the Arab nationalist orbit—was a short-lived one indeed. The 1950s proved challenging to those who did not toe the traditional Arab line, who did not noisily flaunt or feign Arabist credentials, and who did not commit rhetoric, manpower, and lip service to the Arabs of Palestine and those espousing their cause.[20]

The price that Lebanon and Lebanon's Maronite establishment (and by association those who embraced the Maronites' vision) had to pay for their recalcitrance was a dear one indeed: two civil wars, one in 1958 and another in 1975 the effects of which still linger to this day; large-scale emigration and changing demographics; and more importantly loss of sovereignty and the transformation of Lebanon from a vaunted "Switzerland of the Middle East," a vibrant commercial, cultural, and intellectual entrepôt, a state that had never officially been at war with anyone let alone Israel, to a lawless gateway for motley "rejectionists," international criminals, petty revolutionaries, irregulars, and other armed bands waging the Arabs' proxy wars—against each other *and* Israel—from and *on* Lebanese territory.

But the Lebanese who bore the brunt of those changing fortunes were the Jews, even though the Maronites would soon follow. After all, the Arabic adage "first Saturday, then Sunday"—with its ominous

---

[20]Note that that *cause célèbre* of the Arab nation, that is to say the "Palestinian cause," was not referred to by those terms in Arabic and Arab nationalist discourse until at least 1969. Those Arabs of British Mandate Palestine who left or were expelled from their homes after the establishment of the State of Israel in 1948, were referred to in Arabic as "Arab Filisteen" ("the Arabs of Palestine") or "Arab Thamaaniya w Arbra'een" ("The Arabs of Forty Eight") and not Palestinians as such. See, for instance, this 1969 Thames Television documentary, *Lebanon, Middle East, Road to War,* for a statement on the history, evolution, and meanings of the term "Palestine" and "Palestinian." Note in this documentary, not a single time, in neither of English or the Arabics used throughout, was the term "Palestinian" used, or used to mean "Arab" exclusively. In English, "Palestinians" are invariably referred to as "Palestine Arabs" and "guerillas," and in Arabic, they are "Fedayeen" and "resisters." https://www.youtube.com/watch?v=N2rj5QcM5xY.

Muslim triumphalist connotations suggesting "first we dispose of the Jews, *then* we come for the Christians"—this patently religious apocalyptic exhortation, trotted out by ostensibly "secular" Arab nationalist revolutionaries, had its first run in Lebanon of the second half of the twentieth century. This was long before there was anywhere in the world anything resembling an ISIS establishing a Caliphate and reinstating *dhimmi* laws regulating the unequal patterns of relationships between Muslims and others.

In a predatory Middle East, where Ham striking Shem and Japheth had been a custom for generations upon generations, Lebanon stood, perhaps for a fleeting moment in time, as an exquisite exercise in tolerance and pacifism and diversity and multiplicity. But that exercise was perhaps vain optimism, doomed to failure from its inception. The late Fouad Ajami noted in this regard that one needed not be overly old or nostalgic to recall with affection a multicultural Lebanon; a Lebanon where eighteen different communities jostled and feuded for power and influence and relevance—where Lebanese beholden to the creed of Arab nationalism met their match in "Lebanese who thought of their country as a piece of Europe at the foot of a splendid mountain mimick[ing] the ways, and savor[ing] the language of France."[21] Alas, in Ajami's telling, these relatively innocuous feudings of old were child's play compared to the hell that would soon be visited on Lebanon in the name, and for the sake, of Arab nationalism.[22] Those who dismissed Lebanon's hybrid Levantine heritage "and looked Eastward to Syria, and the bigger Arab world" for identity and memory and inspiration, those who sauntered and swaggered preachifying the canon of Arab nationalism triumphed in the end, and the Lebanon of the varied cultural and human composition, the open, humanistic, pacifist, diverse Lebanon was made to succumb to the Middle East's atavisms and the vain zealotry of a resurging Arabism.[23]

And that's where the last chapter in the life-saga of Lebanese Jewry would begin.

---

[21] Marius Deeb, *Syria, Iran, and Hezbollah: The Unholly Alliance and Its War on Lebanon* (Stanford, CA: The Hoover Institution Press, 2013), xiv–xv.

[22] Deeb, *Syria, Iran, and Hezbollah,* xiv–xv.

[23] Deeb, *Syria, Iran, and Hezbollah,* xv.

THE NOT SO *NIFTY FIFTIES?*

The 1950s for Lebanon began with the resignation of President Bechara El-Khoury and the ascent to power by Camille Chamoun; the first two Maronite presidents of post-independence Lebanon who could not be more at odds with each other in vision and temperament and in design and ambition for the country. Khoury was a pragmatist, an accommodationist Christian, an architect of the country's infamous National Pact, which essentially spawned the young state's system of power-sharing between Muslims and Christians. Khoury's National Pact likewise bestowed upon Lebanon an "Arab face," safeguarding for the country's Christians—albeit tenuously—their vaunted specificity and the "non-Arab" character that they professed. It also assuaged the country's Muslims—who were never really enamored of the "idea" of Lebanon as a sovereign entity separate from the Arab world—palliating them with the notion of a state with an "Arab complexion" in solidarity with the neighborhood's dominant culture.

Chamoun on the other hand, a "revisionist" nationalist, would espouse an unapologetically Western-oriented trajectory, promoting Lebanon's discretely "Lebanese identity," setting his administration at loggerheads with the region's Arab nationalists and their passions, provoking in the process the indignation of local Muslims, and laying the groundwork for the future conflicts that would ensue over Lebanon's identity and its place in the "Arab world."

This decade, the 1950s, would also coincide with the settlement on Lebanese soil of some 300 thousand Arab refugees from the defunct British Mandate Palestine. This would entail an alarming demographic shift that would further fuel the fires of Lebanon's identity politics, as most of the refugees were Sunni Muslims in tune with Lebanon's own Sunnis in their devotion to Arab causes and an "Arab Lebanon" *tout court*—rather than the one with its spurious "Arab face." In later years, an exquisitely representative slogan of this culture negating Lebanon's *raison d'être*, one brandished proudly by the Palestine Liberation Organization, became "the road to Palestine passes through Jounié and Tarshish"—the names of a coastal city and a mountain village in the center and north of Lebanon, both with predominantly Christian populations, both in the polar opposite direction from the actual "road to Palestine."

Thus would the fires of Arab nationalist activism begin consuming the country, assailing its Christian foundations and symbols, dismantling the "confederation of minorities" that the Maronites had put in place, and hurling a polity that had stayed on the sidelines of the Arabs' grievances, into the middle of the Arab–Israeli conflict. This also meant that Lebanon's Jews would now be offered as sacrificial lamb, to be burned at the altar of Arabism in oblation and atonement for the losses visited by an "arrogant" upstart "Jewish entity"—a "foreign body," as it were, germinating where an "Arab state" should have taken shape.

In the beginning of the 1950s, Arab nationalist sloganeers, stunned and stunted as they had become by the spectacular defeats dealt them by a nascent Israel, were largely left hectoring and grandstanding from Lebanon. They were unable to face their Israeli tormentor head-on on the battlefield. They were likewise unwilling to sit at the negotiating table. So they opted to seek retribution from one of Lebanon's "weakest links," the country's apolitical, tiny Jewish community.

Yet the Lebanese state and its spokespersons and representatives did attempt a defense—of themselves primarily, but of their Jewish citizens as well—and they did issue firm public rebukes at the manner and method of local Arabist agitators. But the "Christian state" was weak and muzzled by that time, and the Arabist provocations would not relent. And so, in early winter 1951, as Arab nationalist partisans were busying themselves harassing members of Lebanon's Jewish community, the response came swiftly and caustically from one of the country's most talented francophone pens at the time. A founding member of the "Young Phoenicians" group, a close associate of Charles Corm's, a co-author of the 1926 Constitution upon which Lebanon's multiethnic coexistence formula was founded, and by 1951 one of the country's leading political thinkers and "cerebral" journalists, Michel Chiha's castigation came unremitting. His defense of Lebanon's Jewish community was an impassioned tribute to Israel's accomplishments—a tongue-in-cheek takedown of Arab and Arabist resentments and misdirected retaliations in face of steadfast Israeli triumphs and Lebanese Jewish diligence, loyalty, and integrity of character.

Israel is moving apace, wrote Chiha on the pages of Lebanon's leading French-language daily Le Jour in February 1951, while Arabs and Arab nationalists still languish in old resentments and unsated dreams of retribution. Chiha's reprimand was clearly directed at Arab nationalism and its preoccupation with matters of atavistic interests rather than dynamism and movement and progress and improvement. But his immediate target was the Lebanese government itself, its laxity vis-à-vis the Arab nationalists' violations of Lebanese sovereignty, and the impunity with which Arabists tormented Lebanese citizens who didn't share their views, or didn't dance to their tunes—namely Lebanon's Jewish community, which like the country's Christians, preferred to remain aloof from the disputes pitting Arabs and Israelis.

Large segments of Chiha's text deserve being reproduced in their entirety here, as they are an exquisitely representative specimen of the enigma that was the Lebanese social, political, and intellectual climate at the time. Likewise, it offers a glimpse into Israel's own advancements juxtaposed to the Arabs' regressions and bitterness. "Israel's population has already exceeded 1.7 million," wrote Chiha;

> Our neighbors to the South are moving forward at breakneck speed, and the massive effects of immigration are adding tremendously to other local conditions favorable to Israel's high birth rate. [...] We ought to pay our respects to this, Israel's powerful urge towards living, and being alive. [...] In what is being written herewith, in the stress that we are placing on the admiration and unease that Israel's accomplishments may inspire, there is neither envy nor resentment. [...] Let us think about this for a while: Israel has generated a worldwide immigration process; worldwide material, intellectual and moral support; Israel benefits from an unparalleled work ethic and an eagerness to serve; it is imbued with a mystique saturated with ambition and love of land and earthly goods; Israel's virtually unlimited range of expertise in the art and practice of technology and innovation is mind-blowing; Israel's efficient presence in all of the crucial ventures of this planet, and the beautifully selfless work that it puts forth in all fields are all awe-inspiring. [...] We learned recently that three Jewish personalities appointed to administer major branches of Israel's Ministry of Industry and Trade refused to be remunerated for their service. In other words, instead of plundering this vital sector of their society [as politicians on our side of the border take pride in doing], they served their government free of charge, and they lived within their means, regardless of the modesty of those means. Such is the virtue and high ideal of true citizenship; such is the sublime lesson of religious, political and social conviction. There is, in all of this, the glowing primary ingredients of greatness. [...] Meanwhile... meanwhile,... we praise ourselves **not** on account of the activities and accomplishments of our men in power, but on their indolence and lethargy and deceit. [...] We go on living and thinking in obsolete archaic notions, in the fatal laziness of bygone centuries. The best of the Lebanese, the most gifted among them, in all fields possible, are scarcely up to the task at

hand. Let us not forget this painful reality if we do not wish this country of light to lapse into the twilight.[24]

But Chiha was blowing in a broken bagpipe. The assaults then being mounted against Lebanon's Jewish citizens were on the rise, deliberate, methodical, and multi-thronged, making effective use of anti-Semitic propaganda, leveling false accusations against the Jews and bolstering deception gambits with physical attacks. One such instance of these sorts of tactics came in the form of multiple articles, printed in a number of Arab nationalist media outlets in the early 1950s, claiming that the *Alliance* Jewish school in Beirut had its campus walls plastered with posters of David Ben Gurion, Israel's first Prime Minister. *Bayroot al-Masa* of January 25, 1951, for instance, ran a headline that read "A Picture of Ben Gurion Graces the *Alliance* School."[25] The paper further wrote in its lead story that

> Mr. Izzeddin al-Baydarane, a civil servant in the City Beirut Municipality, affirms having seen in his own two eyes multiple posters of the Israeli Prime Minister, the so-called Ben Gurion, hanging in the classrooms of the Alliance Israélite School in Beirut. Beirut al-Masa wonders, where is the Inspector of the Ministry of National Education in all of this? Why does he not visit this school and witness how the sanctity of the homeland is being violated? Where is [Minister of Education] Ra'iif Bellamaa in all of this, a Minister who claims that all foreign schools are subject to rigorous government inspections?[26]

The claim was of course pure unfounded defamation. The school director Elie Slivert was quick to deny it, writing to the editor of the newspaper the following morning, that the allegations about pictures of Ben Gurion being displayed at the *Alliance School* were "utter nonsense and falsehood":

> The pictures in question are those of the great French Jurist, René Cassin, current President of the Paris-based Alliance Israélite Universelle. Furthermore, I wish to draw your attention to the fact that our institutions are dedicated to the education of Lebanese citizens, teaching them love

---

[24] Michel Chiha, "Progression d'Israël," *Le Jour* (Beirut, February 24, 1951).

[25] *Bayroot al-Masa*, "A Picture of Ben Gurion Graces the *Alliance* School" (Beirut: January 25, 1951).

[26] *Bayroot al-Masa*, "A Picture of Ben Gurion."

of country and inculcating in them noble republican values, which in turn make of them loyal citizens of their country. Therein dwell the supreme goal and mission of our schools.[27]

But the dye was cast. The Jews of Lebanon were stuck in the whirl-wind of the Arab nationalists' defamations. And when defamation did not work, physical violence followed. There were even attempts by Arabist elements in the Lebanese Parliament itself to legalize perse-cution as official state policy vis-à-vis the country's Jewish citizens. In one instance, during a debate in the Chamber of Deputies in February 1952, representative of the Chouf Mountains and Deputy of the Druze dominated Socialist Party, Emile Boustany, slipped into an anti-Semitic rant (perhaps representative of his "Arab Socialist" constituencies and his own Protestant origins and Presbyterian formation),[28] demanding that the Lebanese government take strict measures against the coun-try's Jews "who are natural allies of the State of Israel and who, amaz-ingly, still have unhindered freedom of movement within Lebanon."[29] When reminded by his parliamentary colleagues that "Lebanon [was] a democracy and a country of laws and tribunals," and that discrimi-natory laws specifically targeting Lebanese Jews "who are subject to, and indeed enjoy, the same constitutional rights and the same legal protections as any other members of any other Lebanese community," Boustany stormed out of the Chamber, and in the foyer of the assem-bly house resumed his attacks against fellow parliamentarians who opposed him, screaming at the top of his lungs, accusing his colleagues of high treason. "The Jews here," he claimed, "have nothing Lebanese about them except their national identity cards; they are crypto-Israelis, equally Israeli as the inhabitants of Israel proper. That is why it is abso-lutely incumbent upon the Lebanese authorities to initiate measures against them so as to limit their ability to harm the state."[30]

---

[27] *Bayroot al-Masa*, "Letter to the Editor" (Beirut: January 27, 1951).

[28] Although the Boustany's of the Chouf Mountain are overwhelmingly Maronite, Emile Boustany's ancestros converted to Protestantism were all products of American education, primarily at the Syrian Protestant College (later the American University of Beirut), ultimately falling under the spell of Arabist sympathies.

[29] *L'Orient*, "Le Cas des Libanais Israélites" (Beirut: February 29, 1952).

[30] *L'Orient*, "Le Cas des Libanais Israélites."

Representatives of the Phalanges, who came to the defense of the Jews in Parliament—as they had done all along on the streets and on the pages of their newspapers—deemed it "regrettable that the loyalty and patriotism of the Jewish members of the Lebanese family be put into question, and that the Parliament tolerate that such absurd diatribes be allowed in its Chamber."[31] "Lebanon is a land of liberty and freedom, and must remain so for all of its citizens," stressed the deputies of the Phalanges, and such actions by misguided parliamentarians, "aimed at disfiguring and deforming Lebanon's face, and seeking to compromise our national unity, ought not be permitted on the Parliament's floor."[32]

It is interesting to note here that when accused of racism by his parliamentary colleagues, Boustany retorted with a patently anti-Semitic argumentation, which went as follows:

> Hear me out please, this is not a question of religion. I must tell you up front that Jesus-Christ himself was Jewish. My objection is to the Zionist Israelis (sic.) I know, and all of you know, that the Jews of Lebanon, like Jews everywhere else in the world, are Israeli agents, paid by Israel, and doing Israel's bidding.[33]

Although Boustany's offensive discourse was countered with vehement objection in the Chamber of Deputies, it may be said that Lebanon as a whole was split over the question of Lebanese Jews, with the great majority of vocal Arab nationalists following Boustany's lead and translating his inflammatory language into violent deeds, and with the great majority of Lebanese nationalists—in the main Phoenicianists and Lebanonists, and among them many Muslims—taking up the defense of the Jews and mounting an aggressive media and information campaign against their tormentors.

The Syrian Social Nationalist Party, for instance, with its openly anti-Semitic doctrine and its Arab nationalist leanings, took Boustany's defense, skirting the same racist diatribes that he had himself touted as

---

[31] *L'Orient*, "Le Cas des Libanais Israëlites."

[32] *L'Orient*, "Le Cas des Libanais Israëlites."

[33] *L'Orient*, "Le Cas des Libanais Israëlites" (sarcastic interjection and parentheses in the original text).

"common knowledge." In its organ newspaper, *Sada Loubnan*, the SSNP noted that

> Wherever they go, wherever they reside, the Jews never assimilate into another national community; they always opt to remain a separate group within their host societies. Today, given that they have created an independent state in Palestine, a state that is at once religious and racist, all of the world's Jews now consider themselves connected to this new homeland, to this promised land, even as they might have acquired the various citizenships of their current countries of residence. [...] It is therefore a duty incumbent upon the Lebanese government to keep a close watch on the Jews who, there is no doubt, constitute an Israeli fifth column.[34]

This sort of screed would become a salient feature of Arab nationalist public and "intellectual" discourse in Lebanon for years to come and long into the 1960s. But going back to the 1950s and to the Émile Boustany affair (sarcastically dubbed *"le problème d'Émile"* or "Émile's Problem" in some journalistic circles),[35] perhaps the coup de grâce dealt this case came from journalist and (otherwise) friend of Boustany's, Kesrouan Labaki. Labaki was a committed Lebanonist, who as Chief Editor at *L'Orient* in 1949 had to serve a brief prison sentence for having dared publish an editorial denouncing Arab nationalism and excoriating the Lebanese National Pact that had "codified" the mantra of Lebanon's "Arab Face."

In February 29, 1952, in a *Le Soir* editorial titled *They are Damn Good Lebanese*, Labaki lambasted Boustany and his allies: "Everybody knows the solid friendship that binds me to Mr. Boustany," began Labaki's piece;

> I have nothing but respect for his person. However, the position that this deputy of the Chouf Mountain has taken vis-à-vis the Lebanese Jews—and I stress here 'Lebanese Jews' and not 'Jews of Lebanon'—his position is unbecoming of his person, to say nothing of the fact that no clear-sighted Lebanese patriot can ever bring himself to accepting such a deviant attitude. Émile Boustany wants to exact revenge from the Lebanese Jews! Why? Why, because Israel allegedly refuses to grant the right of return

---

[34]Reproduced in *L'Orient*, "Avec Émile Boustany" (Beirut: March 1, 1952).

[35]This is perhaps an allusion to Jean-Jacques Rousseau's, *Émile or the Treatise on Education*.

to Arab refugees. Well, likewise Émile Boustany refuses to distinguish between Israelites and Israelis. In his view all Jews—the Jews of America, the Jews of Europe, the Jews of the Arab world, as well as the Jews of Lebanon—are all, if not Israelis, then at least Zionists. 'When all the Jews of the world deem themselves first and foremost citizens of Israel,' claims Boustany, 'there is no objective reason to believe that the Jews of Lebanon are an exception, and that they, therefore, consider themselves Lebanese first and foremost.' Well, to accept such perverse reasoning, one must be able to first prove that indeed all Jews are Zionists. For our part we do not subscribe to this mode of thinking. […] Furthermore, what exactly is the accusation that Mr. Boustany is leveling against Lebanese Jews? Well, absolutely nothing, except that they are Jewish! What is Mr. Boustany's shoddy rationale based upon to justify his demands for retaliation against Lebanese Jews? Well, nothing there either, except so-called 'base feelings' and nefarious 'ulterior motives' that he attributes to the Jewish community. Well, it is nobody's business to judge anyone, or any group, based on so-called feelings and ulterior motives. And to Mr. Boustany's delusions, Mr. Hamid Frangié provided in our names, and in the same Chamber of Deputies, the only logical answer exuding common sense and justice. And so, alongside the former Foreign Minister's comments we shall add the following: We are not in a primordial tribal counsel here, Mr. Boustany! We are a civilized nation, a member of United Nations! We have a modern Constitution! We are a country of laws! We were active participants in the elaboration and authorship of the United Nations' Universal Declaration of Human Rights![36] We are, additionally, an infinitesimally small state whose very raison d'être throughout the ages has been, and continues to be, that of a refuge for all religions and all belief systems! Mr. Boustany ought to understand that it is not in Lebanon that a Jew will be persecuted today, or any other day, on account of being Jewish. […] In view of the heinous campaign that Mr. Boustany remains so desperately intent on waging against Lebanese Jews, we have a duty here, I believe, as Lebanese patriots, to make public our tribute and the debt of gratitude that we owe to a Lebanese community that has always made proof of exquisite character and vitality and courage and initiative and discipline that are all worthy or our highest praise. The Jews of this country have at all times and for all times been exemplary Lebanese. […] All else does not matter.[37]

---

[36] It is interesting to note in this regard that Charles Malik, Lebanon's Ambassador to the United Nations and the USA until 1955, and one of the co-authors of the UN's Universal Declaration of Human Rights, was a good friend of Abba Eban. Eban himself was for close to a decade (from 1950 to 1959) Israel's ambassador to the USA.

[37] Kesrouan Labaki, "De bons libanais," *Le Soir* (Beirut: February 29, 1952).

Unfortunately, this impassioned *J'accuse*, though it had for a time galvanized Lebanese public opinion against the slippery slope toward which some demagogues were dragging the country, it was ultimately ineffective in turning the tides of acrimony and suspicion and eventually war. All manners of provocation and harassment would escalate throughout the 1950s. Arab nationalists would gain increased dominance and impunity within Lebanon, and their rhetorical, psychological, and physical attacks would grow more brazen—cornering Lebanon's Jews into silence, secrecy, and eventually exile, and by 1958, throwing the country in the throes of civil war.

By the end of 1957, the Chamoun administration was growing more aggressive in its handling of the situation. But "The Attacks Continue" noted Lebanon's French-language daily *L'Orient* in its Sunday, November 3 issue.[38] Yet Beirut's chief investigative prosecutor, Georges Mallat, had declared earlier in the day that a recent probe into a string of bombings targeting Jewish interests had resulted in the arrest of twenty persons, all members of an organization calling itself "For the Recovery of the Despoiled Fatherland."[39] But more political, psychological, and material damage would ensue. One of the latest Jewish targets had been the venerable Selim Tarrab School, possibly in reprisal for the recent arrests.[40] The presumed mastermind, Beiruti engineer Ibrahim Mneimné, was already behind bars on multiple charges connected to other recent attacks. Appeals were being filed by Mneimné's legal team requesting his release. But reflecting Chamoun's muscular policy, all appeals were being turned down by presiding prosecutor, Mallat. Indeed, Mallat was known to have been seeking the death penalty for Mneimné and his accomplices.[41] It is not unlikely that it was this, the government's heavy-handed approach, that led to the recent Tarrab School bombing, suggested *L'Orient* in one of its articles.[42] Still, the growing targets of reprisals remained Jewish, not government interests,

[38] *L'Orient*, "La chaine des attentats continue" (Beirut: November 3, 1957).

[39] *L'Orient*, "La chaine."

[40] *L'Orient*, "La chaine."

[41] *L'Orient*, "Peine de mort requise contre les terrorists et leurs complices" (Beirut: December 3, 1957).

[42] *L'Orient*, "La chaine."

and at that point in time, the Jews of Lebanon seemed to have resigned themselves to their increased scapegoating. They would for long remain in their assailants' crosshairs, until their final forced exit in the decade to come.

Two bombs were diffused in the Beirut Jewish Quarter of Wadi Boujmil early in 1958—one of which targeting the neighborhood's *Alliance* school. This was barely six months after prosecutor Mallat's courageous stand. But as would become the case, for each diffused bomb there were many more lurking, waiting to wreak havoc on Lebanon's embattled Jews. And so, another bomb would go off this time at the entrance of the eminent Dr. Nessim Chams's medical practice, causing considerable damage to the clinic itself and defacing a number of neighboring residences.[43] The demoralizing effect of this attack in particular cannot be overstated, specially in light of the reputation that Dr. Chams had earned over the years, as an altruist and a humanitarian; the "healer of the poor."

THE SIXTIES AND SEVENTIES; WITHER JEWISH LEBANON

Historians have described the decades of the 1960–1970s as the beginning of the dismantlement of Lebanon. Kamal Salibi called this era "the crossroads to civil war"; Farid el-Khazen dubbed it "the breakdown of the state." Either way, both were making no predictions, but rather reading the writing on the wall. The end of President Camille Chamoun's administration in 1958, which had tried to maintain for Lebanon a semblance of neutrality in the Arab–Israeli squabbles, was followed by a string of pragmatist, often indecisive governments. The hardnosed Chamoun, often inflexible in matters of national sovereignty and unyielding in his opposition to Arab nationalism, gave way to Fouad Chéhab who was reputed for his "impartiality" cool-headedness and integrity, and who was therefore "trusted" by Lebanon's Muslim

---

[43] It should be noted that Dr. Nessim Chams was a legend of sorts in Lebanon; he was known as "the healer of the poor," often treating his patients free of charge, regardless of what community they'd belonged to; he was the doctor of Jews, Christians, and Muslims equally. Although his practice was based in Beirut, he had clinics in Sidon and in Haifa, where he would travel regularly to treat largely underprivileged patients who would otherwise not receive medical care.

component who disliked Chamoun's abrasive "nationalist conceit." However, Chehab's "moderation"[44] was met with increased impunity and intransigence on the Arab nationalist side, culminating in the state's further slide into chaos and disorder. By the time Chéhab's successor, Charles Helou, took office in 1964, Lebanon's authority and sovereignty were being openly challenged by an expanding PLO armed presence, resulting in increased attacks on the Jewish community, intensified armed clashes between the Lebanese army and the PLO, and eventually the all but total surrender of Lebanese national prerogatives to the whims and will of Arab radicalism.

By the early 1970s, with the Palestine Liberation Organization having well established itself as Lebanon's "state within the state," etiolating in the process the country's sovereign authority, acts of violence and vandalism targeting Lebanon's Jewish community would become a near-daily occurrence. That was so, even though some two-thirds of Lebanese Jews had all but concluded their exodus by 1967. Yet there were still Jewish straddlers in the country, some six thousand of them—four thousand of whom lived in Beirut—and the PLO, along with its local Arabist abettors, would have none of that. Jewish life in Lebanon, and the faintest symbols of it, had to be eradicated.

In spite of it all, and among other remaining emblems of Jewish presence, the *Alliance Israélite Universelle* school remained a thriving institute of learning long into the 1970s: It was a bastion of *francophonie* as it were and a coveted beacon of French education avidly frequented by Jews and non-Jews alike. This made it, all the more, a thorn in the Arab nationalist's side—a radiant symbol of vitality and continuity and presence for Lebanon's Jews—muzzled as this "presence" might have become. But a presence it *was*, and a presence that had to be upended.

On January 18, 1970, an Arab nationalist gang planted an explosive charge near the outer wall of the *Alliance*-affiliated Khadduri-Louise Zilcha School, causing considerable damage to the campus itself and shattering hundreds of windows in nearby Wadi Boujmil residential buildings.[45] This latest casualty was a small elementary school, home to some 400 students, and local reports did not register human casualties—at least none besides passersby and medical staff at the nearby Saint-Elias

---

[44] Known colloquially in Lebanon's political language as "Chehabism."

[45] Alliance Israélite Universelle Archives (Henceforth AIUA), *Extrait du Jerusalem Post du Lundi 19 Janvier, 1970* (Paris: AIU, AM Liban E007).

Hospital receiving non-life-threatening injuries caused by flying glass. Residents of the Wadi Boujmil quarter reported at least two truckloads of broken glass being carted off by the Beirut municipality—suggesting damage limited to the bomb's sonic boom.[46]

And so the attack might have clearly not been intended to result in loss of life: The explosive charges were reportedly placed on one of the school's windowsills, going off at exactly 6:00 am, on a Sunday, long before any of the students would have begun shuffling into class. Still, psychologically speaking, the message was clear: The school was one of the last remaining harbors of Jewish life in Lebanon; it provided elementary education to hundreds of Lebanese Jewish children (aged four to twelve), and its language of instruction was Hebrew. That was obviously problematic to the perpetrators, whom the Lebanese Directorate of Internal Security described as "criminals intent on defaming Lebanon."[47] But in Lebanon's stifling climate of Arab nationalist autarchy, semantic-perversions and euphemisms had become the rule of thumb. Official condemnations could no longer be made public without the obligatory opacity and ambiguity. And by this time, the harassment of Lebanon's Jewish community would become not only justifiable, but indeed righteous.

And so, the Lebanese authorities would come to describe such occurrences as "incidents intended to create confusion for exploitation by the enemy in [support of] its propaganda campaign against Lebanon"[48]; or that the attacks were "obviously the work of criminal and stupid elements, seeking to undermine Lebanon's prestige and engender an atmosphere of terror and tension from which only the enemy could benefit; because in the end, these deeds are conceived as part of a deliberate anti-Lebanese propaganda operation."[49] In all, condemnations had become verbiage eerily reminiscent of our times' language of "political correctness," denouncing faceless "violent extremists," without ever calling them by their names. Interestingly, Yasser Arafat's *Fatah* Organization had perfected this craft, often issuing histrionic communiqués denouncing violence they had themselves perpetrated. "We

---

[46] AIUA, *Extrait* (Paris: AIU, AM Liban E007).

[47] AIUA, *Extrait* (Paris: AIU, AM Liban E007).

[48] AIUA, *Extrait* (Paris: AIU, AM Liban E007).

[49] *Le Monde*, "Explosion dans le quartier Juif de Beyrouth" (Paris: January 29, 1970), 3.

strongly condemn this act" began one such communiqué signed by Arafat,

> and we condemn it in the name of the armed Palestinian revolution, whose main struggle is to make battle against racism, in favor of the creation of a democratic state in Palestine, where Muslims, Christians, and Jews can coexist on an equal footing, free from discrimination… We call upon the Arab and Palestinian masses to remain vigilant at all times, and to foil all the Zionists' and the Imperialists' nefarious attempts at terrorizing our Arab citizens of the Jewish faith. These attempts are obviously designed to force Arab Jews to immigrate to Palestine, so as to become—in spite of themselves—foot-soldiers in the Israeli army, and supporters of the Zionist racist aggressor state.[50]

For his part, Lebanon's Minister of Interior during this period, the Druze Kamal Jumblatt, a leader of the Progressive Socialist Party whose Arab nationalist (and anti-Israel as well as anti-Lebanonist) sympathies had become explicitly discernable by 1970, would regularly express his own dismay at such attacks, denouncing their "perpetrators" in the name of the Lebanese government—but again, never naming them by name. During a January 19, 1970, visit to the Jewish Communal Council of Beirut, accompanied by the City Mayor and the Director General of Lebanon's Internal Security Forces, Jumblatt condemned in very strong terms one particular attack on Lebanon's Jews, noting that "the Jews of Lebanon are considered full citizens of the Republic," and that he personally "makes a clear distinction between Zionism and Judaism," underlining the fact that "Judaism is a religion that [he] venerates."[51] Jumblatt further stressed the Lebanese government's valorization of its Jewish citizens, noting how especially and extraordinarily attentive it had been to their well-being and physical security over the past few years.[52] Jumblatt further noted that such attacks cannot be anything if not "the deed of foreign operatives aiming to disrupt our public order and the peaceful coexistence among all or our country's constitutive communities."[53] The Lebanese people are

---

[50] *Le Monde*, "El Fath dénonce l'attentat contre l'école Israëlite à Beyrouth" (Paris: January 21, 1970), 2.

[51] AIUA, *January 20, 1970 Memo from the Beirut Alliance Director to the President of the Alliance Israélite Universelle in Paris* (Paris: AIU, AM Liban E007, January 20, 1970).

[52] AIUA, *January 20, 1970 Memo* (Paris: AIU, AM Liban E007).

[53] *L'Orient*, "Le Ministre de l'Intérieur chez la communauté Juive" (Beirut: January 21, 1970).

all "children of the same national family," he stressed, "and our interests are the same."[54] He further reminded his interlocutors that the Jews have been living in Lebanon since time immemorial, and that his own venerable Druze ancestors had long maintained friendly relations with the Jews of the Chouf Mountains, who were skilled merchants with whom his own family had long-lasting business and personal dealings.[55]

These ceremonial niceties were routinely reciprocated on the Jewish side, with, in this particular instance, the President of the Jewish Communal Council, Joseph Attié, thanking Jumblatt for the "protection that the Lebanese government continued to provide to the community," assuring him of the Lebanese Jews' "undivided loyalty to [their] beloved Lebanon."[56]

It is worth mentioning that since the conclusion of the Six-Day War in 1967, which resulted in heightened instances of harassment of Lebanese Jews, and consequently in increased Jewish departures from Lebanon, the Lebanese authorities had installed a permanent police outpost within the Jewish Quarter of Wadi Boujmil, as well as a 24-hour police detail at the entrances of all Lebanese Jewish schools—the *Alliance* school included—so as to insure the community's security and prevent further migrations.[57] In this context, the respected "elite" paramilitary *Unit-16* of the Lebanese National Police was charged with the mission of pro-tecting the Jewish Quarter. But the government's vigilance had clearly proven to be no match to the attackers' determination.

Security and police contingents were, therefore, routinely increased. Plain-clothed members of the Phalanges, a political party that had taken upon itself the responsibility of protecting Lebanon's Jews since at least 1948, *also* regularly increased deployments in the Jewish Quarter (providing adequate backing and protection where official security was deemed deficient).[58] What's more, demonstrating their own resilience and determination to remain in their homeland, Lebanese Jews who

---

[54] *L'Orient*, "Le Ministre."

[55] *L'Orient*, "Le Ministre."

[56] AIUA, *January 20, 1970 Memo* (Paris: AIU, AM Liban E007).

[57] AIUA, *January 19, 1970 Memo from the Beirut Alliance Director to the President of the Alliance Israélite Universelle in Paris* (Paris: AIU, AM Liban E007, January 19, 1970).

[58] AIUA, *January 19, 1970 Memo* (Paris: AIU, AM Liban E007).

were members of the Phalanges joined forces with their party comrades patrolling their neighborhoods, while others made haste cleaning up the damaged areas whenever an attack was carried out, so as to prevent school closures and expedite return to normalcy.[59]

But this was a losing battle: The decade of the 1970s would witness the triumph of Arab nationalists determined to turn Lebanon into a confrontation state: The Lebanese people and polity would fall captive to extortionism; the Lebanese Republic would willy-nilly surrender bits more of its sovereignty with each passing day; and Lebanon the entrepôt and the crossroads of ideas and peoples and cultures would abdicate in favor of a lawless entity, under Palestinian rule, left in abandon to the animus and whim of Arab nationalism. The already-etiolated Lebanese Jews would therefore be pushed further along on the road of exile, mutism, and slow, silent, solitary extinction.

CONCLUSIONS

'What good is it for Lebanon to have a thousand Christians, and a thousand Muslims, and for it to end up being a stranger to itself?'[60] This is a sentence attributed to Phalanges leader Pierre Gemayel who was committed to the idea of Lebanese unity as one based on diversity, and whose political party had been a major pole of attraction for Lebanese Jews, through the 1970s and beyond. "Lebanon is not a country for Muslims," insisted Gemayel, "nor is it one for Jews or Christians"; rather, Lebanon is a place where "Man can be free to believe, *or not*, as he wishes, and where he can worship the god of his own choosing, or *not* worship one at all; [...] Lebanon is a country that we have conceived of as a model for the entire world, not only for the Arab states, to emulate."[61]

Sadly, this Lebanon of Gemayel's proved unfaithful to the mission with which it was entrusted; it failed itself as a self-proclaimed "confederation of minorities," just as it failed those of its children who had placed their wager on its multicultural vocation. Most of all, Lebanon was unable to uphold its end of the bargain with regard to its own millennial

---

[59] AIUA, *January 19, 1970 Memo* (Paris: AIU, AM Liban E007).

[60] Nantet, *Pierre Gemayel*, 174.

[61] Nantet, 175.

Jewish community; another brilliant strand in a rich patchwork of cultures, deserted, abandoned, left behind with colors bleeding, and memories and lives fading. Lebanon's Jews, arguably the oldest, perhaps *the* most "indigenous" of the country's communal groups—"the ones who were there first" as it were—have left, were made to leave, perhaps never to return.

But there isn't bitterness—or very little—in the voices and in the memories of many of those who left and kept in their hearts a soft spot for Lebanon. There are only regrets and longing and searching gazes smiling bittersweet smiles at "places of memory" that still beckon, and still live within a banished offspring of the Lebanese family.

Memories of events and places from our past, wrote Marcel Proust in *À la Recherche du Temps Perdu*, "are but regrets over lost moments in our lives; and the homes, the houses, the roads, and the avenues of times past are, sadly, ephemeral and elusive, like the years of our lives."[62]

Much of what remains of this volume consists of "fragments of lives arrested"—pictures of homes, roads, lives, and times clinging to the memories and personal testimonies of Lebanese Jews—some at home, others in exile—who still have not given up on Lebanon, who "still dream of Lebanon"[63] and who both emotively and physically never ceased "going back" to Lebanon, even as Lebanon, it seems, might have long since abandoned them.

Lebanon was a delectable jumble of cultures and ethno-religious groups, wrote Amin Maalouf in his 2012 novel *Les Désorientés*.[64] As Lebanese, he claimed, "we belonged to multiple poles of attraction," and it had become almost a national duty of ours "to make light of ourselves and each of our respective communal identities, before gently mocking the ethnic communities of our counterparts."[65] Lebanon's diversity was "the blueprint of humanity's future," wistfully affirmed Maalouf, "but alas, this future, was doomed to remaining a blueprint."[66] Wars came and went and crushed in their wake Lebanon's ecumenism. It was "the

---

[62] Marcel Proust, *À la Recherche du Temps Perdu*, Volume I (Paris: Éditions Gallimard, 1987), 420.

[63] Moïse Chams, Interview (Newton, MA, USA: November 30, 2014).

[64] Amin Maalouf, *Les Désorientés* (Paris: Grasset, 2012), 36.

[65] Maalouf, *Les Désorientés*, 36.

[66] Maalouf, *Les Désorientés*, 36.

end of the world" in Maalouf's telling; the end of a civilization; "our civilization" as he put it; "the Levantine civilization":

> An expression that brings a scornful smile to the lips of the ignorant, and makes the partisans of triumphalist barbarity cringe; those children of arrogant tribes who make battle in the name of the one and only God, and who know no worse enemy than our subtle, fluid identities.[67]

Lebanese of Maalouf's generation proudly upheld these noble ideals of diversity and urbane multiculturalism; they proclaimed themselves the enlightened children of Voltaire, Camus, Sartre, and Nietzsche, disciples of Surrealism; yet "they quickly faded back into the primordial Christian, Muslim, and Jewish molds" of old when trouble came knocking.[68] In the early 1970s, "we were young," noted Maalouf; "it was the dawn of our lives; but the dawn had already become twilight."[69] "War was looming," he wrote ominously:

> It was coming closer, slowly crawling in our direction, like a radioactive cloud; we had no time to stop it; we had time only to flee... Our country, with its delicate system of power-sharing, was drowning, and it would rapidly go unhinged; we soon discovered, in the middle of the floodwaters submerging us, that Lebanon was well-nigh irreparable... The first of my friends to flee was Naïm—his entire family, his mother, father, two sisters and grandmother all left, quickly, quietly. They were certainly not the last remaining Jews in the country, but they surely were part of a small dwindling minority, which, up until then, had resisted abdication. The 1950s and 1960s witnessed a muted hemorrhaging of Lebanon's Jews; in a slow drip, without much fanfare, the community had begun melting away. Some of its members had gone to Israel—by way of Paris, Istanbul, Athens, or Nicosia; others chose to settle in Canada, the United States, England, or France. Naïm's family opted for Brazil. But they left relatively late in the game, in 1973.[70]

Although written in the form of a novel, Maalouf's story is a real one, his protagonists more archetypal than imaginary, drawn from his and

[67] Maalouf, *Les Désorientés*, 36.
[68] Maalouf, *Les Désorientés*, 36.
[69] Maalouf, *Les Désorientés*, 37.
[70] Maalouf, *Les Désorientés*, 37.

their Lebanon's past and dreams and regrets and aspirations, as much as from remembrances and experiences and events of lives lived. It is in this context that this chapter has sought to bring to light the history and saga of the Jews of Lebanon.

And so, among the themes to be examined in the pages to follow are not only the history of the Lebanese Jewish community in its own voice, but also the attitudes of the Lebanese in general vis-à-vis an important— albeit a small and disappearing—component of their country's ethno-religious fabric. Also passed in review will be the space and place of the Jews in Lebanese society, their role in the country's ethnic makeup, and finally the cultural, social, political, and intellectual contributions that they made to twentieth-century Lebanese life.

As an important ingredient in an already complex and richly textured ethno-religious patchwork, an argument was made that the Jews of Lebanon were part of a generation that literally created the modern Lebanese Republic as a confederation of minorities—if not politically, then at least conceptually, emotively, socially, and culturally speaking. In that sense, the erasure of Lebanese Jews from modern Lebanese collective memory—and their personal testimony highlighting this point—shall read like a travesty of history. Lebanon without the Jews seems certainly like a distortion of the country's modern political and cultural history, just as much as it may be a betrayal of the Jews' own millennial "native"—not to say "indigenous"—association with Lebanon—and the Levant as a whole in more general terms.

The canon of modern Middle Eastern history is replete with—indeed dominated by—narratives of the "Nakba"—the dispossession of some one million Arabs from British Mandate Palestine in 1948, on the heels of the establishment of the State of Israel. Yet, little is hardly ever mentioned about the expulsion of millions of "oriental" Jews from Muslim- and Arab-defined lands parallel to the Nakba. Less still is reported on the silent exodus of the once vibrant Lebanese Jewish community between 1948 and 1975. Dany Liniado, a Lebanese Jew now living in Mexico, speaks with hardly contained melancholy of a "golden era" of a past Lebanese existence; a life cut short by Arab nationalist resentments, decimated by perverse prejudices putting an end to a once diverse Lebanese fabric forcibly expunged of its native Jewish character.

Dany's father, Desiré Liniado, a successful Beirut lawyer, leading public intellectual and author, and friend of Raymond Éddé, son of Lebanon's Maronite President Émile Éddé (1936–1941), is an eloquent and heartbreaking voice in this sad narrative of loss and exile. Dany recounts the heartache of her family's history being sacked, their memories assailed, and their Beirut home squatted by PLO and Arab nationalist radicals in 1975—without the slightest chance to collect a modicum of the family's personal effects (or "recollect" pieces of their memories).[71] Her father nevertheless attempted to return to their home, to fetch some of his own elderly father's clothing and personal belongings. But he was instead abducted by the PLO members occupying the house, and subsequently subjected to a grueling cruel regime of torture.[72] By the time his friend Raymond Éddé was able to "buy" his life back and secure his release some five hours later, Desiré Liniado had already begun dying. He would succumb to the grief and heartache of exile three years later, in 1978. It was on Raymond Éddé's advice that he had resolved to leave Lebanon: "You must leave," Éddé had told him; "this country no longer wants you," recalled Dany Liniado with tears in her voice.[73]

Snippets of Dany's recollections are reproduced in detail later in this volume. With others, her story and the lessons drawn from it stand as a "restorative" bit—a bid at correcting a lacuna of exclusion and omission vis-à-vis the Jews of Lebanon, mending their memory, and restoring them to their rightful place in Lebanon, as a foundational element of modern Lebanese history and sociocultural production.

[71] Danielle Liniado, Interview (Mexico City, Mexico: August 28, 2015).
[72] Liniado, Interview.
[73] Liniado, Interview.

CHAPTER 4

Rootedness and Exile:
Holocaust and Aftermath

Que le désespoir nous inspire du courage.

Sénèque ca. AD 47

As stressed earlier in this volume, Lebanese Jews are a long-standing Lebanese community which may more legitimately than others claim precedence and deeper roots in Lebanon. Likewise, as a "minority" in a Lebanese "federation of minorities," Lebanese Jews are both similar to *and* distinct from other Lebanese communities, just as they may be similar to and *distinct* from neighboring Jews of "Arab lands." For one, the Lebanon of the first half of the twentieth century was not an "Arab state" in the traditional connotations of the term and did not consider itself to be an "Arab state"—indeed, many Lebanese to this day still take great umbrage at being considered "Arabs" in an "Arab world."

Therefore, what might have befallen the "Jews of Arab Lands" in "the shadow of the Holocaust" certainly did not apply in the case of Lebanon, and Lebanese Jewish life appears to have been markedly different from Jewish life elsewhere in the Arab-defined Middle East.

Consequently, Lebanese Jews, their stories, their status, their sociocultural production, and their political allegiances cannot, and indeed *ought* not, be folded into the same complex of events and circumstances as other Jews of the Middle East.

In this sense, although naturally preoccupied with the goings-on in the nearby *Yishuv*, the Zionist project, and news of the destruction of European Jewry, Lebanese Jews of the first half of the twentieth century

© The Author(s) 2019
F. Salameh, *Lebanon's Jewish Community*,
https://doi.org/10.1007/978-3-319-99667-7_4

had "their own fish to fry" so to speak: They were by and large invested in *their* Lebanese experiment, competing for *their* place in Lebanese society, and preoccupied with issues pertaining to securing *their* own piece of the "pie" in Lebanon's fractious system of power-sharing.

LEBANON OF THE JEWS AND THE FRENCH MANDATE

Much evidence reveals that, not unlike Lebanon's Christians, the Jews of Lebanon were heavily invested in the idea of the Lebanese Republic as a "confederation of minorities" rather than an "Arab state" in the making. Lebanese Jews therefore played an important role—albeit perhaps at times a discreet one alongside the country's more vocal Christians—in the establishment of modern Lebanon as it came into being socially, culturally, and politically during the first half of the twentieth century.

On September 1, 1920, General Henri Gouraud, the High Commissioner of the French Republic, Governor of the French Mandated territories of a Levant recently wrested from a defeated Ottoman Empire, would bring into being a modern Lebanese Republic intended and expressly designed as a refuge for Near Eastern minorities. "Greater Lebanese," thundered Gouraud's solemn act of state creation:

> I assured you a few weeks ago, at a crucial time in your history, that "the day is near that your ancestors had in vain hoped for, and that you, more fortunate than they, will no doubt see shining through." Well, that day is now upon us! And so, before all the people gathered here, peoples of all regions once dominated by Mount-Lebanon; peoples, who had once lived as neighbors and who shall from this day forward be united under the auspices of a single nation, rooted in its past, eminent in its future. In the presence of the Lebanese Authorities, children of the country's most venerable families, representatives of all faiths and all rites, among whom I must greet with special veneration the great [Maronite] Patriarch of Lebanon, who has descended form his mountain sanctuary to celebrate this most glorious of days crowning his life's struggles [...] Before all of these witnesses to your aspirations, your struggles, and your victory, and in sharing your pride, I solemnly proclaim Greater Lebanon, and in the name of the French Republic, I salute her in all her grandeur and all her power. [...] Behold this beautiful country arising. Free, breaking away from the heavy hands that have for centuries tried to stifle it, this country will finally be able to employ, for its own development, the character and skill that you and your ancestors have often—way too often—deployed

and expended abroad. [...] Behold, Greater Lebanese, the sacred lot of hopes and sacrifices that this solemn moment carries with it. [...] Greater Lebanon was conceived to benefit everyone, and is in place to harm and disadvantage absolutely no one.[1]

This was the Lebanon to which Lebanese Jews had staked their claims, pledged their loyalty, and pinned their hopes and their future: a refuge and national home for Middle Eastern minorities where Jews would play the role of a *primus inter pares* partner, within an independent sovereign state distinct and separate from "any Arab state that may come into being" in the Levantine region; a "home" where, in the words of Maronite Patriarch Elias Peter Hoyek (1843–1931), Jews and others would be free to practice the rituals of their cultural, spiritual, and historical accretions, *even* and *especially* those setting them apart from neighboring groupings "in terms of language, customs, trends, and [...] cultural orientation."[2]

It is in this spirit, and in order to celebrate and serve *this* Lebanon specifically, that the first issue of *Al-Aalam al-Isra'iili* (the mouthpiece of Lebanon's Jewish community) was published—remarkably, on Thursday September 1, 1921, one year to the day following General Henri Gouraud's memorable address. Indeed, all three columns of the newspaper's front-page were dedicated to its inaugural editorial; a "mission statement" as it were, and a moving authoritative prolegomenon paying tribute to this Lebanon of the Jews. "Following the Great War," began the article,

and on the heels of all the destruction and ruin that it wrought in its wake, almost obliterating all landmarks of civilization and human life and accomplishments, man has finally been given respite, ridding humanity from the claws of injustice and oppression, and inaugurating a new era raised in peace, predicated on the noble principles of human rights.[3]

[1] Charles Corm Archives (henceforth ChCA), *Texte de la déclaration du Général Henri Gouraud, 1er Septembre 1920* (Beirut: Lebanon, September 1, 1920); See also Adel Ismail, *Le Liban, documents diplomatiques et consulaires relatifs à l'histoire du Liban*, vol. xix (Beirut, Lebanon: Éditions des oeuvres politiques et historiques, 1979), 81.

[2] Archives du Ministère des Affaires Étrangères (henceforth MAE), *Les revendications du Liban*, Volume 266 (Paris: Série E-Levant, 1918–1940, Syrie-Liban, Sous-série Syrie, Liban, Cilicie, Correspondence Politique et Commerciale).

[3] *Al-Aalam al-Isra'iili*, "Prolegomenon" (Beirut, Lebanon: September 1, 1921), 1.

The editorial went on to praise the outcome of the Great War, a "war to end all wars" as it called it, applauding the ensuing peace settlement's verdicts favoring the notion of self-determination for newly awakened and rising nations.

In light of this, *Al-Aalam al-Isra'iili* submitted itself to its readers as a medium of information, and a conduit for the truth—albeit a truth issuing from a distinctly Lebanese Jewish landscape.[4] To this point, the journal's first editorial stressed that, given that each of Lebanon's various communities already reaped the benefits of a publication of their own, speaking in their names, and providing a service to their community in particular, the Jewish community had no alternative but to follow suit and walk in the footsteps of its non-Jewish compatriots.[5]

And so, with the object of keeping Lebanese Jewry abreast of current events, and with the express purpose of goading them along the path of political and literary awakening—as a sign of their own specific cultural and intellectual renaissance—this distinctly Lebanese Jewish periodical willed itself into being.[6] "In these uncommonly auspicious times" concluded the editorial, "as peace and security and freedom abound under the aegis of French Mandatory Authorities and their heroic men," the Lebanese Jewish community's calling "had to be consummated, and had to materialize" in print.[7]

The chosen name of the periodical, *Al-Aalam al-Isra'iili*, the "Israelite Universe"—an Arabic rendition of the venerable French *L'Univers Israélite*—was meant to convey to Lebanon's Jewish community news of their coreligionists from around the world, which might not have reached them otherwise. As regards the journal's orientation and content and affiliation, the editors took great care to stress their "scientific, critical, informative, and scholastic" vocation, conveying "political events and accounts and testimonies from East to West, specific in the strictest sense to the Jewish community."[8] And so, local and regional events that did not directly touch or affect Lebanese Jewry were generally left to other local periodicals specializing in such features. The inaugural editorial closed out with an entreaty "to God and the readers to

---

[4] *Al-Aalam al-Isra'iili*, "Prolegomenon," 1.

[5] *Al-Aalam al-Isra'iili*, "Prolegomenon," 1.

[6] *Al-Aalam al-Isra'iili*, "Prolegomenon," 1.

[7] *Al-Aalam al-Isra'iili*, "Prolegomenon," 2.

[8] *Al-Aalam al-Isra'iili*, "Prolegomenon," 2.

bless the newspaper's quest in the service of the [Jewish] community and the [Lebanese] motherland."[9]

For upwards of fifteen years, the *Al-Aalam al-Isra'iili* was unhindered, openly fulfilling its mandate and eloquently honoring its mission statement as a "Jewish," *but* "Lebanese" publication. Stylistically, the newspaper's Arabic language was a weekly literary tour de force, revealing not only the erudition of its writers and editors, but also the intellectual sophistication and high standards of education and general knowledge of its readers. Thematically, and in terms of substance, content, intellectual, creative, and political interests, the newspaper lived up to its reputation as a Jewish *but* Lebanese newspaper. It was didactic, delving into histories relevant to Lebanon, and the Jews; speaking of Phoenicians and Hebrews (and therefore of modern Lebanese Jews and non-Jews) being a kindred people; publishing articles on the origins of the Alphabet and Phoenician maritime trade, and other such stories of general interest appealing to the sympathies of Lebanese of those times— non-Muslims in the main—who were especially sensitive to myths of origin and historical narratives valorizing ancient Canaanite seafarers, deeming them modern Lebanon's progenitors and ancestors.

The newspaper also headlined cutting-edge rubrics on literature, the revival of Arabic *belles lettres*, biographies of major Zionist and Lebanese intellectual figures (Jews and non-Jews alike), a wealth of interviews on Hebrew language revival, and special spotlights featuring conversations with politicians and luminaries of the time, including, among others, Ze'ev Jabotinsky (1880–1940), "father" of Revisionist Zionism, Ahad Ha-Am (1856–1927), founder of the "cultural Zionism" movement, Chaim Weizman (1874–1952), first President of the State of Israel, Emir Faisal (1885–1933), son of the Sharif of Mecca, Taha Husayn (1889–1973), the doyen of modern Arabic *belles lettres*, and Ithamar Ben-Avi (1882–1943), the first native speaker of modern Hebrew, and son of renowned linguist and Hebrew language revivalist Eliezer Ben-Yehuda (1858–1922).

The September 8, 1926, issue of *Al-Aalam al-Isra'iili*, celebrating the sixth anniversary of the establishment of Greater Lebanon (what the newspaper referred to as "Independence Day,") featured a patriotic ode by Lebanese Jewish poet Haim Jamous, parts of which read as follows:

---

[9] *Al-Aalam al-Isra'iili*, "Prolegomenon," 2.

O hallowed day of September 1, may God keep you for us an eternal day of hope / O holiday pregnant with memories and meaning, [...] / Will God's earth ever have men as noble, as heroic, as my bold countrymen [...] / Lebanon's peasant, on his dazzling landscapes, dons the winds of eternity for clothing [...] / Today, joyous, we shall celebrate our country's independence, / and tomorrow, we shall weep in solemn remembrance of those who died for our sake [...] / And as I look up, awed, at the fluttering flag of my country's cedar tree, I see glory flickering, hidden in its folds...[10]

Incidentally, *Al-Aalam al-Isra'iili* was among the first Lebanese newspapers to have published the original full text of the Lebanese national anthem, in November 1926, almost a full year before a final version was officially adopted by the Lebanese government.[11]

In that sense, the newspaper can be said to have lived up to its mission statement: It was unapologetically Jewish; it was unreservedly Lebanese; and when the circumstances demanded, it was obstinate in its determination that Jewish rights within the Lebanese polity be respected.

To wit, in late Summer 1931, celebrating its eleventh year of publication, on the week following the eleventh anniversary of the September 1, 1920, establishment of Greater Lebanon, *Al-Aalam al-Isra'iili* inaugurated its "National Day" issue with a compelling, strongly worded editorial calling to task Arab nationalist propagandists in Lebanon. Aptly titled "As a Matter of Principle," the editorial excoriated the deceit and opportunism of those Lebanese politicians doing the bidding of Arabs, willing to immolate the country's Jewish community for the sake of ingratiating themselves to the Arabs, and assuaging Arab compulsions about Jewish presence in the Middle East.[12] "Why should there be a problem with Jews struggling for a place among the nations?" wondered the editorial:

Why is it a problem to some that the Jewish nation is struggling to put an end to its exilic existence and its age-old dispersion? Why is it a problem that Jews should unite and unfurl their flag and fly it aloft [like other nations]? Why is it a problem that Jews should redeem themselves and

[10] *Al-Aalam al-Isra'iili*, "They Say My Country Is Free" (Beirut, Lebanon: September 8, 1926), 5.

[11] *Al-Aalam al-Isra'iili*, "The National Anthem" (Beirut, Lebanon: November 4, 1926), 2.

[12] *Al-Aalam al-Isra'iili*, "As a Matter of Principle" (Beirut, Lebanon: September 11, 1931), 1.

restore their erstwhile dignity and glory? [...] Yes, this publication shall
and ought to continue furnishing every effort on behalf of Jewish dignity! We shall spare no sacrifice to keep this newspaper going and growing,
[...] to uphold its principles for the sake of our principles, which a great
many people in this region take great pleasure demeaning and suppressing—for the simple reason that our principles may be deemed contrary
to the nationalist and political creeds of others [...] We have struggled,
and we shall continue to struggle, because our principles remain the same,
unchanged, immutable. For, we are and shall remain, above all, Jews,
proud of our history and identity and the teachings of our fathers. But we
are equally importantly Lebanese, living in a Lebanese homeland, to whose
dignity and prosperity we shall ever and forever struggle and aspire. Yes,
and we shall continue to serve Lebanon and play our role impartially and
conscientiously in order the safeguard the bonds of brotherhood among
all of Lebanon's children; our own brothers and compatriots [...] And
let those peddling noxious rumors and spreading discord and false propaganda, let them fear God's retribution for the alienation and animus that
they are sowing between Arabs and Jews! [...] Indeed, there exists, in
Palestine today, a motley crew of [Arab] leaders insidiously making trouble and instigating disorder and inciting violence. They are indeed doing
the bidding of the British, to the detriment of Arabs and Jews alike. We,
in Lebanon, are fighting against those criminals, and we ask that our Arab
brothers, in Palestine proper and elsewhere, recognize that their interests,
as much as our own, remain in working together hand in hand, to keep
the Machiavellians and their machinations at bay. Let us work, truly work,
together to moderate the hearts and actively take part in the construction
[not the destruction] of Palestine.[13]

But the world—and with it the Middle East—was undergoing a rapid
transformation during the 1930s and 1940s. And conciliatory Lebanese
Jewish voices were—it seems—blowing in a broken bagpipe.

Gathering Winds of World War II

Yet, Lebanon would still try clinging to its well-cultivated reputation
(and *raison d'être*) as a confederation of minorities; a place unencumbered by the Arabs' identity politics and the resentments of an Arab–
Israeli conflict in the making.

---

[13] *Al-Aalam al-Isra'iili*, "As a Matter of Principle," 1.

As noted earlier, in 1936, as the "Arab Revolt" was gathering steam in nearby British Mandate Palestine, and as the Mufti of Jerusalem was more vociferously assailing Jewish claims to that disputed territory, Lebanese political leader Pierre Gemayel was asserting equally emphatically to his own Jewish compatriots, *and* to the world at large, that Lebanon was different, liberal, humanist, in a region riven by authoritarianism, animus, and bigotry. Lebanon, he noted,

> this Lebanon of the Phalanges, is neither the Greater Lebanon [established by the French,] nor is it merely the Mount-Lebanon [of Christians.] Our Lebanon is the Lebanon of an illustrious history, a Lebanon 6000-years young. It is the Lebanon of the early Lebanese who came to this land in order to till it into the homeland of liberty and freedom, the homeland of humanism, the homeland of all of those ancestors of ours who were smitten by a lust for sovereignty and freedom. Lebanon is not a Christian country; nor is it a Muslim or a Jewish country for that matter. Lebanon is not merely a piece of territory; nor is it only a constitution. Lebanon is the stuff of dreams, it is the stuff of human conscience and spiritedness and kindness. And it is in this spirit of Lebanon's that we have conceived our own principles of being Lebanese.[14]

Again, this sentiment reflected Lebanese-Jewish worldviews and public stances throughout the 1930s and 1940s. In this sense, one ought to recall from earlier in this volume a famous 1937 visit by Maronite Patriarch Antony Peter Arida to a Jewish center in Beirut, during which community president Joseph Farhi brandished the Jews' ancient bonds to Lebanon. "For us Jews," said Farhi, "our attachment to Lebanon is not a modern phenomenon";

> It has existed for thousands of years. Already Moses solicited god's favor to see the promised land—the enchanting Lebanon. Later our biblical poets celebrated the marvelous sites, the majestic cedars which Solomon preferred for building the Eternal Temple. Time has not diminished our attachment to the land which we inhabit; [it] has nothing but fortified our feelings of loyalty and devotion to Lebanon [as a land] of liberty and justice for all its citizens without distinction of race or confession.[15]

---

[14] Jacques Nantet, *Pierre Gemayel* (Paris: Éditions Jean-Claude Lattès, 1986), 173.

[15] Kirsten E. Schulze, *The Jews of Lebanon; Between Coexistence and Conflict* (Brighton: Sussex Academic Press, 2001), 39.

Arida himself, a spirited spiritual leader known locally as "the Patriarch of the Jews," never missed an opportunity to "offend" Arab nationalist sensitivities, publicly flaunting his commitment to Jewish rights—in Lebanon proper, and beyond.

During a late June 1933 pastoral visit to flocks in Beirut, Damascus, and Aleppo, Arida fiercely denounced Nazi Germany's mistreatment of German Jews. And in solidarity with the Jews of Lebanon (*and* their coreligionists around the world), he dispatched a message to leaders of the World Zionist Congress condemning both Germany and local Middle Eastern leaders insensitive to the plight of world Jewry. Arida further addressed an encyclical calling on Maronite churches throughout the world, the Levant in particular, to dedicate their Sunday prayers and homilies to the Jews of the world.[16] Hitler's Germany has distorted Christian teachings, began the Patriarch's encyclical:

> The Jews' only sin, in the eyes of this Germany, had been simply their being Jewish. Where are in all of this those [Arabs and Muslims] who noisily vaunt their so-called admiration for freedom of conscience and religion? Yet, we witness our Catholic brethren throughout the civilized world voice their strong condemnation [of Hitler] and offer their devotion to the persecuted Jews. We indeed share with them their goodwill and warm affection, which stem from the spirit and the letter of the Gospels. We ought to never forget that the Jews are our brothers in humanity, and that Almighty God has chosen them, and no one else, as keepers of His Divine Oneness and His Eternal Truth.[17]

This last section of Patriarch Arida's message had particular resonance and generated a particular wave of euphoria among the Jews of Lebanon. It was in line with a series of memoranda that the Patriarch had begun dispatching to various Lebanese, French, and, Jewish organizations, beginning in May 1933. In one such message, addressed to the director of the *Alliance Israélite Universelle* in Beirut, Arida reminded his correspondent how the Jews of Lebanon and France had once shared in and "assuaged the suffering" of Lebanon's Christians, and that the Maronites among them "shall never forget the compassion shown them

---

[16] *Al-Aalam al-Isra'iili*, "The Echo of His Holiness the Maronite Patriarch's Affection Toward the Jews of Germany" (Beirut, Lebanon: June, 26, 1933), 3.

[17] *Al-Aalam al-Isra'iili*, "The Echo of His Holiness," 3.

[…] especially now as the Israelites of Germany are being subjected to all manner of oppression and injustice."[18]

Many in the Lebanese Arabic-language press rushed to denounce the Patriarch's favorable public stance vis-à-vis the Jews—especially his encyclical, which the majority of Arab nationalist and anti-Jewish periodicals excoriated. This question of someone's compassionate stance vis-à-vis the Jews—a Maronite–Christian prelate to boot, in an Arab-defined universe, daring to lend public support to Jews presumably sympathetic to the Zionist movement—was considered so combustive, so anathema, that rumors began circulating in the Arabic-language press suggesting a "mutiny" in Maronite ranks—obviously a propagandist effort to discredit Patriarch Arida. In one such hoax, a Damascus-based Arab nationalist tabloid published a letter allegedly written by the Archbishop of Beirut, Monsignor Ignatius Mubarak (d. 1951), rebuking the Patriarch for his pro-Jewish sympathies, and shaming him publicly. In this, the newspaper, *Alif-Baa'*, alleged Mubarak had told the Patriarch that,

> When we elected you, we had not done so for you to become the Patriarch of the Jews. You have shirked your duty to your community and neglected the Maronites in order to tend to the Jews. […] God has punished us because we have elected you.[19]

The authenticity of this letter was later denied, and those circulating it were publically denounced by Mubarak himself, who called the words attributed to him "absolutely unfounded rubbish."[20] Indeed, later developments throughout the 1930s and 1940s would reveal not only an Archbishop Mubarak who was sympathetic to the Jews of Lebanon, but indeed a Maronite spiritual leader very much in the image of the bulk of his community, even emitting very public, unapologetic, straightforward pro-Zionist positions. On the other hand, it is worth mentioning that some of the newspapers circulating Mubarak's alleged mutiny against the Maronite Church, were notoriously shoddy outfits, openly anti-Semitic

---

[18] Letter reproduced in *Al-Aalam al-Isra'iili*, "His Holiness the Maronite Patriarch and the Afflicted Jews" (Beirut, Lebanon: June 12, 1933), 3.

[19] MAE, *Presse Syrienne et Libanaise du 2 au 8 Juillet, 1933*, Paris: Série E-Levant, Syrie-Liban, Volume 527.

[20] MAE, *Presse Syrienne et Libanaise du 2 au 8 Juillet, 1933*, Paris: Série E-Levant, Syrie-Liban, Volume 527. For a profile of "another," "pro-Zionist" Mubarak at odds with the *Alif-Baa'* depiction, see the Archbishop's 1947 letter to UNSCOP in Chapter 1 of this volume.

and vehemently opposed to the very notion of a Lebanese entity distinct and separate from the yearned for "Arab Kingdom"—Let alone were they opposed to a Lebanese leader espousing a Jewish cause.[21]

[21] For a summary and brief report on Lebanese newspapers in circulation between 1920 and 1933, see for instance MAE, *Presse-Propagande; Presse Syrienne et Libanaise*, Paris: Série E-Levant, Syrie-Liban, Volume 525–526, E-417-1. The major Lebanese newspapers are classified as follows:

French-language Lebanese Dailies:

Le Reveil: founded in 1906; directed by A. Coury;

L'Orient: founded in 1924; directed by Gabriel Khabbaz; 3700 print-run;

Arabic–language Lebanese Dailies and Weeklies:

Al-Ahrar (The Liberals): founded in 1923; directed by Gibran Tuéni; 3500–4000 print run; organ of the Masonic Lodges; critical, political, moderate;

Al-Ahwaal (The Circumstances): Founded in 1890; directed by Khalil Badaoui (Christian); 1800–2000 print-run; Mr. Badaoui was censured by the military tribunal in 1920 "for publishing tendentious articles." He has since "shown more rigorous journalistic integrity, and a more friendly stance vis-à-vis France";

Al-Barq (The Lightening): founded in 1908; directed by Bechara el-Khoury; Francophile leanings;

Al-Bayraq (The Flag): founded in 1929; directed by Assaad Akl; 1200 print-run; Francophile leanings;

Al-Istiqlaal (Independence): directed by G. Awad; 700–800 print-run; Francophile leanings;

Lisan al-Haal (The Voice of the Circumstances): founded in 1878; directed by the Boustany family and Checri Dagher; 1200–1300 print-run; moderately Francophile leanings;

Al-Bachir (The Herald): founded in 1869; directed by Fr. Makhlouf; 3000 print-run; organ of the Society of Jesus; Francophile leanings;

Al-Maarad (The Exposition): founded in 1920; directed by Michel Zaccour; 2300–2500 print-run; Lebanese nationalist; supportive of the French Mandate and Lebanese independence;

Al-Raaya (The Flag): founded in 1926; directed by Daoud Nassar; 700 print-run; former editor-in-chief Joseph Saouda; a radical Lebanese nationalist, Francophile but opposed to the Mandate; wrote a series of articles extolling the traditional Franco-Lebanese bonds and celebrating the Crusades, which provoked the ire of the Muslim press;

Al-Aalam al-Isra'iili (The Israelite Universe): founded in 1920; directed by Selim Mann; Israelite organ; 600 print-run; Francophile leanings; Zionist tendencies; particularly concerned with questions relative to the Jewish community;

Arzet Lebnaan (The Cedar of Lebanon): Founded in 1914; directed by Joseph Hitti, 1200 print-run; Francophile leanings; proponent of the French Mandate and continued French presence in Lebanon;

Lebnaan (Lebanon): founded in 1924; 500 print-run; Armenian language; organ of the Armenian-Catholics;

Pukik: founded in 1925; 500 print-run; Armenian language; organ of Armenian-Jacobites.

It is worth mentioning that in acknowledgment of the Maronite Church official policy and public mood vis-à-vis the Jews of Lebanon and elsewhere, the Jewish communities of Beirut, Damascus, and Aleppo issued a formal statement naming the Maronite Patriarch "an honor to humanity, a cornerstone of world peace, a defender of human rights, a bulwark protecting the powerless and persecuted of this world, and a shelter to those whose humanity is profaned."[22]

At any rate, these events of the 1930s, and the public exchanges of goodwill and praise and affection between Maronites and Jews, trumpeted as they were by the Maronite Patriarch himself, had an important antecedent. In late May and early June 1933, as waves of Jewish immigrants escaping Nazi persecution were beginning to make their way east across the Mediterranean, in the direction of British Mandate Palestine, a number of Arabic-language Lebanese newspapers ran inflammatory news-stories, expressing editorial displeasure at the prospects of Lebanon offering sanctuary to at least a fraction of those refugees.[23]

Some of those periodicals were known to publish exhortations issuing from anti-Jewish Koranic Suras and Prophetic Hadiths calling for the "crucifixion of the Jews, and dealing them the final blow."[24] Yet those same purveyors of cruelty, noted *Al-Aalam al-Isra'iili* in one of its 1933 responses, would in the same breath trot out compassionate tolerant Koranic passages—to wit, Koran 11:118, about "had your Lord wanted to, He would have made all mankind a single nation," and that "all creatures are Allah's children, and those dearest to Him are the ones who treat His children kindly."[25]

---

[22] *Al-Aalam al-Isra'iili*, "The Echo of His Holiness," 3.

[23] With the rise of the Nazis to power in January 1933, incidents of persecution against German Jews increased, in an attempt to drive them out of the country. This was long before 1939 and Kristallnacht. Nevertheless, anti-Jewish boycotts began in earnest on April 1, 1933, and as a result Germany's Jewish community began being ostracized from the rest of society; Jews were removed from government positions, universities, and hospitals, restrictions were placed on Jewish businesses and Jews in liberal professions, and Jewish institutions and places of worship were systemically vandalized in an effort to purge Germany of its Jewish citizens.

[24] *Al-Aalam al-Isra'iili*, "The Children of Christ in the Service of Christ; They Work According to His Teachings and the Guidance of His Book; Kharijites Lecture the Chief Among the Maronites' Pontiffs" (Beirut, Lebanon: July 17, 1933), 1.

[25] *Al-Aalam al-Isra'iili*, "The Children of Christ," 1.

Yet those same ostensibly righteous Muslims would go on instigating violence against those of "God's children" who were Jewish, simply on account of their being Jewish. Some of their trademarks included common anti-Semitic canards often reading like pages straight out of the *Protocols of the Elders of Zion* playbook. One such story spoke of a Jewish cabal whereby a "massive swarm of Jewish immigrants descended on Tripoli" (a Sunni-dominated port-city in northern Lebanon), "embarking on large-scale land purchases," and "secretly meeting" in Beirut's swanky Saint-George's Hotel "plotting their upcoming moves to conquer and dominate both Lebanon and Syria."[26]

These sorts of stories compelled Patriarch Arida to publicly denounce the organs of Arab nationalism in Lebanon, speaking his indignation, and bluntly asking those involved to "get off the backs of the Jews."[27] The Patriarch further demanded that the French Mandatory authorities in Lebanon at that time, under the leadership of the Maronite Church, expend every resource at their disposal to settle Jewish refugees in Lebanon and facilitate their assimilation into Lebanese society.[28] In recent times, noted the Maronite Patriarch, some 300 thousand new refugees, victims of the Great War, Armenians, Chaldeans, Syriacs, and others, were settled in Lebanon with nary the complaint issuing from any sector of Lebanese society; yet the grievances and protests mount when the dispossessed are Jews.[29] The Patriarch stood firm, insisting that those bragging about their own "compassionate and merciful attributes dispense them for the sake of a suffering humanity," and offer sanctuary to the oppressed Jews of the world, *in* Lebanon proper.[30]

This sentiment was reiterated in a June 5, 1933, editorial in *Al-Aalam al-Isra'iili*, in which the author extolled Lebanon's mission as a refuge for persecuted minorities, and reminded readers—and vicariously

---

[26] *Al-Aalam al-Isra'iili*, "They Came, They Disembarked, They Colonized: Same Melody, Same String; Will You Ever Change Your Tune?" (Beirut, Lebanon: July 24, 1933), 1.

[27] *Al-Aalam al-Isra'iili*, "They Came, They Disembarked, They Colonized", 1.

[28] *Al-Aalam al-Isra'iili*, "His Holiness the Maronite Patriarch Dotes on the Jews of Germany" (Beirut, Lebanon: June 5, 1933), 1.

[29] *Al-Aalam al-Isra'iili*, "His Holiness the Maronite Patriarch Dotes," 1.

[30] *Al-Aalam al-Isra'iili*, "His Holiness the Maronite Patriarch Dotes," 1 (emphasis in original text).

French and Lebanese authorities—that the German Jewish refugees were
not destitute paupers, and would not be living on sufferance or at the
government's expense (were they to be granted asylum in Lebanon).
Indeed, many of them were rich industrialists, entrepreneurs, and highly
educated resourceful pioneers, who may turn out to be a boon to
Lebanon were they to settle and build industries and bring capital and
know-how to Lebanon's emerging economy.[31] "It is worth reminding
our fellow Lebanese of a germane historical event that may put things
into perspective," prefaced the editorial:

> Our fellow Lebanese ought to recall a pertinent event that took place
> some seventy-three years ago, when in the midst of the unrest of 1860,
> French Parliamentarian and founder of the Alliance Israélite Universelle,
> Adolphe Crémieux, gave a moving address in the French Chamber of
> Representatives, in support of Lebanon and the Lebanese. In his talk,
> Crémieux appealed to all Frenchmen, and French Jews in particular,
> to come to the aid of the suffering people of Lebanon. Within hours of
> Crémieux's address, French Jews had collected upwards of 1500 golden
> Liras, promptly sending the monies to Lebanon to be distributed among
> those affected by the tragedies of 1860. We are recalling this episode
> not to boast of the humanitarian spirit of fellow Jews from France, nor
> to praise them and thank them for their benevolent action, because what
> they did was, after all, a human duty pure and simple, incumbent upon
> any human being endowed with a modicum of compassion toward fellow
> human beings. [...] No, we recall this incident to note that history often
> repeats itself, and to remind ourselves of our Lebanese people's celebrated
> high morals, and noble humanism, and gracious hospitality.[32]

---

[31] *Al-Aalam al-Isra'iili*, "Jewish Immigrants in Lebanon; We Should at Least
Reciprocate Their Humanism" (Beirut, Lebanon: June 5, 1933), 1.

[32] *Al-Aalam al-Isra'iili*, "Jewish Immigrants in Lebanon," 1. It is worth mentioning that
Crémieux's actions were those of a humanitarian, not strictly a Jew. And he was indeed
instrumental in prompting French authorities to dispatch troops to Mount-Lebanon, to
put an end to the Druze-Maronite wars, which had all but decimated the Maronite population of the Mountain, subjecting them to a well-orchestrated Druze slaughter, and a
willing Ottoman endorsement. Crémieux's actions also led to the establishment of a special régime for Mount-Lebanon, the *Règlement Organique*, which ultimately led Lebanese
autonomy, within the Ottoman Empire, under the protection of a concert of European
powers led by France.

The editorial went on to prod the Lebanese of the 1930s to not only answer the call of history by giving assistance to those who helped them seventy-three years prior, but also indeed to heed history and "live up to Lebanese history," which, "from time immemorial has known the Lebanese to be a lot of upright, noble, generous humanists."[33] *Al-Aalam al-Isra'iili* concluded by quoting Lebanese writer and future president of the Lebanese Press Association, Alexandre Riachi (1888–1961), who had recently written along similar lines. In his periodical *The Itinerant Journalist* (al-Sahaafi al-Taa'ih), Riachi reportedly stressed that the Lebanese "have an obligation to receive the aggrieved Jews of Germany," paying tribute to "all those Lebanese who remember and honor the kindness done to them three-quarters of a century earlier by meeting the friendship and benevolence of others with gratitude of their own."[34]

It is worth mentioning in this regard that Crémieux's actions were those of a humanitarian, not a Jew strictly speaking. And Crémieux was ultimately instrumental in prompting French authorities to dispatch expeditionary troops to Mount-Lebanon, putting an end to the Druze-Maronite wars of 1860. Incidentally, this conflict, which had all but decimated the Maronite population of the Mountain, subjecting them to a well-orchestrated Druze slaughter, had the Ottomans' endorsement, and French involvement ultimately weakened Ottoman suzerainty setting Lebanon's Christians on a path to independence. Indeed, it may be argued that it was Crémieux' s actions that led to the establishment of the 1860 special régime for Mount-Lebanon, the *Règlement Organique*, which resulted in Lebanese autonomy, within the Ottoman Empire, under the protection of a concert of European powers led by France—all culminating some sixty years later in the establishment of Greater Lebanon.

1938–1946; Foreshadow and Shadow of the Holocaust

The Lebanese Jewish community's changes of fortune can indeed be plotted by way of the language, content, and tenor of the community's mouthpiece, *al-Aalam al-Isra'iili*, through its fifty-year life span.

---

[33] *Al-Aalam al-Isra'iili*, "Jewish Immigrants in Lebanon," 1.

[34] *Al-Aalam al-Isra'iili*, "Jewish Immigrants in Lebanon," 1.

Initially an assertive outspoken periodical with a respectable standing in the Lebanese press and a 600 print-run at its founding,[35] *Al-Aalam al-Isra'iili* became a leading credible news-source, holding its own among Lebanon's best, in a Levantine marketplace of ideas boasting an old venerable journalistic tradition. Lebanon was, after all, heir to the Phoenicians of classical antiquity, the presumed inventors of the Alphabet, and the Jews, kindred Canaanite blood-relatives of the Phoenicians, had no better place than this "cradle of the Alphabet" to revive and maintain *their* tradition as humanity's first "literate people."

Al-Aalam al-Isra'iili was therefore on good solid ground in Lebanon. Its *raison d'être*, political bent, and cultural and communal missions were part of the natural order of things Lebanese; part of Lebanon's diverse ethno-religious fabric. In that sense, the newspaper's role was not only viewed to be legitimate and necessary, but also indeed existential to Lebanon's very mode of being—not only to the life of its Jewish community. It was after all established in the quintessential printing-press capital of the Middle East, in 1921, in the shadow of the French Mandate, at a time when France was to many Lebanese deemed an emancipator, a "protector of the meek, civilizer of nations, mother of all sacred liberties" in words popularized by Jewish and Christian writers of the time.[36]

In this context, *Al-Aalam al-Isra'iili* was intended as a non-partisan, vocal, socially engaged, "Political Cosmopolitan Independent Newspaper" (Ar. "Jariida siyaasiyya jaami'a hurra")—as the front-page caption under its official logo and name proudly described it for close to two decades.

But by 1938, *Al-Aalam al-Isra'iili* had morphed into a cagey, rather politically diffident "Illustrated critical weekly literary newsmagazine" (Ar. "Majalla adabiyya ikhbaariyya intiqaadiyya usbuu'iyya musawwara") according to the now opaque, overwrought language of its front-cover motto. Indeed, during that era, and notwithstanding occasional political forays, the periodical can be said to have distinguished itself more by its weekly "Medical Corner" dealing with such trivialities as "The Scientific Explanation of Sneezing" and "The Origins of Kleptomania." It also ran regular "Dear Abby"-style advice sections and similar, rather superficial

---

[35] MAE, *Presse-Propagande; Presse Syrienne et Libanaise*, Paris: Série E-Levant, Syrie-Liban, Volume 525–526, E-417-1.

[36] Charles Corm, "L'Ombre s'étend sur la montagne...," *La Revue Phénicienne* (Beirut, Lebanon: Éditions de la Revue Phénicienne, July 1919), 11.

rubrics, characteristic of the "gossip magazine" genres and racy tabloids of early twentieth-century America. Gone from *Al-Aalam al-Isra'iili* were its previous, rather instructive, cutting-edge, mordant journalistic feats.

Deteriorating further during the World War II era and its aftermath, and reflecting Lebanon's and the Jews' changing fortunes, *Al-Aalam al-Isra'iili* would sink into further insignificance—or, let's say neutrality—emitting only brief bashful attempts at regaining some political voice. The interlude between the Vichy period in the Levant (July 1940), and Charles De Gaulle's Free French retaking the upper hand in August 1941, in effect marked the end of the French Mandate and the weakening of France's role as a world power sympathetic to Lebanon's Maronites and *their* vision of the Lebanese polity as a haven for minorities.

The British by now had become the "superpower" calling the shots in the Levant, and France had at best become a junior partner, yielding to Great Britain's Arab nationalist sympathies. Subsequently, Lebanon would gain independence from France in 1943, would get sucked deeper into the orbit and resentments of Arab nationalism, and *Al-Aalam al-Isra'iili*, although still billing itself a "Critical Independent Political Newspaper" (in different iterations of its journalistic life) would now add a prominent preface to its "identity," describing itself as a "Mission for Understanding Among Nations, and a Means of Brotherhood Among Men."

By 1948 (coinciding with the date of the establishment of the State of Israel), *Al-Aalam al-Isra'iili* would altogether change its name into a subdued *Al-Salaam* (Ar. "Peace"), reflecting a diminished Jewish community (and voice) and pointing to the toxicity and animus that the Arabic adjective "Isra'iili" had now come to carry—meaning both "Israelite" and "Israeli" in Arabic, and therefore making no distinction between the two.

A representative sampling of articles and news stories from that time period offers a rare glimpse not only into the history and decline of Lebanon's Jews; it also sheds light onto Lebanese society as a whole, revealing the inner-workings of Lebanon's complex identity politics, offering answers to such questions as Lebanon's place in the Middle East—queries into what is Lebanon's nature, and questions as to whether it is Arab, Christian, Eastern, Western, Mediterranean, a sanctuary for minorities as some might have imagined it, or a temporary illegitimate entity "torn" from a putative "Arab whole" awaiting reunification as Arab nationalists contended?

More importantly perhaps, *Al-Aalam al-Isra'iili* offers a unique perspective into the Lebanese Jews' attitudes vis-à-vis their country, their Lebanese identity, Arab identity, Middle Eastern and world Jewry, Zionism, Nazi Germany, *and* eventually the Holocaust and the destruction of European Jewry, and ultimately—on a local level—the end of an age-old Lebanese Jewish life.

Notwithstanding its low-profile during the World War II era, *Al-Aalam al-Isra'iili* still did not shy away from taking the defense of Lebanese Jews as the situation necessitated. One such instance took place in early February 1938, when free copies of an Arabic translation of the *Protocols of the Elders of Zion* were being distributed as a "bonus supplement" to the Saint-Vincent de Paul's monastic journal *Al-Masarra*.

This was a period during which the infamous Hajj Amin al-Husseini (1895–1974) had taken refuge in Lebanon. Wanted by British authorities for his role in the Arab rebellion in Palestine, he slipped away in late 1937 and settled in central Lebanon; in the Maronite coastal town of Jounié to be exact; at a stone's throw from the headquarters of the Saint-Vincent de Paul society where *Al-Masarra* and the Arabic translation of *The Protocols* had been published. This is not to suggest that Husseini might have played a role in this incident—he was after all under tight French surveillance. Still, as one of the most strident anti-Semitic Arab bullhorns of the times, his involvement in stoking up anti-Semitic sentiments would not have been out of character. Indeed, the Beiruti Muslim and Arab nationalist press of those days, from the late 1930s on, had all but embraced Husseini's biases and objectives—in style, prose, and tenor he would only be proud of.

Yet, *Al-Aalam al-Isra'iili* did not mince words, calling to task those behind the *Masarra* incident, even alluding to Husseini in its rebukes. In a strongly worded article titled "Enemies of Arabs and Friends of Evil," the magazine lambasted the Pauline journal for what it called the promotion of vile Nazi propaganda and anti-Semitic canards of the most outlandish kind.[37] Even the Arab nationalist newspaper *Alif-Baa'*, noted *Al-Aalam al-Isra'iili*, not exactly a friend of the Jews, and an otherwise

---

[37] *Al-Aalam al-Isra'iili*, "Blood in Religion: Enemies of Arabs and Friends of Evil" (Beirut, Lebanon: February 18–28, 1938), 11.

"depraved openly anti-Semitic publication," denounced the circulation of the *Protocols*, noting that,

> Our intense hostility toward the Jews notwithstanding, we have to accept and profess in all frankness that the Jewish religion is innocent of these charges; the alleged use of human blood for the purpose of religious rituals. This is an allegation utterly unacceptable to the human mind. We do not believe in these fairytales, and we do not expect a reasonable human being, endowed with a sound mind and a modest intellect, to believe in such nonsense. [...] However, this is by no means attesting to the Jews being the finest from among those lovers of humanity.[38]

By all interpretations, this ostensible denunciation of *The Protocols* can hardly be read as anything less than a poisoned apple, noted *Al-Aalam al-Isra'iili*. It was at best an Arab nationalist publication's feigned indignation at a Catholic publication's anti-Semitic screed; a pot calling a kettle black, of sorts; Arab nationalists denouncing both Jews and Christians—both presumed enemies of Arabism—and in the process casting doubt on the Jewish people's humanity. But *Al-Aalam al-Isra'iili*, in spite of having resigned itself to an apolitical path beginning in the late 1930s, still spoke truth to power at times, and still pointed its sharp pen in the direction of those defaming Lebanese and other Near Eastern Jews. "We are here to defend the persecuted whatever their creed," came a rarely political editorial in the March 1938 issue of the newspaper,

> But, above all, we are here to defend the oppressed Jew, because the Jew is a human being with rights no less legitimate than those of others. And we are indeed more qualified than others to speak on behalf of Near Eastern Jewry, for the simple reason that non-Jews, in countries mired in intolerance and hatred, are often reluctant to take up the defense of their own Jewish countrymen. [...] We may be minorities in this Middle East. But we are vibrant minorities. Indeed we are the heartbeat of minorities in these lands of the Arabs. We speak the language of the Arabs. And under the domination of Arabs, we ought to be allowed our own free press, to express our own opinions, and our own enlightenment, and our own feelings toward the lands of our fathers, in the language of the countries ruling over us. [...] Alas, we have become a tempting prey, targets of a motley ignorant fanatics; targets of hack journalists regaling themselves and their

---

[38] *Al-Aalam al-Isra'iili*, "Blood in Religion," 11.

readers with anti-Jewish defamation campaigns, sold to the highest bidder, in a press-world of mercenary journalism-for-hire. [...] Our journalistic inertia can unfortunately turn into intellectual death. This is precisely what opened the door to deceitful fraudulent journalists to gratuitously demean and abuse us. The weak shall no longer be the scapegoat of the bully and oppressor. [...] We shall fight for our rights and our history. And let it be known that our journal is not the mouthpiece of anyone or any political party; it is the mouthpiece of Truth and Fairness and Justice; and come what may, we shall always and with all of our strength and determination remain defenders of these values, which are ultimately the very principles and foundations of human values.[39]

But the Arabists's attacks on the Jews of Lebanon would not relent, soon to span the physical, economic, and emotive, in addition to the (by now all too familiar) informational and intellectual. To wit, the Arabic-language daily *Bayroot al-Masa*, an unsavory tabloid which had made a career out of badgering and defaming Lebanon's Jewish community, wrote its indignation in the summer of 1938 at the notion that "the journalistic world would tolerate an Arabic-language Jewish newspaper," allowed to publish in Lebanon.[40] *Bayroot al-Masa*'s main objection was to *Al-Aalam al-Isra'iili*'s reporting that "Arab rebels had assassinated four innocent Arab-Jews on the first day of Pesach," on April 16, 1938, and the Jewish magazine's "daring refer to the perpetrators as 'killers' rather than 'Mujahiduun'" (Ar. wagers of Jihad or "freedom fighter").[41] The *al-Masa* further stressed that *Al-Aalam al-Isra'iili* was a publication not authorized to engage in "political reporting," demanding the Lebanese and French authorities mete out appropriate sanctions on the publication and its owners.

The Lebanese government of course did no such thing, and indeed informed the editors of *Al-Aalam al-Isra'iili* that owners of *al-Masa* had filed a formal complaint with the authorities to muzzle the Jewish publication—a sad reflection of how Arab nationalists were now seeking not

---

[39] *Al-Aalam al-Isra'iili*, "Wake Up and Take Heed: Inertia Is Death" (Beirut: March 18, 1938), 6–9.

[40] *Al-Aalam al-Isra'iili*, "Freedom of the Press" (Beirut: June 4, 1938), 11. It is worth noting that *Bayroot al-Masa*, founded by the Beiruti writer Abdallah al-Mashnuq, had garnered a wide reputation as a shrill voice of Arab nationalism, "raising high the flag of Arab causes, in defense of Muslim rights."

[41] *Al-Aalam al-Isra'iili*, "Freedom of the Press," 11.

only an oversight of what news gets reported, but indeed what semantics may be used in reference to the activities of those Arabs and Muslims opposed to Jewish presence in British Mandate Palestine.[42]

Al-Masa and other likeminded Arabist mouthpieces eventually pressured the Lebanese government into issuing a decree shutting down the Jewish journal in late November 1938—an interruption that lasted only a few days, but one that demonstrated the weakness of a Christian-dominated Lebanese state in the face of rising Arab radicalism. Arabist organs had previously been badgering *Al-Aalam al-Isra'iili* into "proving its loyalty to Arabism"; a request which the journal derided, asking its tormentors "before demanding proof of anything, from anyone, others ought to adduce evidence of their own political, cultural, and intellectual maturity, respecting the freedoms of communities living under Arab rule, speaking the language of the Arabs, and contributing to the language of the Holy Koran."[43] This act of public defiance of a brash political movement on the rise left the Lebanese government no alternative

---

[42] In fairness, *Al-Aalam al-Isra'iili* also recognized the "righteous gentiles," most notably among them Muslim *Ulema* who reprimanded those spreading false rumors against the Jews. One such righteous Muslim, a sheikh named Mohammed al-Zoghbi, published in a March 30, 1938, issue of *Al-Aalam al-Isra'iili* scathing remarks against those engaging anti-Semitic canards, noting that,

God Almighty has privileged the Children of Israel, as humanity's first monotheists. [...] All prophets, from Moses to Jesus have been true to the Torah. Anyone who runs through the Books of the Torah will note that the Jewish people have never in their history hurt a single being, let alone have they spilt the blood of innocents [for ritual purposes.] Indeed, the Jews are notorious for their cleanliness, dedicated to a fault in their observance of their rituals. [...] How can anyone possibly believe that the Jews would engage in such crimes [attributed to them,] involving spilling human blood for the purpose of mixing it in their foods? We have been living for hundreds of years with these peaceful people, people whom we would be hard pressed to see in any of the jails of Syria. [...] It is all the more surprising that Christian prelates should engage in spreading such nonsense about their brothers; Christians who consider the Torah to be part of their own scriptures, referring to it as attestation and prediction of the coming of Jesus. How can Christians admit to the sacredness of the Torah, and yet unleash their vicious aggression against the children of the Torah, the keepers of their own [Christian] traditions?

See *Al-Aalam al-Isra'iili*, "O Muslims, Fight Strife and Sedition in Your Countries" (Beirut, Lebanon: March 30, 1938), 19–20.

[43] *Al-Aalam al-Isra'iili*, "Freedom of Expression Prisoner of the Law" (Beirut, Lebanon: January 2, 1939), 1–2.

besides yielding to the blackmail—even if arguably *pro forma*, to buy and bide its time.[44] But the challenges to Lebanon's Jews kept mounting. And notwithstanding those difficulties, and the cataclysmic shifts later brought along by World War II, Jewish presence and history and ascendency in Lebanon continued. And throughout World War II and its aftermath, Jewish refugees from Aleppo, Damascus, and Baghdad would come to swell the relatively healthy numbers and station of Lebanese Jews. Jews are carriers of noble Lebanese and French values came the courtly commentaries of French High Commissioner Gabriel Puaux during an official visit to Beirut's *Alliance* school on February 13, 1939,

> You are here to stay, in this beautiful Lebanon. You are here, in this beautiful country where tolerance reigns, where unhindered freedoms of conscience and belief are respected. Know that, in this land of yours, you are respected, by all those around you. And so, I remain persuaded [...] that you shall remain loyal friends of France, and in that sense exemplary Lebanese.[45]

During that visit, *Alliance* director Elie Penso bragged about his Beirut school being home to some one-thousand-fifty students, in 1939, whereas that number had barely exceeded five-hundred a mere twenty years earlier, in 1919.[46] This was certainly testimony to the rising influence of the *Alliance* itself and the expansion of its educational mission; but it was also a reflection of rising Jewish demographics in Beirut, and Lebanon as a whole. Lebanese Jews would indeed continue to grow in their physical, social, and intellectual influence throughout the WWII era, despite their sometimes precarious security situation—often entailing an increasingly hushed political voice. But they kept a proud place and space and station in Lebanese society, even as the political honeymoon

---

[44] President Émile Éddé made sure that only an interval of days, not months, separated the "Shut Down" decree (Presidential Decree 3472) and its subsequent "Annulment" (Presidential Decree 3572).

[45] *Al-Aalam al-Isra'iili*, "Discours-Réponse de son Excellence Monsieur Gabriel Puaux" (Beirut, Lebanon: February 22, 1939), 11. (Reproduced in the French original.)

[46] *Al-Aalam al-Isra'iili*, "Allocution de Monsieur E. Penso, Directeur des Écoles de l'Alliance Israélite à Beyrouth" (Beirut, Lebanon: February 22, 1939), 12. (Reproduced in the French original.)

that Lebanon had been would soon turn sour on those who dared opt out of Arab nationalist worldviews, and their resentments.

Indeed, it was not World War II, nor was the eventual loss of Lebanon's specificity as a "confederation of minorities" during the 1950s and 1960s that would lead to the etiolation of Lebanese Jewry. It was the 1970s that planted the last nail in the coffin of Lebanese Jewish life—that is to say, the rise of the Palestine Liberation Organization as a major political and military force in the region; the PLO's inauguration of a "state within the state" in Lebanon; and the attendant extortionism and loss of sovereignty that would ensue. Thus the idea of Lebanon as "entrepôt" and crossroads for ideas and peoples and cultures would surrender to a lawless entity, dominated by PLO and Arabist animus, determined to turn a fragile republic whose very *raison d'être* had been an existential—indeed a congenital—neutrality, into a confrontation state caught in an apocalyptic struggle *hardly* of its choosing.

"My country is at war with my people" is an adage often attributed to Arab-Israelis who—all things considered—might have done fairly well for themselves without an "Arab-Israeli" conflict hanging round their necks. With some tweaking, one may argue that there is perhaps no better adage than the above to illustrate the predicament of Lebanese Jewry, hindered as it was by the posturing of Lebanese "countrymen" at swords' points with Jewish "kinsmen", all in the service of an alien ideology that proved noxious to the very notion of Lebanon.

CONCLUSIONS

And so, there may be no "happy returns," no "Odyssey-ian" homecomings in the future of Lebanon's Jews. Indeed, there may only be roads and movement and peregrinations and exile in their future; a future made up of nostalgia in Amin Maalouf's telling; "nostalgia for a bygone era," as he put it in *Les Échelles du Levant*:

> a bygone era where men of all origins confused lived side by side on their Levantine ports of call, and blended all their languages together. Would this be a reminiscence of times past? Or is it a foretelling of a future yet to come? And what about those who persist in their attachment to this dream? Are they backward-looking reactionaries? Or are they the true visionaries?[47]

[47] Amin Maalouf, *Les Échelles du Levant* (Paris: Grasset, 1993), 49.

As the Lebanese Republic inches closer to the centennial anniversary milestone of its modern life, and as new columns of Middle Eastern refugees snake around the world, changing landscapes and exchanging homelands, one hundred years after the birth of the post-Ottoman Arab-defined Middle East, Maalouf's words ring so eerily familiar. This chapter, like its antecedents and the ones yet to come, is an attempt to initiate a corrective to a lacuna of exclusion with regard to Lebanese Jewry, restoring a people to their rightful place in the sun—and out of the shade—recovering, rehabilitating, and memorializing their lives. The chapters that follow relate stories to that effect; stories told in the voices of human subjects, some of them Lebanese Jews, others not, all of them issuing a summons to Lebanon, calling on the Lebanese to redeem to their national memory suppressed fragments of their history.

CHAPTER 5

Lebanese Jewish Memory and Memorial: Personal Recollections

La parole est moitié à celui qui parle,
moitié à celui qui écoute.

Michel de Montaigne (1533–1592)

As mentioned at the outset of this study, besides being a research-based work of history, this book's aim was to also contribute a modest little brick to the edifice of "a memorial" to Lebanon's Jewish community; an act of remembrance as it were; and a sanctuary and place of reflection dedicated to a foundational Lebanese community—arguably the oldest and most "indigenous" of "indigenous Lebanese" communities—and one well-nigh expunged from the normative scholarship on modern Lebanon.

Their miniscule numbers notwithstanding, Lebanese Jews are not a marginal community, even as they might not have benefitted from adequate treatment in the corpus of Lebanese history. What's more, Lebanese Jews themselves are not unaware of their venerable age-old lineage in Lebanon. Their written "profiles" of themselves, their internal communal memoranda, their official and informal correspondence with foreign and Lebanese interlocutors, their public commentaries and official stances, and their own self-narratives in the Lebanese press as well as in a variety of private contexts all attest to their keen awareness of their deeply rooted connection to Lebanon. In one such profile dating back to

© The Author(s) 2019
F. Salameh, *Lebanon's Jewish Community*,
https://doi.org/10.1007/978-3-319-99667-7_5

1964, hidden in the confines of the World Jewish Congress Collection, a Lebanese Jewish correspondent proudly flaunted the presence of Jews in Lebanon going back to classical antiquity and Biblical times: Long before there were Christians and Muslims in Lebanon, wrote this correspondent,

> Jewish communities were to be found in the interior as well as on the coast, and they led a most active cultural and commercial life. There are records of exchanges, both cultural and trade, between [the Phoenician] King Hiram of Tyre and King Solomon. An Old Testament Hebrew prophet is buried on Lebanese territory in Sujod, which has become a place of pilgrimage [for Lebanese Jews and others.] In later days, it is known that St. Paul went to visit the Jewish community of Damascus [by way of Lebanon.] In more recent times, in the days of the Emir Bechir [Prince of autonomous Ottoman Mount-Lebanon] Jewish communities of merchants and artisans flourished at Deir al-Kamar, Saïda and Tripoli, and in Beirut, where ancient synagogues bear witness to an active Jewish life in those times.[1]

Yet, in the vast academic literature on Lebanese history and memory, and especially on the history of Lebanese "expansion" and migration—in the words of Philip Hitti a venerable "chapter in the history of emigration and colonization worthy of [the Lebanese] as descendants of Phoenicians"—there is nary a mention of Lebanese Jewry or Lebanese Jewish communities, whether at home or in expatriate colonies.[2] Yet, true to their Phoenician lineage, and in the tradition of their seafaring Phoenician ancestors, noted Hitti, Lebanese of every stripe, undoubtedly Jews among them, have

> planted settlements in Italian, French, and other European cities whence were exchanged the products of Asia and of Europe. Modern Lebanese settlements flourish at Cairo, Marseille, Paris, Manchester, New York, São Paulo, Buenos Aires and Sydney. Nineteenth-century Lebanese were the first among Arabic-speaking peoples to respond heartily to intellectual Western stimuli.

---

[1] Anonymous, *Profile of the Lebanese Jewish Community* (Beirut, Confidential, June 1964), Jacob Rader Marcus Center of the American Jewish Archives, The World Jewish Congress Collection, Series H: Alphabetical Files, 1919–1981, Box: H235, File 3, Lebanon, 1960–1969, 04.031.

[2] Philip K. Hitti, *A Short History of Lebanon* (New York: St. Martin's Press, 1965), 64.

They mediated the new acquisition to their neighbors and thereby enhanced the renaissance of the entire area. Currently they enjoy a measure of democracy and practice a system of free enterprise probably unequalled in the Near East.[3]

And yet the story of Lebanese emigration remains strangely silent on Lebanese Jewry—just as Lebanese history proper is quiet on native Jewish communities at home. Attempting to fill this lacuna of omission, and complete this act of remembrance—a duty to memory as it were— the remaining chapters of this book are meant to consist exclusively of testimonies of Lebanese Jews—as well as the recollections of *other* non-Jewish Lebanese—weighing in on lives and times when there was still a sizable vibrant Jewish community in Lebanon.

Although many interviews were conducted for this purpose over the span of four years, there were many snags in attempting to publish them. Indeed, some of the main responders, at different stages of this volume's iterations, have had a change of heart, sometimes demurring with regard to granting permissions to use their narratives verbatim, or refer to their personal accounts by name. Without those responders, the research-based chapters of the book would have required major rewrites and omissions. This has led to an expansion of the circle of informants, with interviews and various meetings being conducted in France, Israel, Mexico, and even Lebanon—although in the latter case the remaining emaciated members of the Jewish community remained at best cagey, reticent, not to say mute, and so, provided accounts that will be referred to *only* occasionally, in passing, and anonymously. Likewise, and for want of space, only a fraction of the testimonies collected over the years will figure in this section.

And so it begins.

On July 20, 2017, a last trip to Israel was finalized to wrap up the last series of interviews for this volume. Leaving Paris on August 8 at midnight, and arriving in Tel Aviv at 5 a.m. on that same day, I was scheduled to meet with Ambassador Yitzhak Levanon on that very same morning, at 11 a.m., in Herzliya.

Ambassador Levanon, born and raised Yitzhak Kishik-Cohen in Beirut, son of renowned Beiruti merchant Joseph Kishik-Cohen and his wife, socialite Shulamit (Shula) Cohen, left for Israel in 1967. His adopted patronym, Levanon, seems to have been a nod to his

[3]Hitti, 6–7.

Lebanese past even as it relinquished the venerable (priestly) last name of his Lebanese father—a past, that given his family's experience in the Lebanon of the 1960s, Levanon might have wished expunged from memory. Yet, this past seems to still linger on, cling to him, live with and within the ambassador, whispering to him in Lebanese inflections that still seep into his spoken languages—Lebanese and French alike—speckling his mannerisms, his idiomatic expressions, and his linguistic habits with the sound of an intimate last name redolent with Lebanon—Levanon...

At any rate, the ambassador seemed to be keen on meeting with me. I wouldn't say he was eager. Diplomats are usually diplomats because they are sober, deliberate, unsentimental, the very opposite of "eager"; political animals adept at keeping personal feelings and emotions at bay. In fact, only I might have been the anxious party in this affair, "eager" to engage this *"retour en arrière,"* this "going back in time" in the direction of Lebanon, memorializing perhaps notable nuggets of the ambassador's Lebanese past—a part of his life that he might have otherwise not wished be recalled; or perhaps remembrances that might very well have lapsed from his memory—or that he may be reserving for his own autobiography, should there be one in the works.

But was I in for a surprise.

Certainly, this section of the book aims at preserving and memorializing an oral history that will have otherwise receded into oblivion. It is a quest after Lebanese Jewish stories. A *"travail de mémoire"* to be sure, indeed perhaps even a *"devoir de mémoire"* toward, for, and about Lebanese Jews and non-Jews alike. But this may be before anything else an act of discovery (or excavation and rediscovery); an inquiry into Lebanon and a "censored" piece of Lebanese cultural, social, and political history; a blend of history, memory, politics, and nostalgia that are not a staple of the traditional normative literature on Lebanon today, and that may at times read too intimately personal, perhaps even too uncomfortably lyrical for a work of history. But that's perhaps to be expected in an endeavor preoccupied with human subjects, informed by a human experience.

In preparation for what may lay ahead for me in Israel, I had written to Ambassador Levanon on July 29, 2017, from Paris, to reconfirm our upcoming August 8 meeting. I recalled in the text of my e-mail an old Lebanese habit, an idiomatic register of sorts whereby upon parting company, or preparing to meet someone, the Lebanese—instead of opting for the customary "so long" or "hello" or "see you soon"—simply ask "baddak shee?" i.e., "do you need anything?" or "may I bring you anything with me for next time?" The cultural connotation here is a simple one indeed; it says "there is no final goodbye" and "no lasting separation"; "I shall return in no time," and so, "what shall I bring with me for next time?" Likewise, in anticipation of meeting someone—whether a new acquaintance for the first time or an old intimate friend that we'd just left—the query is often the same; *not* "hello" or "good to see you" or "looking forward to seeing you," but rather "baddak shee?" (again, "do you need anything?"). The common rejoinder to this query is usually "Baddé saléémtak" ("all I want is your wellbeing") or "Tijé/Tuwsal bis-saléémé" ("may you come/arrive safely"). The latter was exactly Ambassador Levanon's clipped reply to my e-mail: "Tuwsal bis-saléémé," or "arrive safely."

The reason I mention this story is twofold: Firstly, these sorts of idiomatic registers do not exist in any of the cultural rituals that I am familiar with—whether Arab, Israeli, American, or French. Indeed, those are dyed in the wool Lebanese modes of being—similar to the way the Lebanese may bid farewell or Godspeed to a traveler with "truuh w tirja' bis-saléémé," which is to say "may you go and come back home safely," suggesting, again, that no separation is everlasting, and no journey (for a culture of émigré seafarers) is a one-way trek. The second reason ambassador Levanon's reply struck me and stuck out to me dwells in its perspicacity. As a cultural historian, I found it fascinating that a 73-year-old Israeli—albeit a foreign-service veteran attuned to multicultural minutiae, but nevertheless an Israeli who left his native Lebanon more than fifty years ago—still had not shed very much of the more perceptible cultural markers, linguistic habits, and idiomatic registers that only those "old hands" intimate with Lebanon's ways are capable of keeping alive. Fifty years of imbibing other cultural norms did not, it seems, dampen ambassador Levanon's "Lebanonness," reminding me of a passage from the doyen of Francophone Lebanese poets, Charles Corm (1894–1963) paying tribute to the Lebanese emigrant's tenacity and the persistence of the linguistic "lebanonisms" that he keeps tucked inside his memory's vault. Addressing those resilient, distinctly Lebanese linguistic habits, Corm wrote

Your soft and graceful inflexions, still slip their ancient drawl / In all the modern languages swarming on our shores [...] And I still can feel your faithful fingers, gently knock on memory's door, awakening my heart [...] / For Man here below, in spite of having learnt / His brute oppressor's tongue, has kept the looks, the tone, / Has kept the pitch, the pulse, of his forefather's inflections, of his old ancestors' voice! / Exiles and vaga- bonds, through all their ports of call, / Still bring along their language, still cling to their old brogue / Still pilfer its perfumes, still tinge it with the hues, of their first mother's voice...[4]

Although I initially did not ask him—so as not to spoil the poetic license with which I explained it to myself—I am almost certain that Ambassador Levanon's chosen patronymic was meant as a homage to his Lebanese past. And though I must stress that the ambassador's affections for Lebanon were palpable during our meeting, I must also stress that his disappointments were equally apparent. Perhaps the adage about "those who love a lot expect a lot" (and maybe ultimately lose a lot) is not with- out truth. After all, Lebanon, the ambassador's ancestral homeland, one in which—and for which—his family had lived and built and committed for centuries, was the same Lebanon that abused and banished his family. And so it goes without saying that those who love a lot are perhaps jus- tified having higher expectations. And expect the Kishik-Cohens proba- bly did and might have had every prerogative to do. But what they were dealt in return was a rotten hand. And for this, Lebanon stands alone, naked, to answer to history's reckoning. For one hundred years of its modern existence, Lebanon has tangled and angled to have its cake and eat it too, maintaining itself as a sovereign independent entity "*distinct*" from what is normatively referred to as the "Arab world," but at the same time paying lip service to Arab phobias and often falling prey—and ultimately paying tribute—to them...

Lebanon's Maronites, who from 1920 to 1958 attempted to put in place a state in their own image, pride themselves on having never suc- cumbed to Islam's dhimmi system and on having never lived as a deval- ued tributary people beholden to the sufferance, benevolence, and fickleness of Muslim overlords.[5] Indeed, Philip Hitti stressed that for the better part of thirteen centuries of Muslim dominance in the Near

---

[4]Charles Corm, *La montagne inspirée* (Beirut: Éditions de la Revue Phénicienne, Third Edition, 1987), 105.

[5]Philip Hitti, *Lebanon in History; From the Earliest Times to the Present* (London and New York: St-Martin's Press, 1957), 244–46.

East, the Maronites were manifestly the only native Christian people to have exacted tribute from the Muslim rulers, rather than succumbing to their authority.[6] Yet, those same Maronites still managed to "dhimmify" themselves in their modern Lebanon, becoming willy-nilly the "party organs" and "spokespersons" for Arabs and Arab nationalists, espousing the Arabs' *causes célèbres* and intellectualizing them and lending them international legitimacy and airtime. By making the case for Arabism and Palestinianism—in the hope that Lebanon's "experiment" would be spared the wrath of both—the Lebanese, the Maronite political class in particular, forfeited their obligations to Lebanese Jews, delivering them to the acrimony and animosity and resentments of Arab nationalists intent on making Lebanese Jewry pay the price for Israel's successes— on the battlefield, in the arena of nation building, on the world's stage of economic and technological development, and in the court of world opinion. A case in point is Michel Chiha, a paragon and chief ideologue of the notion of Lebanon as a "merchant republic" and multicultural polyglot Mediterranean hub; a mediator negotiator indifferent to the quibbles of doctrinaires and nationalists, engaged in building bridges and commercial entrepôts, and acting as conduits—not nursing old wounds and leaving them to fester. Even *this* Michel Chiha opted to leave Lebanon's Jews high and dry. Indeed, Chiha's sapient form of "intellectual" journalism of the 1940s and 1950s produced some of the most vehement (almost venomous) critiques of Zionism, even as he might have been sympathetic in earlier times to what may be deemed a Christian Lebanese version of Zionism.[7]

---

[6] Hitti, *Lebanon in History*, 244–46.

[7] See, for instance, Michel Chiha's "Progression d'Israël," *Le Jour* (Beirut: February 24, 1951). In this, Chiha praises Israel's accomplishments, while shaming the undisciplined opportunistic Lebanese for not following Israel's example. Both his introductory and concluding sentences offer an exquisite summation of his despair and yearning—if not the outright admiration (even if also the envy) he had vis-à-vis Israel. "Our neighbors to the South are moving forward at breakneck speed," he wrote "we ought to pay our respects to this, Israel's powerful urge towards living and being alive. [... Yet, we, the Lebanese] go on living and thinking in obsolete archaic notions, in the fatal laziness of bygone centuries. [...] Let us not forget this painful reality if we do not wish [Lebanon,] this country of light to lapse into the twilight." By any measure, read from the purview of the twenty-first century and in light of what has befallen a Lebanon bereft of Jews, Chiha's words are nothing if not painful, premonitory, and woefully prophetic.

Things were likewise with Saïd Akl (1912–2014) one of the main cantors of Phoenicianism, who, betraying a hint of "intellectual bondage" at a particular juncture of his intellectual life, surrendered his literary talent in the service of Arabist sensitivities. Following the 1967 War and the reunification of Jerusalem, Akl produced a poetic screed denouncing what he described as Jewish "barbarity" (Ar. *Hamajiyya*); a "rousing" lyrical anti-Jewish invective that Akl put to the angelic voice of Fayrouz, Lebanon's diva; a song that before too long was to become the anthem of Arab anti-Jewishness as it were; polite, veiled, "principled" anti-Jewishness.[8] One wonders how Lebanese Jewry must have felt, with such vile anti-Jewish hectoring and lip service issuing from Lebanon's Maronite establishment—one, as we saw earlier, ordinarily sympathetic to Jews, and supportive of Israel.

In a sense, Lebanon's Christians' wager might have been the following: "we make the case against the Jews' right to self-determination in Israel, and maybe the Arabs will spare us *their* repudiation of our own rights to a Lebanese entity distinct from those of the neighborhood's Muslims." But things did not pan out as planned: Lebanon's Jews were sacrificed on the altar of Maronite opportunism, and in the process, the Maronites themselves lost their hold on the Lebanon of 1920, the "confederation of minorities" that had been *their* creation. A premonitory article in the French periodical *Information d'Israël*, dating back to 1968 and aptly titled "The Beginning of the End of Lebanese Judaism," perhaps sums up the dire situation confronting Lebanese Jewry: Lebanon, where a bevy of national and ethnic minorities mingle and coexist in harmony, began the *Information d'Israël* piece, this Lebanon was relatively and surprisingly successful in maintaining and safeguarding the security of its Jewish community—compared to the situation of Jews in other parts of the Arab world:

[8]The poem and song in question are titled *Sayfun fa-liyushhar* (A Sword, Let it Be Drawn). There is a dispute and a great deal of fuzziness regarding the poem's authorship. Some argue Saïd Akl wrote it. Others affirm it was the Brothers Rahbani, the musical duo behind Fayrouz who also worked in partnership with Saïd Akl through most of Fayrouz's career. What is certain, however, is that Saïd Akl himself assured this author, during an interview in 1999, that the poem was indeed his own, even if it does not figure in any of his published works. What's more, he also noted that even when they wrote their own Modern Standard Arabic texts, the Brothers Rahbani always consulted with Saïd Akl who often edited, corrected, and augmented their texts. This is apparent in the thematic, linguistic, and symbolic parallels any casual reader can draw between *Sayfun fa-liyushhar*, and another poem titled *Zahratu l-Madaa'in* (The Flower of Cities) treating a similar topic, and which is an established component of Akl's corpus.

This, however, does not mean that in Lebanon—even if much less so than in other neighboring countries—the Jews do not feel targeted, bullied, pressured, blackmailed. Indeed, and since July of last year [1967], Lebanese Jews have become more amenable to the advice admonishing them to immigrate. And the numbers corroborate these circumstances: from a population of 6000 according to communal records prior to the Six-Days War, Lebanese Jews have dwindled to 3000 mere months following the war's end. [...] Add to that the continuous anti-Jewish incitements in some of the Lebanese press [...] and the constant harassment by many Arab businessmen withholding payments owed to Jewish debtors and traders, and the picture of a Jewish purge becomes complete. [...] Lebanese Jews are acutely conscious of the dangers menacing them. And although many are staying put, aware of the free access they still enjoy to an outside world alert to their situation, they could very well, overnight, find themselves completely isolated, cut off, submerged in a climate of hatred and violence.[9]

And so, the erstwhile liberal, libertine, diverse, and tolerant Lebanon of the Maronites would sell its soul and surrender its *raison d'être*, pandering (*into* the twenty-first century) to the phobias of the neighborhood's Muslims, trying to court their favors, arrogating itself the function of their advocate and enabler, and the international "voice" and mainstay of their hang-ups. Even today, under the watchful gaze of Hezbollah (the infamous Party of Allah), a purveyor of cruel mediaeval ideals, Lebanese politicians, journalists, and public intellectuals, many Maronites among them, seldom miss an opportunity to feed the old uncouth anti-Semitic tropes of times past, engaging a variety of hackneyed canards about some endless international Jewish conspiracy, and most of all, discharging barrages of verbal hectoring and public denunciations of the "offense" that is the Jewish state, driving further underground the last remaining relics of Lebanon's emaciated, muzzled Jewish community.[10]

In this context, in early August 2017, Lebanon's leading francophone daily, *L'Orient le Jour*, published the story of a Brooklynite Beiruti, Raymond Sasson, a personage that fit the bill of the "good Jew" who

---

[9] "Le commencement de la fin du Judaïsme libanais" (The Beginning of the End of Lebanese Judaism), *Information Israël* (Paris: May 17, 1968), the Jacob Rader Marcus Center of the American Jewish Archives, The World Jewish Congress Collection, Series H: Alphabetical Files, 1919–1981, Box: H235, File 3, Lebanon, 1960–1969, 04.079.

[10] This last term, "offense," is an English rendition of the Arabic "Udwaan" (literally "aggression"), a mainstay of Arabic political, journalistic, and academic writing describing the State of Israel.

is not Israeli. The son of a Lebanese Jewish mother, Sasson holds the Lebanon of his birth in special affection we are told: In August 2017, at almost fifty years of age, he was on his sixth trek to Beirut, part of an annual summer pilgrimage that he had begun nine years earlier with his elderly Lebanese mother. Although a moving testimonial by any measure—a nostalgic "going back in time" for a man who left Lebanon at the age of four—the *OLJ* journalist's rendering of Sasson's story was not without condescension and infantilization of Lebanese Jewry. To wit, and for good measure, the article informed readers that Sasson was not a Zionist and never been to Israel, as if repudiating the notion of Israel as a home for world Jewry was the only way a Lebanese Jew is able to burnish his Lebanese credentials and assuage the anxieties of those who have yet to come to terms to the reality of a "Jewish state" still, in many Arab quarters, never referred to by name.[11]

What's more, the patronizing, often venomous "Readers' Commentaries" that the *OLJ* article generated—mostly by Lebanese Christians—suggested that the idea of a Jewish conspiracy still had its adherents in the Lebanon of today. Thus, the "Jews of Lebanon" some of the *OLJ* readers took care to tell us—rarely "Lebanese Jews" as such, but rather the sterilized alien "Jews of Lebanon—left Lebanon willingly, stealthily. Indeed, Lebanese Jewry, we are told, a varied and complex group as any of Lebanon's ethno-religious groups, had prior knowledge of the looming Lebanese war of 1975, and therefore left beforehand, quietly, undercover, leaving the other Lebanese to fend for themselves. Otherwise, the indignities, harassment, abuse, physical violence, and persecutions that Lebanese Jews have suffered since 1948, often at the hands of bands of Arabist marauders and Palestinian paramilitary groups functioning outside and above legal Lebanese authorities, are disregarded or glossed over. History in general is glossed over, doctored up, distorted in modern Lebanon to suit the sensitivities and prejudices of the current powers that be. In fact, there *had been* a proud sanguine Jewish life in Lebanon prior to the modern obscurantist Hezbollah era and its predecessor, often jaundiced Arab nationalist one; an era where Lebanese Jewry could be unquestionably Lebanese and openly sympathize with Zionist thought.

---

[11] Patricia Khoder, "De Brooklyn à Beyrouth; L'histoire d'un retour," *L'Orient le jour* (Beirut: August 8, 2017). https://www.lorientlejour.com/article/1066187/de-brooklyn-a-beyrouth-lhistoire-dun-retour.html.

That had indeed been the case for as long as there was a confident "Christian Lebanon" in the early twentieth century, upholding a "diversity of perspectives" and promoting a pluralist multicultural conception of the Lebanese state as a "confederation of minorities." A case in point confirming a healthy unhindered Jewish life in Lebanon that could openly uphold Zionist principles is a commemorative article in the first issue of *Al-Aalam al-Isra'iili*. In this September 1, 1921, edition of Lebanon's Jewish mouthpiece, published on the first anniversary of the establishment of Greater Lebanon, an honest, pellucid, Arabic encomium celebrating the life and works of Theodor Herzl (1860–1904) read as follows:

> *This past July brought us back the commemoration of the passing of the founder of modern Zionism, Theodor Herzl. It is therefore more than appropriate for us on this auspicious occasion, and in view of the definitive and resounding successes met by the Herzlian project, to enumerate the great achievements of this great man who injected his fearless spirit into the Jewish nation, who accommodated all its disparate aspirations rendering them all a single concrete reality. Prior to Herzl, Jewish existence was exilic, drifting among the nations and wandering aimlessly from one country to the next; indeed the Jewish being before Herzl was persecuted in one place, oppressed in the next, even as it had never lost hope in an impending redemption. Like the Jewish self, Jewish hope had also attempted to accommodate to the shifting circumstances, taking shape at times in the form of religious fervor, at other times blooming in the guise of poetic yearnings giving birth to impressive universal literary forms like the ones elaborated in the "Zionism" of the great Yehuda Halevi (1075–1141). At other times still, Jewish hope would crystallize in the form of renewed Messianism as was the case with Shabbetai Zevi (1626–1676). Yet, the dream of Israel's return to Palestine did not take its scientific and indeed its practical operational dynamic until that remarkable thinker, Theodor Herzl, came along. Still, his beginnings did not prepare him for that momentous task. Early on in his life he was a foreign correspondent of one of the most important European publications, living a life of bliss and prosperity. He was also a moderately successful playwright with a number of successful "impressionist" plays to his name. But in Paris, where he was stationed for a time, there was a sudden eruption of reactionary movements instigated by the Dreyfus Affair, which began in 1894. During that time, the French authorities, in this country of "Human Rights," stripped a military officer of his high military rank on charges of high treason, even as this officer always insisted he was innocent; claims of innocence that were met with collective mockery and ridicule by the French public. These events had*

the deepest effect on Herzl, who then felt in himself burgeoning the compulsion to "find a solution to the Great Eternal Jewish Question." It was then that Herzl came to the realization that there was no salvation for the Jews in pursuing European ideas and European lives and European arts. It was likewise not enough for the Jews to be more patriotic than the greatest of patriots. "Whatever he does," noted Herzl, "the Jew shall remain a Jew, at best a 'tolerated guest,' at worst a 'scorned and hated stranger'." Alongside these modern forms of Jewish hatred, Herzl began also recalling the oppressions and persecutions of times past, to which the Jews were the perennial victims. His conclusion was that his people had endured fire and bloodletting across the ages; he remembered the past, and witnessed the present, animating in him powerful emotions leading him to pen his watershed Der Judenstaat, *his "roadmap" to us all on the path of patriarchs and ancestors, to the land of Abraham and Isaac and Jacob [...]; to Palestine, the only homeland that the Jews ought to recover and reclaim as the world persists in denying them a homeland anywhere else on this earth. This became Herzl's lifelong struggle [...] He faced and lobbied kings and potentates and emperors and sultans for the purpose of making his dream a reality. He met with unspeakable adversity in his quest, but he remained undaunted, soliciting the help of intellectuals and politicians and superpowers. Finally, the first great nation to take notice of Herzl's cause, giving the Zionist idea its due, was Great Britain. "Uganda" was therefore offered to the Jews, as a palliative, but that proposal was rejected, and Herzl persevered in his quest for Palestine, despite the material and emotional, and ultimately the physical hardships that all his struggles entailed [...] Herzl died [on July 3, 1904] before seeing the fruit of his labors ripened. But the Jewish people reaped those delectable fruits. Tell us then, with what tongue and by way of what pen could the gifted orator or the eloquent writer render back to Herzl, this rare genius, our debt of gratitude? Nay, neither tongue nor pen can be adequate enough for this task. [...] So let his remains rest in peace, for we have already attained, thanks to his inestimable efforts, much more than material gains.*[12]

But perhaps there will be a reckoning of history some day. Perhaps there will be accountability in the future of those Lebanese who sought to erase, suppress, or distort Jewish life in Lebanon; perhaps they will be called to task one day, those stood on the sidelines while their Jewish countrymen paid the price of their own cowardice and political expediency, suffering the exactions of Arab phobias and Arabist anti-Jewish compulsions.

---

[12] *Al-Aalam al-Isra'iili*, "Theodor Herzl" (Beirut: September 1, 1921), 3–4.

But there are Lebanese Jewish personal stories bereft of politics and political score-settling. To wit, another Lebanese Jew featured in this section, Alain Abadie, *also* a Beiruti by birth like Ambassador Levanon and Raymond Sasson, but currently living and singing in Tel Aviv, insisted we completely left politics out of our encounter. Indeed, as I shall elaborate later, our meeting turned out to be a bacchanalia of food, music, and memories. Incidentally, the Alain of Bat Yam[13] today, a youthful (almost baby-faced) seventy years old, remains a spitting image of the Blues-smitten guitar-playing adolescent on the balcony of his parents' Beirut home, belting out an eclectic (electric) blend of R&B and Michel Sardou serenading the neighborhoods of Wadi Boujmil and beyond. A mere teenager in Beirut, he had become a fixture of Télé-Liban's 1970s talent shows, a celebrity of sorts in Beirut's nightlife and musical scene, and an accomplished musician, songwriter, and recording artist that at the time could have rivaled France's best from his small port city in the Eastern Mediterranean.[14]

Alain still lives on the Eastern shores of the Mediterranean, at a stone's throw (a mere two-hour car ride) from his native Beirut; yet, he lives worlds away from the port city and the fragrances of his youth. Still Beirut breathes and heaves within him, in the impeccable French that still seeps out of his daily Hebrew, in the exquisite Beiruti inflections that still betray his spoken Lebanese, in his mannerisms, his cultural affections, and his culinary habits, but most of all in the guarded archive of old photographs that he keeps handy, stored in the cramped memory of

---

[13] Bat Yam is a coastal southern "suburb" of Tel Aviv. It is home to sizeable communities of Turkish Jews and other Jews of Muslim-majority countries.

[14] One of Alain Abadie's hits, his 1973 *Aime* (Love), was a local sensation that, had Lebanon not been less fortunate in the years that followed, might have rivaled France's best, namely Michel Sardou's *La maladie d'amour* and others, which had been fixtures of the Beirut music and artistic scenes of the time. See Abadie's *Aime* here, with excerpts of the lyrics:

https://www.youtube.com/watch?v=bMprirR406E.

Caresser un visage, avoir une main dans ta main, / Un sourire qui vous aime, en se réveillant le matin, / Une voix, un murmure, et quelques mots d'amour, / Quand tu t'amuses entre mes bras, je te dis bis au petit jour... / Aime, aime, aime, aime....

Aime la nuit et le jour, aime la vie et l'amour, / Aime l'hiver et l'automne, aime tout ce que je te donne, / Aime le vent et la mer, aime les fruits de la terre, / Aime la vie, les oiseaux, et le ciel quand il fait beau... / Quand ta voix me murmure, autour de mon oreille, / Les mots que j'attends de toi, chaque fois tu m'emverveilles...

his smartphone, ready to be flaunted at the drop of a hat, at the mere mention of Lebanon: Here, there is a photograph of a 14-year-old Alain, guitar strapped around his neck, singing at Beirut's famous *Caves du Roy* nightclub; there, one sees a picture of a younger Alain, in shorts and t-shirt, the ubiquitous guitar in hand, singing on the balcony of a Beirut apartment building (probably his own), or sitting alongside a schoolmate (most probably Yitzhak Levanon) in the middle of an AIU school classroom; there still, there is a Beatlesque Alain, wailing into a microphone, on the set of *Studio el-Fan's* talent show; another photograph still shows Alain and his mother at some remote village on Mount Lebanon, with a snow-capped peak as their backdrop.

Alain is a lover of life, music, people, and food. One can see that from the ease with which he connects to people, the ease with which he acclimates to alien surroundings—in this case Israel—and recreates within them his own Lebanon with all its cultural, linguistic, culinary, and emotive accretions. He is not a doctrinaire. And so I deferred to Alain's wishes, leaving politics completely out of our discussions, sticking strictly to his life as a child-artist in Lebanon and his activities post-Lebanon.

Alain left the land of his birth fairly late in the game, in 1975, much later than other Lebanese Jews preceding him by almost a decade—and around the same time Amin Maalouf's Naïm, in the *Les désorientés* narrative, left. But instead of Naïm's Brazil, a typical destination among Lebanese Jews in those days, Alain's family settled for (and *in*) Tel Aviv—an unlikely and uncommon destination among Lebanese Jewish exiles who, notwithstanding the bad taste that Lebanon might have left in their mouths, still dreamt of a happy return. And although I never really learned the exact circumstances of Alain's journey south, his affections for Lebanon and his fond memories of his native Beirut pervaded his being, and our conversations. His Facebook friends list, exceeding a thousand, is dominated by Lebanese, expats and residents alike, old friends from Lebanon mostly, Jews and non-Jews alike. Likewise, Alain's Facebook posts, when not relevant to his musical performances in Tel Aviv, his life as an artist and musician in Israel, are populated by old faded photographs of the Beirut of his youth, or scratchy renditions of old musical recordings, or some worn footage of some performance of his—here on some balcony in his Wadi Boujmil neighborhood, there on some jetty salt-sprayed by the Mediterranean, often in sun-whipped bushy hairdo, happy, smiling, always a guitar in hand and a song on the lips...

Although I yielded to Alain's wishes to stay away from politics, politics is a strange avocation and an inveterate adversary that always finds a way to intrude on good company. And so, from being initially cagey, reticent, reluctant to speak to me about his erstwhile Lebanese life, Alain became suddenly a Beiruti well worth his salt, garrulous, animated, eager to share his life.

On August 8, 2017, at noon, he picked me up from my Tel Aviv hotel for a lunch of Falafel and Hummus at Abu Hassan's, in the Old Port of Jaffa. That same evening, it was "open mic." at Alain's favorite Tel Aviv haunt, where he and I were both slated to take the stage for an "impromptu" jam-session: Two voices "from Lebanon" as it were, in Tel Aviv, one Jewish and one Maronite; both yearning for some "home" in song, from afar; a mere 100 miles from Beirut, yet worlds apart and away from her; banished in a port city that might as well have been Beirut's twin sister-city; yet still in a kindred cultural, ethnic, social, and linguistic duplicate of Beirut that remains forbidden to most Beirutis.

In the following narratives, there are also stories of *other* Lebanese Jewish expatriates that I've met in Israel; Lebanese Jewish exiles who opted to settle in France, the USA, Canada, Mexico, and Italy, but who make annual pilgrimages to Israel, probably in order to be the nearest possible to the land of their birth; to gaze at their native Lebanon from a safe distance; not very near at hand, but very close to the heart. "I live with the memories and smells of Lebanon, […] I *dream* of Lebanon" came an especially poignant revelation from one of my older responders from Canada; a venerable, gentle medical doctor who did well for himself in the past fifty years of his exile, but a man from Lebanon who still "dreams" of his forefathers' home, of the summer home that his father built in the resort town of Bhamdoun in Mount Lebanon, of their Beirut flat on top of his father's bustling medical practice… The question that emerges from these old faded memory snapshots is whether or not Lebanon herself still dreams of her banished children, still thinks about them, or still contemplates what went wrong and what may be done to make things right again.

And so, what come next are the testimonials of those banished children of Lebanon, expatriates and residents alike, Jews and others excavating memories and reflecting on times in their lives seldom considered in the vast, normative literature on Lebanon and Lebanese Jewry. In this, and save for minor stylistic intrusions to maintain some textual fluidity, I have brought nothing of my own into the testimonies given me. However, the reader will note that occasionally, where commentary and clarifications were judged useful, and so as to still leave my responders' train of thought undisturbed, I have provided footnoted annotations (sometimes heavily so) to their personal narratives, often with the purpose of buttressing the historicity of their stories and bringing factual confirmation to their recollections. Otherwise, the present testimonies, whether given me in English, French, or Lebanese, are being reproduced verbatim, the way they were entrusted to me.

THE AMBASSADOR

In her groundbreaking *The Jews of Lebanon Between Coexistence and Conflict*, Kirsten Schulze, the doyenne of Lebanese Jewish history, argued that unlike other Jews in the Muslim-majority countries of the Middle East, the Jews of Lebanon were a foundational Lebanese community of millennial existence—an essential ingredient in what is today the Lebanese Republic.[15] They were well adjusted, stressed Schulze, well organized, well connected, prosperous, safe, comfortable, and indeed, she noted, they witnessed a demographic surge after the establishment of the State of Israel—countering the large-scale exodus of Jews from Muslim-majority countries during that same time period.

To a large extent—and the historical section of this volume echoes and substantiates that claim—Schulze's glowing appraisal of Lebanese Jewish life is not necessarily a faulty one. But it is not an ironclad archetype reflecting a consistent mode of being either. There were exceptions to this rosy picture. Indeed, as we saw earlier, Lebanese Jews *did* suffer the exactions of Arab nationalism and Near Eastern Muslim (*and* Christian) anti-Semitism, often under the indifferent gaze of Lebanese authorities beholden to Arabist compulsions. Consequently, Lebanese Jewry has indeed all but disappeared from Lebanon's political, cultural, and social landscapes of the late twentieth and early twenty-first centuries, in spite of Lebanon having been a homeland for Jews for upwards of 2000 years, and despite the Lebanese Republic being in principle a "confederation of minorities" hospitable to Jewish presence, Jewish life, and Jewish aspirations.

---

[15] Kirsten E. Schulze, *The Jews of Lebanon; Between Coexistence and Conflict* (Brighton and London: Sussex Academic Press, 2009), 12–30.

Ambassador Yitzhak Levanon, born in 1944 Yitzhak Kishik-Cohen, and heir to a venerable Beiruti family issuing from a priestly line,[16] is also a trained political scientist with a historian's instinct and the raconteur's talent. So it is important at this juncture to give voice to his own rendition of Lebanese Jewish history. The Lebanese Jewish community, he argues, although a very small group historically speaking, is a very old community, and one of the best organized in the communal context of Lebanon, and indeed in the context of Jewish life in Arab lands overall. The italics in the narrative that follows are the ambassador's own words albeit in paraphrase; non-italics are my interjections and questions, which the reader will note I have kept to a minimum, relegating my own commentaries, clarifications, and supporting evidence to detailed, often unwieldy, footnotes. However, it is important that the notes be treated, and read, as a "companion" to the main text.

So, "tell me about the Lebanon you know" was a good starting point, I thought:

Let me tell you about the Lebanon in which I was born, in which I grew up, and which I ultimately left in 1967, at the age of twenty-one.[17]

---

[16]The patronym Cohen, a rendition of the Hebrew Kohen/Kahen, clearly suggests a priestly lineage.

[17]As mentioned earlier in this volume, 1967 was a particularly trying year for Lebanese Jewry. Christian-dominated Lebanon was an idea on the wane by then; Arab nationalism was becoming increasingly vocal and increasingly hostile to Lebanese specificity and Lebanese neutrality. As a result, Lebanese Jewry suffered the repercussions. It is "The Beginning of the End of a Lebanese Judaism" read one heading of the French periodical *Information Israël* in June 1968; "Lebanese Start to Leave" read another, a year earlier, in London's *Jewish Chronicle*. Many members of Lebanon's estimated 5000 strong Jewish community were absconding their country noted the *Jewish Chronicle*: "undeceived by the deceptively calm atmosphere prevailing there at the moment, and not completely reassured by the Lebanese Government's announced determination to maintain law and order," Lebanese Jewry had begun its exodus. "There is now a permanent police guard on the Jewish quarter of Beirut, where most Lebanese Jews live, as well as on their synagogues and other buildings. What the Jews are afraid of, however, is a clash between Christians and Moslems over the Middle East situation. If this occurs, and there are signs that it is brewing, the Jews will be caught in the middle, they fear. Almost to a man, Lebanese Moslems are pro-Nasser and fiercely anti-Israel, whereas the Christians (mostly Maronites) take a realistic attitude. They feel that, now that a ceasefire is in operation, everyone concerned should calm down and take a long hard look at the situation as it really is, without any illusions. The Moslems, who make up something over half the total population, are firmly in favour of a climb-down by Israel, and they fully support Arab intransigence. The first 20 Jewish families from Lebanon arrived in France this week, en route for the United States, Brazil, Canada and Australia. They and their coreligionists who are still leaving have been

Look. Let's be honest with ourselves. We, the Jews, had a good life in Lebanon. Generally speaking, and with all of the limitations—and let us not kid ourselves, there were limitations, which might have been condoned, or accepted, or glossed over by the Lebanese government at times—we did have a good life in Lebanon despite everything else. You have to understand that at that time, our Lebanon, the Lebanon in which we lived, was a completely different place, a completely different state than the one in existence today. The main political powers in the Lebanon of the 1920s and into the late 1950s were in the hands of Lebanese Christians, specifically Maronite Christians. Muslims, namely the urban Sunnis, had nominal powers in government, and were (albeit not willingly perhaps) adherents to "political Maronitism." The Shi'ites on the other hand, those who are holding Lebanon hostage today, and who are trying to mold the country and its culture into their own image, were well nigh absent from Lebanon's political life. So, the driving power behind Lebanese politics for almost half a century of Lebanese statehood were the Christians. And Lebanese Jews had very tight, very close, very friendly relations with Lebanese Christians, and their affinities spanned the political, cultural, social, and intellectual arenas. Indeed, Lebanese Jews, their small numbers notwithstanding, were active participants in Lebanese political and social life; they were involved in Lebanese (Christian) political parties, they formed alliances with parliamentary blocs, they socialized with multiple segments of Lebanese society, they

able to transfer their assets abroad and take with them all their belongings." See the *Jewish Chronicle*, London, June 30, 1967, in the Jacob Rader Marcus Center of the American Jewish Archives, The World Jewish Congress Collection, Series H: Alphabetical Files, 1919–1981, Box: H235, File 3, Lebanon, 1960–1969, 04.061.

Relative to this, and true to the Arabic adage "Egypt writes, Lebanon publishes, and Iraq reads," there have reportedly been some 300,000 copies of the *Protocols of the Elders of Zion*, published in Lebanon during the summer of 1968. This sizeable production of this "infamous and hoary anti-Semitic forgery" was reportedly being circulated throughout Lebanon and the world, and according to "reliable sources," the printing and distribution of this tract were being subsidized by King Feisal of Saudi Arabia. Likewise, some 200,000 copies were reported to have been printed in French and destined to French-speaking majority Muslim African countries, while another 100,000 copies were rendered in English, Italian, Arabic, and Spanish, and destined for distribution, through the good offices of the Arab League, in various Arabophone countries and other Spanish-speaking, English-speaking, and Italian-speaking lands with a sizeable Muslim expatriate community. See *The Jerusalem Post*, July 5, 1968, in the Jacob Rader Marcus Center of the American Jewish Archives, The World Jewish Congress Collection, Series H: Alphabetical Files, 1919–1981, Box: H235, File 3, Lebanon, 1960–1969, 04.090.

frequented Lebanese Christian schools and institutes of higher learning, they served in the military and police forces, and they had a marked presence in the diplomatic corps, the civil service, the educational system, and generally speaking in Lebanon's cultural and intellectual life.[18]

[18]Things were still tenuous for Lebanese Jews, namely beginning in the 1950s, and harassment had become the lot of their daily existence, especially as Arab nationalists and "Muslim fanatics" emboldened by the growing weakness of Lebanon's Christians, began exacting stricter controls over the movements and activities of Lebanese Jews. However, things took a turn for the worst in the aftermath of 1967, as the Lebanese Jewish community grew increasingly concerned about its well-being and its security. This ultimately led to the shuttering of Jewish businesses through 1967–1969, contributing to heightened urgency among Lebanese Jews to leave the country. "The hostile attitude towards the Jewish community in Lebanon has increased with the growth of the influence of the terrorist organizations there," wrote the *Jerusalem Post* in July 1969. And hard as the Lebanese government—and armed vigilante elements of the Maronite-dominated Kataëb Party—tried to safeguard the security of their Jewish compatriots and their urban quarters, their efforts seemed always offset by radical Muslim elements. Those Jews who opted to stay put, resisting emigration, were in the main small businessmen, shopkeepers, teachers, and craftsmen according to a *Jerusalem Post* report from September 1969. But the Lebanese government itself, under the conciliatory—not to say "weak"—leadership of the Maronite Charles Helou, was overly beholden to Arab phobias and Arab obsessions vis-à-vis Israel—a kind of "national frailty" that often translated into a dereliction of duty vis-à-vis Lebanese Jewry. Jews were therefore apprehensive about their future in Lebanon, and the tensions between Lebanese Christians and Lebanese Muslims with regard to the Arab–Israeli conflict and the presence of a large Palestinian (Muslim) refugee community in Lebanon often impacted Lebanese Jews negatively. It is worth stressing, again, that the Lebanese government's record toward Jews was always favorable and discrimination as such—let alone persecution—was non-extant. But the Christians in government were under pressure to burnish their "Arab" credentials, which often led to less than "enlightened" policies vis-à-vis the Jews; Muslims were gaining in influence and strength in Lebanese public life, and during the Six-Day War Muslim mobs expressly began fomenting anti-Jewish feelings, harassing Jewish persons, attacking and boycotting Jewish businesses, and ordering Jewish shopkeepers to shutter their stores. Ultimately, these sorts of attitudes began getting formalized in "official" policy. To wit, "no new civil servants are taken from the Jewish community," noted the *Jerusalem Post* in the summer of 1967, even as "those who are already in government employ are kept on so far." Still, some Lebanese Jews opted to stay put at the behest of their Christian compatriots. Allegedly, some Lebanese tend to "think of the Jews as a barometer of world opinion. If [they] are well treated, then Lebanon is still [considered] a civilized place." However, Lebanese Jewry lives a precarious existence; their attitudes toward Israel are often a mixed bag of pride and apprehension; pride in Jewish resiliency and accomplishments, and apprehension of what may befall Lebanese Jewry should there be a more radical shift in Lebanon's political and religious balance. Yet, Israeli visitors to Lebanon were common throughout the 1960s, and Hebrew was often heard in Beiruti cafés and restaurants; Israeli interlocutors were only asked "not to mention Israel by name"

To the preceding must be added that the Lebanese Jewish community was very well organized. We ran our own synagogues, schools, community services. We observed holidays, celebrated weddings, mourned at funerals, etc., in full view of Lebanese society and on an equal footing to any other Lebanese community, Muslim, Christian, Druze, or other... We had our own social movements, the Maccabi Youth Movement, and the Jewish Scouts. I myself was a member of the Maccabi, and we held annual public parades, organized athletic competitions, and put on display various palettes of activities that were always attended by official representatives of the Lebanese government whose presence was always center-stage and front-row, often delivering laudatory speeches praising our activities and contributions to Lebanese society and Lebanon's diversity.[19]

In addition to the Talmud Torah schools, which were basically "religious schools," we also had the Alliance Israélite Universelle schools, which formed the bulk of Lebanese Jewish youth.[20] Our Chief Rabbis were among the

---

in public and refer to it euphemistically only, as "over there." Otherwise, "being Jewish" in post-1967 Lebanon was not a particularly "curious" affair, suggesting that even at the height of anti-Jewish radicalism, Lebanese Jews "being Jews" and conversing publically in Hebrew was not a matter looked upon askance. See "Lebanese Jews in Danger" and "Jews in Lebanon," in *The Jerusalem Post*, July 21, 1969, and September 12, 1969, in the Jacob Rader Marcus Center of the American Jewish Archives, The World Jewish Congress Collection, Series H: Alphabetical Files, 1919–1981, Box: H235, File 3, Lebanon, 1960–1969, 04.126, and 04.128.

[19] According to a confidential profile of the Lebanese Jewish community, community events were always well attended by high state dignitaries representing the political and civil authorities, especially so during Jewish holidays. Indeed, Yom Kippur and the first day of Passover figure in the Lebanese state's official list of public holidays. See "Confidential Profile of the Lebanese Jewish Community" in the Jacob Rader Marcus Center of the American Jewish Archives, The World Jewish Congress Collection, Series H: Alphabetical Files, 1919–1981, Box: H235, File 3, Lebanon, 1960–1969, 04.042.

[20] According to the *Cahiers de l'Alliance Israélite Universelle*, N. 135, February 1962 (at that time, Ambassador Levanon would have been sixteen years of age), the number of students at the Beirut *Alliance* school for academic year 1961–1962 was 1026 students—589 girls and 437 boys. The Beirut Selim Tarrab School on the other hand had 193 students, while the Sidon *Alliance* school, a much smaller operation, had a total of 82 students. However, only 36 students of the Sidon *Alliance* school were Jewish; the rest were Muslim (24) and Christian (22). See the *Cahiers de l'Alliance Israélite Universelle*, N. 135, February 1962, in the Jacob Rader Marcus Center of the American Jewish Archives, The World Jewish Congress Collection, Series H: Alphabetical Files, 1919–1981, Box: H235, File 3, Lebanon, 1960–1969, 04.028.

best and most respected in the region, in terms of influence, erudition, and spiritual authority. In addition to that, Lebanon's Jewish community ran its own communal social and humanitarian institutions, often operating under Hebrew names (such as the Bnai Brith Lodge, the Bikur Cholim Committee, the Talmud Torah Committee, the Synagogue Committee, and the "Foyer de Jeunesse" youth center and "Club de Familles" adult center), but providing services to all those in need and spanning the entire Lebanese society—not only limited to Jews—and assisting with such services spanning the medical, financial, educational, cultural, recreational, alimentary and suchlike. So in a sense, this was a highly organized society, dispensing services worthy of welfare and social security benefits that ought to otherwise be provided by state institutions. At a maximum, the Jewish population of Beirut after 1948 was around fourteen-thousand, yet that community's limited private social and humanitarian institutions were able to fulfill the needs of society as a whole, regulated and administered by an infinitesimally small segment of Lebanese society.[21]

Yet, as I mentioned earlier, there were limitations placed on the Lebanese Jewish community; limitations instated, if not by law, then by convention and practice.[22] To wit, Jews were well nigh absent from the Lebanese diplomatic

---

[21] For this purpose, the communal structure was organized under the supervision of the Jewish Community Council—an elected body of twelve members whose duties, among others, included the levying of taxes known as "arikha" (or "assessment taxes") in addition to those ordinarily excised by the Lebanese state. The "arikha" was collected from all members of the Jewish community, was commensurate with each member's means, and was used primarily to cover communal needs. To wit, in 1929, one of the few periods for which statistics are currently available, the medical services provided by one of the Jewish communal institutions, the Bikur Cholim, covered some 5000 persons, fifty of whom were hospitalized, and thirty of whom were cared for at maternity wards. It is worth noting that long into the 1960s, the Bikur Cholim dispensary was staffed by at least one registered nurse and one medical doctor, three times a week, providing medical services to an average of fifteen patients per day of operation. For more on this, see the Jacob Rader Marcus Center of the American Jewish Archives, The World Jewish Congress Collection, Series H: Alphabetical Files, 1919–1981, Box: H235, File 3, Lebanon, 1960–1969, 04.035-6.

[22] Indeed, according to a 1957 *World Jewish Affairs* memo, the official Lebanese attitude vis-à-vis Lebanese Jews was "definitely not hostile" and markedly "more liberal than that of any other Arab country." Many Lebanese Jews, noted the report, had "if not power, then at least a considerable degree of influence" on Lebanese society. They were full-fledged citizens, with the right to vote and to participate in the country's political and cultural life. They had synagogues, Jewish kindergartens and educational institutions, a mikvah, and a Maccabi movement for recreation... Yet, the Jews of Lebanon were always made to be aware of an undercurrent of anti-Jewish bias, and they were acutely sensitive to their tenuous status in Lebanon even if by law they were on equal footing with other Lebanese citizens and had full recourse and access to the protection of Lebanese law. Lebanon remained aloof from

corps. They were blocked from reaching the higher echelons of government and civil service. A personal example may be illustrative; my own uncle had to move heaven and earth to get a position as an engineer for the Beirut City Hall. Even those Jews who were members of the police force, the army, the internal security, they were all viewed with circumspection, and they were all subject to limitations in authority, promotion, and the rest of it. Can we call this "persecution"? Probably not! But it is certainly a form of "restriction" and "limitation," and unfortunately human beings ordinarily acclimate and resign themselves to these sorts of restrictions; a condition that had its parallels in the educational system as well, where Jews might have been readily accepted in "Christian" institutions, but not so readily so in "Muslim" institutions.[23] Likewise, all—or let us say the majority—of the Jews were confined to the Wadi Boujmil neighborhood of Beirut, with very few residing outside of that city quarter.[24] As Jews, we could of course mingle with non-Jews

the "Arab–Israeli" conflict, and the Lebanese-Israeli border was notorious for being the most tranquil in the region. This often placed Lebanese Jewry in an awkward situation: With Lebanon not being at war with Israel meant that should the Arab states accuse Lebanon of "leniency toward Israel," Lebanese authorities may opt to "clarify their attitude at the expense of the local Jews." See *World Jewish Affairs*, London, August 20, 1957.

[23] The educational system in Lebanon is largely private, even if governmentally regulated. Otherwise, private schools constituted the bulk of educational institutions and had much autonomy with regards to programmatic and curricular matters. Although Lebanese Jews would have been hard-pressed opting for secondary or higher education at "Muslim-dominated" institutions, they still gravitated toward Anglophone and Francophone institutions of higher learning—namely the American University of Beirut and the Jesuit Saint-Joseph University. That being said, things were about to change dramatically in the aftermath of 1948 and on the heels of the massive exodus of some 13,000 Syrian Jews and their settlement in Lebanon. The Syrian government demanded that the Lebanese refrain from naturalizing Syrian Jews and often insisted they be altogether expelled from Lebanon. At any rate, by 1969, out of the roughly 15,000 Jews residing in Lebanon (many of whom refugees from Syria), only about 3000 had remained. During that period Syrian Jews and Jews in Lebanon in general were often refused work permits, acceptance into educational institutions, or participation in social or recreational activities. Even at institutes of higher learning, the American University of Beirut, government ordinances (often extorted by the Syrian government) called for the "expulsion of Alien Jews" from university and ultimately from the country.

[24] Contrary to popular belief and the normative depictions in the traditional scholarship on Lebanon and Lebanese Jewry, the Wadi Boujmil neighborhood of Beirut, sometimes referred to as "Wadi l-Yahood" (the Valley of the Jews), is a relatively small neighborhood. In American terms, it does not exceed two city blocks. Abutting the Bab-Idriss commercial sector of Beirut, Wadi Boujmil is never colloquially referred to as "The Valley of the Jews"

outside of the neighborhood, form friendships with Muslims and Christians and others. But basically, the bulk of our contacts and connections outside of the community were with the Christians—the Maronites specifically. And this for a variety of reasons, among them cultural and political affinities, as well as mutual recognition and tolerance. In that sense, as Jews, we would have been hard-pressed socializing in a Shi'ite environment—the Shi'ites being viewed as "second class" citizens in a Lebanese context—or for that matter fraternizing in a non-urban Sunni environment—as Sunnis were tradition- ally viewed to be anti-Israeli, anti-Jewish, pro-Nasser, and pan-Arabists. So in sum, we were not geared, nor were we naturally inclined to gravitate in the direction of those particular environments. Therefore, we tended to "escape" and avoid being in touch with potentially hostile Lebanese com- munities.[25] *This of course did not mean that no efforts were furnished for a*

in Lebanon. As far as the neighborhood's Jewish population, by most optimistic estimates the number of Jews residing in this neighborhood could not have exceeded 500, out an esti- mated total of 3000 by 1970. Those numbers are of course estimates and approximations. However, they constitute the maximum possible demographic numbers. Therefore, the Jewish population of Wadi Boujmil would have been at most a fraction of the total numbers of the Lebanese Jewish community—one-sixth to be exact, which is to say 16% of the coun- try's Jewish population. What's more, and contrary to other places in the world—Europe included and not necessarily so *only* Muslim-majority countries—Lebanese authorities never attempted to confine Lebanese Jews to exclusively Jewish neighborhoods, even if some 90% of the community resides in Beirut. For more on this, see "La situation des Juifs au Liban," *Le Monde* (Paris: January 1, 1970).

[25] In this context of Lebanese Jewish circumspection, it is worth noting that Lebanese Prime Minister Rachid Karamé never missed an opportunity throughout his tenure in the late 1960s to excoriate Israel and browbeat Lebanese public opinion with his trademark bluster and hectoring about "Lebanon's unreserved support for the cause of the Palestinian Commandos." Never mind that there was no such explicit policy in Lebanon at the time— indeed "official" Lebanon took great care to protect and flaunt its neutrality. But public stances such as Karamé's, issuing from the office of the Prime Minister no less, had the com- pelling effect of riling up Muslim public opinion (against Lebanese Jewry *and* those other Lebanese unmoved by Arab causes), and consequently cowing Lebanese Jews into submis- sion and mutism. To wit, in a December 1969 story filed from Beirut by the French daily *Le Monde*, Karamé is described to have declared in the Lebanese Chamber of Deputies that his government had every intention of unreservedly backing Palestinian Commandos in their activities against the State of Israel. "The Palestinian cause," he noted, "is the *cause célèbre* of the Arabs; not only because Zionism is a danger to our very existence, but because the Arab cause in Palestine is a fundamentally just and righteous cause." One can only imagine the effects of this declaration on a besieged dwindling Jewish community, coinciding with the funeral processions of a Palestinian Fedayeen at the Omari Mosque of Beirut, attended by upwards of 3000 demonstrators and complemented by bursts of machine-gun fire filling

rapprochement with Lebanon's non-Christian communities. Many were, and we indeed did attempt overtures toward the Muslim communities. Still it remained that the Maronites were the Jews' "natural allies," and the bulk of the Jewish community's efforts were geared in the direction of the Maronites and likeminded Christian communities.[26] *And so, rapprochements with the Christian communities took several tacks; they were personal, social, cultural, and political, the latter functioning on the ministerial, governmental, parliamentary, and political party levels. Lebanese Jews were known for instance*

the Beirut skies. See "M. Rachid Karamé declare que son pays appuiera sans reserve la cause des commandos palestiniens," *Le Monde* (Paris: December 6, 1969). Around this same time period, the *Jewish Chronicle* reported Lebanese Jewish businesses being shut down by Jewish owners growing increasingly concerned for their safety. The reports also noted Lebanese security forces cordoning off Beirut's Jewish quarter, but without clarifying whether such measures were put in place "to protect the Jews from Moslem fanatics or to keep a stricter control over their movements and activities." In either case, whether to offer protection from "Moslem fanatics" or restrict the "movements and activities" of Lebanese citizens who happen to be Jewish, the situation can be deemed less than reassuring. See "Lebanese Jews Close Shops in New Scare," *The Jewish Chronicle* (London: July 18, 1969).

[26] It should be noted in this regard that the Lebanese Jewish community's cautious aloofness from Lebanese politics notwithstanding, it was still held hostage of the Arab–Israeli conflict, the Christian-Muslim rivalries in Lebanon, Christian-Lebanese "neutrality" (perhaps even hostility to the Palestinian cause), and Muslim-Lebanese anger and resentment of their Christian-dominated government's distance from the Arabs' *cause célèbre*, which is to say the Palestinian cause. By the end of 1969, Lebanon's Christian leaderships were hastening to contrive a face-saving solution that would spare Lebanon the repercussions of an unresolved Arab–Israeli conflict. In early 1970, Kataëb (Phalanges) Party leader Pierre Gemayel proposed resetting the bulk of Lebanon's Palestinian refugees (some 350 thousand strong by his count) into neighboring Arab countries, in what he called a "functional and equitable" redistribution. This "redistribution" noted Gemayel should be a call to Arabs to show their "Arabist" mettle, rather than wallow in the arenas of rhetoric and empty oratory about Arab unity and solidarity. Arabs should take their fair shares of Arab refugees according to each Arab country's resources, size, and absorptive capacities. This "redistribution process" should serve a twofold purpose stressed Gemayel: raise the standard of living of the refugees and prevent them from establishing themselves permanently in their host countries. It is unfathomable, he stressed, that Lebanon should be expected to bear the lion's share of refugees in spite of its modest means and exiguous territory, while Syria, eighteen times the size of Lebanon, hosts less than half of Lebanon's share of Palestinians. Why doesn't Iraq, Saudi Arabia, or Libya for that matter, with their rich economies and expansive territories assume their responsibility, he wondered? What's more, concluded Gemayel, it is imperative that Lebanon maintain the demographic and communal balance that underpins the foundations of its statehood: With the imbalance brought about by the lopsided Palestinian presence, Lebanon is no doubt heading for disaster, noted Gemayel.

to have filled the ranks of the Lebanese Kataëb (Phalanges) Party, among other Maronite political formations. This is how, over time, we often succeeded in turning social encounters, political alliances—and often ideological and philosophical affinities—into longstanding friendships. All this, of course, was done in a pragmatic mindset, within the limitations of the political handicaps that we were dealt in Lebanon and which we had to navigate. We were realists. We knew what we could fight for, and what we ought to settle for. We understood that we were in no position to fight for visible positions; there was no sense in fighting for the directorship of the Internal Security forces, or the Beirut Municipal Council, or the Governorship of Beirut for instance. Not that those positions were beyond our means or qualifications. They were not impossible to have. They were simply unrealistic. Even the Maronites themselves had their own limitations within the national and ethno-religious fabric of Lebanon, and they were themselves "realistic" about what was attainable and was not—whether for themselves or their political allies from other communities, the Jews included. They recognized that Lebanon's current modus vivendi was the best that they could secure at the time, and that it behooved them to maintain it.

It was this same modus vivendi that suited Jewish life in Lebanon. Just as it worked for the Maronites, it also worked for the Jews. It was convenient for us; we ran our own schools; the Alliance Israélite Universelle college's curriculum lined up with our history, our geography, our languages; we organized our own communal activities; we celebrated our holidays; we went to synagogue and about our daily lives unmolested. The Wadi Boujmil neighborhood was simply a quarter of Beirut. It was not a ghetto. It was not circumscribed, or singled out, or set apart from other neighborhoods. Indeed, it was surrounded by other neighborhoods that were not necessarily Jewish, and an outsider would have been hard-pressed demarcating Wadi Boujmil or pointing out the lines where the Jewish quarter ended and where another one began. But we were snug in our neighborhood; we had all we needed there; we were secure, protected, but we were not defined by it or limited to it. We could (and did) come in and out as we pleased, in safety, and confidence, and—save for times of trouble—we were never stigmatized as Jews. As a youngster, if I wanted to venture out to the Armenian quarter,[27]

---

[27] Known as Bourj Hammoud, the Armenian district is a major commercial, industrial, and residential quarter of East Beirut, inhabited overwhelmingly by Lebanese-Armenians, a large portion of whom are descendants of the victims of the Armenian Genocide during Ottoman times. It is one of the most industrious (and densely populated) districts of Beirut.

to the Hamra district,[28] to Orozdi-Back,[29] I could do so at any time of day, any day of the week, without batting an eye. It was not uncommon for us to go straight to the beach, or Semiramis,[30] following Shabbat services at synagogue. It was safe. We were safe. Nobody bothered you. Nobody chastised you. Nobody questioned you. But you knew that once you did your business, it was best you went back home. Fast. Not because it was not safe. Rather, because it was not your place. That was the atmosphere in which we grew up. And those were the feelings shared by most of the community that lived in Wadi Boujmil.

But when times of trouble came knocking, things came to change. And "trouble" would become more palpable in 1958, during the brief Lebanese "civil war," which was essentially a clash between the Kataëb[31] and the Najjaadé.[32] During those times the Kataëb provided armed protection of the Wadi Boujmil neighborhood, with the assistance of some Jewish members of the Party, but also some of the local Maccabi boys, who were essentially athletes, not armed, but young men, muscular, and in optimal physical shape. So we joined the Kataëb at nighttime, to help out with the protection of the neighborhood. This was serious stuff. There were shootings. People died.

---

[28] In its heyday, Hamra Street was Beirut's trendiest, known as the Champs Élysées of the Middle East. It was dotted with luxury stores, sidewalk cafés, theaters, hotels, nightclubs, and cultural centers attracting the rich, the bohemians, the jetsetters, and the intellectuals and free-thinkers (and freewheelers) of both East and West, the Muslim world, and Europe.

[29] Orozdi-Back was an old high-end Beirut department store established in 1914. Situated near the quays of the Beirut Harbor, next to the Customs Offices and the Port-Authority warehouses, Orozdi-Back like Beirut itself was at the crossroads of continents and traditions; it straddled the Mediterranean—which is to say it wielded luxury goods issuing from Europe—and the Near Eastern hinterland—which is to say access to regionally produced products.

[30] Semiramis was once the cornerstone of Lebanese cuisine and one of Beirut's most famous, most highly rated, and most decadent restaurants, offering the best of Lebanese cuisine's gastronomical delights.

[31] The Kataëb is an overwhelmingly Maronite Christian political party upholding Lebanese specificity and calling for distance from the Arab–Israeli conflict and inter-Arab disputes—firmly opposed to Arab nationalism, Arab identity for Lebanon, and pan-Arab designs for the region.

[32] The Najjaadé was a Sunni Muslim Lebanese political party with strong pan-Arab nationalist and fascist leanings. The party founder was Muhyiddin al-Nusuli, a journalist and Arab nationalist intellectual with great admiration for Hitler and Mussolini, whom he viewed as role models for state building. The party's ideology was vehemently opposed to the Kataëb's vision of Lebanon as a non-Arab non-Muslim state.

It was war. We were instructed by the Kataëb to sleep on the floor, not in our beds, so as to avoid being on elevated surfaces and risk being shot.

We dodged the bullet. But changes were afoot. Nasser was riding the tide of popular support. He succeeded, albeit briefly, in his Syrian-Egyptian union. Pan-Arabism was galvanizing the masses. And Christian Lebanon was losing ground to mounting Arabist pressures and successes. When Fouad Chéhab took the helms of the presidency in September 1958, he put an end to the civil war by advancing the notion of "no victor no vanquished," thus assuaging the warring parties. But this was taken as a setback for the Maronites in Lebanon; a deep concession to Arab nationalists; a setback which would ultimately have a negative effect on the Jewish community and Jewish life in Lebanon. From a low political profile previously, Lebanese Jewry was now forced into political self-effacement and isolation, which would over time lead to severe social, commercial, cultural, and ultimately existential repercussions. From Kataëb protection, the Jews were now in need of express governmental protection and a visible armed police presence in their neighborhoods.

This also led to the first wave of Jewish emigration from Lebanon. The first to leave were the youngsters, many of whom were members of the Maccabi.[33] *There were no persecutions per se to warrant these departures, but the atmosphere was poisoned, people were cocooned in their own neighborhoods, hesitant to venture out of their traditional comfort zones, and so, over the course of a few weeks following the end of the 1958 events, many segments of Lebanese Jewish society came to the realization that Jewish life for them now lay outside of Lebanon.*[34] *By the way, I'll let you in on a little secret: the symbol of Lebanon, al-Arz, the Cedars? I've never been to the Bsharré Cedars region in my life. Not once! The closest I ever got to*

---

[33] The Ambassador opened a parenthesis here for a bit of trivia about the Maccabi and a local beer in Lebanon named Maccabee. He noted that until 1958 the Lebanese Maccabee Beer was marketed and sold in Israel. The brewers, the Beiruti Jabr family, eventually sold it to an Israeli brewer after 1958. This is important to note because it illustrates that not only Lebanon and Israel were never at war, even at the height of the Arab–Israeli tensions, but that in certain quarters they maintained officious relations, and sometimes commercial, cultural, and personal contacts.

[34] According to a report by the President of Lebanon's Jewish Communal Council, Dr. Joseph Attié, by 1958 the Jewish community of Beirut amounted to some 8500 peoples, 5000 of whom were native Lebanese while the rest were recent arrivals from Damascus and Aleppo. Although no official figures on the numbers of departures were made available, Dr. Attié's report noted that entire Lebanese Jewish families had left in the aftermath of the 1958 civil war, after liquidating the bulk of their assets and moving their monies abroad.

the Cedars was Farayya, to ski for two hours, then back home to Beirut.[35]
There were outings of course, to different parts of Lebanon; to the Bekaa,
Baalbeck, the South, but life generally speaking was in the cocoon, in the
communal places and communal events within the limits of Beirut and
immediate environs. But it was frankly scary to even venture into certain
areas of Beirut—for instance the Ma'arad, Suq Sursock, Bab-Idriss and the
rest, of it, areas with next to no Maronite presence, dominated in the main
by Muslims, pan-Arabists, Druze, Kurds, and partisans of the Najjaadé
Arab nationalist Party. My father's business for instance was in the Suq
Sursock quarter, and of course we had to tend to our business, and so we
did just that even though it was scary to do so. But we still went to the store,
stayed in the store, closed the store, went home, and that was that. That was
the daily routine; it wasn't always safe; it wasn't always pleasant; but you
rolled with it; you didn't challenge it; you didn't try to change it; you got
used to it. If nothing bad happened, you counted your blessings and moved
on; if something bad happened, you called it "nassiib" (destiny) and still
counted your blessings and moved on.

All that notwithstanding, I guarantee you that 99% of Lebanese Jews who
left Lebanon, or were made to leave Lebanon—and I am one of them—still
love Lebanon and are still nostalgic for Lebanon. Nostalgic for the plurality
and diversity and pluralism of the place; its liberties; its ways of thinking; its
democratic system, with all its failings; its high culture; its cacophony of lan-
guages; and finally its tolerance and openness to the other—that is to say the
climate of "tolerance" before the good old days got poisoned by the dogmatism
and resentments of Nasserites and other fanatics of similar stripes. Lebanon
was life, essentially. Family! And ultimately, what is life when you're done

These large-scale emigrations, stressed Dr. Attié, were "not due to the current political
situation. The Jews in Beirut are not subject to any form of discrimination, and remain
the heart of the city's commercial life. Indeed many are still doing well for themselves
and their families, some even amassing fortunes. However, what's driving many to leave
the country are anxieties and the lack of confidence in what may be lurking in the future
of the country." That being said, noted Attié, the wave of departures is being offset by a
slower wave of new Jewish arrivals, bit by bit trickling out of Syria. See the Joseph Golan
Correspondence, Jacob Rader Marcus Center of the American Jewish Archives, The World
Jewish Congress Collection, Series H: Alphabetical Files, 1919–1981, Box: H235, File 8,
Lebanon, Joseph Golan, 1959, 09.008.

[35]Farayya is a ski area in the Kesrouan district of Mount Lebanon, in the heart of
"Maronite country," and above the coastal town of Jounié.

with work and your other pursuits? Lebanon was that! Life! A challenge in that regard. But that is life, isn't it? This is the nostalgia that I have. Nostalgia for the challenge that was Lebanon! The soul that it had!

And there is something else that I wish to add to this. Something that I may not be able to explain adequately, but that still needs to be said: When I travel the world, moving between Montreal and Boston and Paris and Milan, and meet all kinds of Lebanese from all walks of life and all backgrounds and age groups; they all seem to have retained something special, sentimental—a soft spot of sorts—for Lebanon and their previous Lebanese lives. To my sense, this may be attributed to the fact that we were all born there and came of age there, in Lebanon. There is certainly something to say to that. It's a very strong, overpowering sensation; we were born and raised in Lebanon, and nobody can ever take that away from us, or change it. But ask me to go back and live in Lebanon now, today, and I'll probably tell you that I cannot. Still, Lebanon is in my heart. When I meet another Lebanese, anywhere in the world, something magical happens; something inexplicable. You start the encounter with random Lebanese words or some traditional banter, anecdotes, remembrances or names of places or some idiomatic expression or turn of phrase, and suddenly we are all transported back in time to that special place that we kept intact in our memories. It's truly magical. And inexplicable.[36]

Sadly for the Jews of Lebanon, form 1958 to 1967 things took a turn for the worse and kept on worsening. The causes were multifold. They were social, political, cultural. They had nothing to do with the Jewish community per se, but they affected the Jewish community very adversely, besieging it with anxiety and apprehension about the future. Yet, all Jewish institutions were maintained, functioning with "skeleton crews" so to speak, but functioning nevertheless—celebrating holidays, going to work, tending to

---

[36] For the cultural historian, sociolinguist, and philologist, there is certainly "something to say" to the linguistic relics that Ambassador Levanon refers to in this section. Immigrants and exiles often preserve linguistic habits, or certain inflections and accents, and even idiomatic expressions and other shared norms that might have otherwise fallen into desuetude in the mother country—a link of authenticity and belonging that is immediately perceptible to other immigrants and that immediately transports them to the places of their birth. An English example may be illustrative: New Yorkers and Southern Britons, for instance, although both English speakers, do not attach the same emotive or social meaning to the English language that they speak; there are sets of norms, knowledge, cultural accretions, beliefs, and values that dwell in a New Yorker's English that are lost on a Southern British English speaker.

the needy, operating dispensaries and social clubs and youth centers, even as society sputtered on against tremendous odds.

But the watershed moment was 1967. Not 1948. Not the establishment of the State of Israel. Now, although most Lebanese Jews might have been sympathetic to the notion of a Jewish State, and the creation of the State of Israel, not all of them were keen on picking up their lives and moving to the State of Israel. Even when things became difficult for them in Lebanon, the bulk of Lebanese Jewry did not end up in Israel, but rather in France and Montreal and South America and the United States. The reasons for that were multifold, but suffice it to say that culturally speaking they felt more connected to those countries—especially France—than to Israel as such. Yet, the Jewish State was the fulfillment of an age-old Jewish dream. We felt emotively linked to that state, even if we preferred to not move there, or advertise our affections for it. Unfortunately there was this guy named Nasser, who in 1967 called for the destruction of the State of Israel; a state, which we considered a divine answer to our yearnings. For us this was an alarming moment, premonitory of, literally, the destruction of the Jewish people.[37] *And it gave us pause. It affected us. Add to that the conflict within Lebanon proper, which augmented our already tenuous security situation in 1967, and the ground becomes riper for another wave of migrations. By that time, it had become crystal clear to us that Lebanese Jewish life was on its last leg. The process was irreversible, and Lebanese Jewry was beginning to resign itself to the bitter reality that "there is no going back," that "the halcyon life that was our past was now in the past."*

At this point people started leaving en masse. Entire Jewish families vanished. Banished. Jewish institutions and communal organizations started shutting down—mainly due to the paucity of manpower necessitated by shrinking demographics, but also because such institutions and their services were becoming increasingly superfluous, perhaps even too visible in an environment that was no longer hospitable to Lebanese Jewish life. Other

---

[37] This is actually a feeling shared by many other Near Eastern minorities—not only Jews—who were negatively affected by the rise and popularity of Nasser, and the austere brand of pan-Arabism that he advanced. His was a merciless dogmatic identity model, loath to diversity, and unforgiving vis-à-vis those upholding (and living) differing standards of selfhood. After all, Nasserism, and pan-Arabism in general terms, represented the liquidation of Near Eastern cosmopolitan societies, which had been the hallmark of places like Beirut, Alexandria, and Aleppo. Indeed, the overriding feature of pan-Arabism was cultural homogeneity and linguistic orthodoxy, which put an end to old venerable cosmopolitan societies on the Eastern Mediterranean.

communities and refugee groups began trickling over to the Jewish quarters, squatting Jewish properties and homes. Among those were the Kurds, but also the Palestinians, many of whom were assigned Jewish property by the pro- Nasserite government of PM Rachid Karamé.[38]

By that time the Christians had lost their hold on Lebanon and the direction of Lebanese politics: Gone was Lebanon's commitment to neutrality in the Arab-Israeli conflict; the Palestinians were now on their way to creating a "state within the state" in Lebanon[39]; *and the Shi'ite community itself was growing demographically, overtaking the traditional Sunnis, becoming more confident, and beginning to demand a closer hearing to their needs and a greater share of the Lebanese political pie. The stage was set for the 1975 Lebanese civil war, which would last for some sixteen years, and would effectively put an end to Lebanese pluralism and to upwards of 2000 years of Jewish life in Lebanon—which might as well be an end of "Lebanese life" tout court. This is so not only because the Jews were part and parcel of the Lebanese social and cultural fabric. Rather, this is mainly due to the fact that Lebanese Jews were indeed a foundational element to the 1920 Lebanese republic, as well as the most longstanding, deep-rooted, "indigenous" population of Lebanon; a population that was still given short shrift and upended.*

Can We Talk About Your Mother?[40]

She was imprisoned for seven years, during which time we were allowed to visit her—although I am not sure we could have called that "visiting" with

---

[38] It is worth mentioning here that Karamé's stock in trade had been extorting from Lebanese society a more active role in the Arab–Israeli conflict, and a more resolute commitment to the Palestinian cause. See, for instance, "M. Rachid Karamé declare que son pays appuiera sans reserve la cause des commandos palestiniens" [Mr. Rachid Karamé Affirms That His Country Shall Unreservedly Uphold the Cause of the Palestinian Commandos], *Le Monde* (Paris: December 6, 1969).

[39] This was a period and a condition referred to as "*Fatahland*" in the literature on Lebanon—*Fatah* (Ar. Conquest) being the dominant faction of the Palestine Liberation Organization, which, under the command of Yassir Arafat, had already set up shop in Lebanon.

[40] Shulamit Kishik-Cohen (1917–2017), Ambassador Yitzhak Levanon's mother, deserves a biography of her own. Although some accounts (Arab in the main) insist she's a native Argentinian, by Ambassador Levanon's account, she was born and raised in Jerusalem. The fourth child of an Egyptian Jewish father who had spent some time in Argentina, and a Jerusalemite mother, the daughter of a Rabbi, Shulamit spent her early childhood in Jerusalem. Due to her parents' financial hardships—trying to tend to a household with twelve children—she was given in marriage at a very young age to a well-known, rich, and much older Beiruti merchant, Joseph Kishik-Cohen. This was early 1936. The

her. We went to see her, almost on a daily basis, to bring her food mainly. She didn't eat prison food, which was dirty and un-kosher. So we cooked for her, and still she didn't eat, or barely ate, our homemade foods. Prison guards often probed even the food that we brought, poking the kibbé and other dishes with their fingers to make sure no secret messages were being smuggled through the food… So, she barely ate. And of course we wanted to see her. But not like that. Not in the humiliating emaciated state of being that she was put in! Not in the manner in which the authorities allowed us to see her, from the vantage point of a staircase, from which we could catch glimpses of her cooped up inside a cage.

She was mercilessly tortured, subjected to electric shock, denailed, and put through a concert of other creative methods of cruelty. There was also the

couple settled in Wadi Boujmil, in a beautiful home very near to the Magen Avraham Synagogue where they raised seven children, among them the future Ambassador Levanon. Shula, as she was known locally, was a woman of extraordinary charm, intelligence, charisma, elegance, and beauty. A socialite of note in the extravagant, cosmopolitan, and libertine Beirut of the first half of the twentieth century, Shula became deeply invested in the local Jewish community, and very active on Lebanon's cultural and social scenes. She taught Hebrew for many years at the *Alliance* school in Beirut. Due to curricular and programmatic requirements established by the Lebanese government, Shula had to intercede on behalf of the AIU school, handle official paperwork, and deal with the ins and outs of Lebanese bureaucracy. Over time, she established close relationships with local politicians, civil servants, foreign dignitaries, and diplomats. At home, her salons often attracted a veritable "who is who" of the local high society, representatives of the various political classes, a bevy of artists and bohemians, and members of the Arab and foreign diplomatic corps. In the late 1950s and early 1960s, she was suspected of spying for the benefit of the State of Israel and was as a result arrested, accused, and convicted of espionage. She was subsequently imprisoned and systematically tortured for upwards of seven years. She was finally released in 1967 as part of a prisoner-exchange deal between the Lebanese and Israeli governments, and later moved with her family to Israel where she spent the remainder of her life. Although her times, life, and work were profoundly more complex than the often lurid sensationalized depictions of her in Arabic-language tabloid exposés—and likewise perhaps overly laudatory in Israeli sources—Shula Kishik-Cohen was above all a wife, a mother, a Beiruti, a Jew, and a Zionist of her times. She, therefore, deserves a more thoughtful, unsentimental, and ideologically neutral examination. Such a project is beyond the scope of this volume. But what is appropriate, I thought, was asking Ambassador Levanon to give his own account of his own recollections of his own mother's life and trials. Telegraphic and abridged a treatment as this important topic was given during our conversation, the Ambassador's reticence is understandable, and as a biographer myself, I am very sensitive to a respondent's hesitation.

psychological torture, the solitary confinement, the isolation, the daily non-stop regime of humiliation. By the time she was released and came to Israel, she might as well have been dead. But she was a strong-willed resilient lady, and she recovered rather quickly—both physically and mentally—leading a healthy happy fulfilling life for another fifty years following that ordeal.[41]

It was the Lebanese Deuxième Bureau[42] *that pushed for my mother to be arrested, charged, and imprisoned. All on trumped up charges. We know that for a fact today. Mom was tried and convicted in a military court, by career military officers, all acting as judge, prosecutor, defense council, and jury, all to assuage pan-Arab anxieties and phobias, all holding Lebanon and the Lebanese captive.*

[41] In her book *The Jews of Lebanon; Between Coexistence and Conflict*, Kirsten Schulze noted, based on interviews conducted with Shula Cohen in 1995, that the latter was very well connected with higher ups in the Lebanese government, that she was a close friend of Sunni Prime Minister Riad al-Solh and many other Muslim and Christian politicians, and that when she was imprisoned, many of her official Lebanese interlocutors left the country for fear of being implicated in the crimes she was accused of. She further noted that during her incarceration many officers, officials, and non-Jewish friends tried to comfort her and her family, including Kataëb Party president, Pierre Gemayel, who visited her often. This arguably contributed to the commuting of what had been initially a capital sentence, to a life sentence, eventually leading to her release.

[42] The Deuxième Bureau is Lebanon's military intelligence. It was made especially powerful during the administration of President Fouad Chehab (1958–1964). A former Commander in Chief of the Lebanese army and heir to an old aristocratic Maronite family, Chehab struck a neutral line in Lebanese politics, assuaging Christian anxieties about rising Arabist radicalism and satisfying Muslims and Arab nationalists who did not see in him a "Lebanese nationalist" as such. His policies were described as measured, pragmatic, and contemptuous of Lebanon's sectarian divides. But generally speaking, the "General-President" was a less assertive "Lebanonist" than his Maronite predecessors, thus ushering in a period of dithering and a weakened Lebanese Christian resolve. His successor, Charles Hélou (1964–1970) was even weaker, giving free reign to Arab nationalist agitation, hostility to Israel and Jews, and ultimately complete loss of Christian-Maronite prerogatives. This may explain Lebanon's tilt toward "Arabism" and the behavior of traditional Lebanese politicians now angling for closer "association" with Arabist causes. It is in this context that the arrest and imprisonment of Shula Cohen ought to be looked at. Indeed, there are still to this day rumors swirling around the Shula Cohen affair, suggesting she was scapegoated and thrown under the bus to protect high-ranking Lebanese officials, politicians, and military officers who, prior to the early 1960s and the Chehabist era, were deeply involved in secret officious relations with Israel. Thus, a change of narrative was in the offing, to cover the tracks of important Lebanese officials. And Shula Cohen was made to pay the price.

Where Are Lebanon and Jewish Lebanon Heading in Your View?
What Is in Their Future?

Lebanon is completely different today; completely alien to its being and its raison d'être as I knew them and lived them. I don't see how Lebanon will be able to return to that period of time; to its heyday as the pluralist, diverse, and open society that Jews and other minorities once called home. Nothing is left of the "liberal" Christian camp to temper Lebanese politics today and distinguish Lebanon from its grim neighborhood. Who has remained in the arena? You have the Kataëb; you have the Lebanese Forces; and you have General Michel Aoun's forces in the Christian Lebanese camp. This is division. This is not unity. There is no Christian Lebanese unity today; there isn't one single Christian camp with a unified vision today—as might have been the case in the 1940s and 1950s and 1960s. Yes, there were differences of opinion and style within the Christian camp back in those days; but it was still a single camp with a single unified vision and conception of the country. Aoun today is not like the liberal Christians of times past. Aoun is a tool of Hezbollah and seems acquiescent in Hezbollah's takeover of the State and its institutions. On the other hand, the Lebanese Forces, who are opposed to the Aounist forces, have neither the numbers nor the means to overtake them or effect any changes. The Kataëb are a façade with nothing of substance behind them. On the opposing side you have a growing and increasingly emboldened, energized, and politically (and militarily) dominant Shi'ite community. In other words, the vision of and for Lebanon today is essentially a Shi'ite vision for a Shi'ite dominated state where others are subservient to Shi'ite interests, way of life, and worldviews. This is what it means to be Lebanese today; at least this is the image that comes to mind at the mention of Lebanon in our time. Gone from this vision are the cosmopolitan, diverse, pluralist Lebanon of yore, where Jews, Christians, and Muslims could lead a fulfilling national life—a challenging and exasperating national life at times—but a fulfilling exciting existence nonetheless.

Ultimately, Lebanon is a complex place, a special place. You cannot learn about Lebanon by opening a book and reading a few pages here and there. You don't learn about Lebanon through the traditional means of learning. You have to have been there, to have eaten Lebanon's foods and drunk its wines and breathed its salt-sprayed winds mingling with the snowy mountains overhead. Lebanon's distinctness and complexities are apparent in its political eccentricities and climatic systems, in its geographic diversity and linguistic habits. Therefore Lebanon's presence and political face, Lebanon's mannerisms and overall conduct—both internally and abroad—are all a function of its anthropological and topological diversity.[43] *I'll give you a simple illustrative example that only a Lebanese can appreciate: Two Lebanese friends meet after years of absence; the first thing they say to each other is "ya akho sh-sharmoota weyn kenet?" ("You brother of a whore, where have you been hiding all this time?")*[44] *An outsider may take offense at the crassness of such language, whereas in Lebanon and among the Lebanese it is an expression of love, affection, endearment. This is the Lebanon that I remember, and that I have kept with me; its foods, its climate, its languages, its high culture; my neighborhood, our nightlife, the corner store, the butcher-shop, the barber, my girlfriends, our social life... All those memories are still with me... No one can take that away from us.*

The Girl from Damascus

My name is Zahava Ganor, née Claire Faour. I was born in Damascus but moved with my family to Lebanon at a very young age, when I was nearly three years old. Although I don't know, nor do I remember Damascus well, I have kept faint memories of it, since I did have the opportunity to return there once or twice with my parents, when Jews were still allowed to go back to Syria. There, in Damascus, my parents once owned a nice house, and my father ran a big successful clothing business where he worked alongside his brothers.

---

[43] Ambassador Levanon in this segment of his narrative spoke with depth and passion and authority reflecting his very intimate understanding of Lebanon. He is on solid historical and sociological ground when he says "you have to have lived there—*been* there—to truly understand Lebanon." This personal testimony is lent confirmation in most serious studies on Lebanon. To wit, the Preface to Philip Hitti's 1964 *A Short History of Lebanon* notes the following:

Of the Near East states, Lebanon is in a class by itself. Its historic experience, mountainous geography and the composition of its population combine to give it an identity and a personality of its own. [...] History knew Lebanon from the earliest times and never forgot it. Perhaps no other area of comparable size, about 3977 square miles, can match it in the volume of historical events [...] Such are the features—geographic, historic, cultural, and political—that make of Lebanon a distinct entity... See Philip Hitti, *A Short History of Lebanon* (New York: St. Martin's Press, 1965), iii and 1–7.

[44] Crude as this example may be deemed in some quarters, it reflects a profound understanding of Lebanon's history, sociology, psychology, and best of all the diversity and colorfulness and optimism of its linguistic habits in their rhythms, music, prosodies, and allegories. It is a social and cultural register that is fundamentally Lebanese, and that is completely lost on outsiders.

In Beirut, we rented a large room in a shared apartment in Wadi Boujmil. My first elementary school was the local Christian school, the Saint Vincent de Paul. Later, I entered the Alliance Israélite Universelle school. My father worked three days a week in Beirut and three days in Zahlé, some forty miles east, in the Bekaa Valley. Like many Beirutis seeking the cooler climes of the mountains, during the summer all my family moved for three months to Zahlé. My childhood memories are divided between those two places; Beirut and Zahlé.

In general, I have kept very good memories from my childhood in Lebanon.

In Beirut we lived a calm communal life in the Jewish neighborhood, not far from the big synagogue, the Magen Avraham. I remember very vividly the main street, the shops, the Arab peddlers, especially those who came after the Pesach holiday hawking the Caek bread.[45] *We were part of a traditional Jewish society that lived in peace and mutual respect alongside the Arab neighbors.*

On Shabbat, my parents used to go to synagogue with my grandmother. My older sister usually stayed behind, getting the rest of us children ready to join them, and then preparing the traditional after-service breakfast, the "ftour." The ftour usually included the time-honored, tasty Lebanese dishes of kibé, sfiha, sambusek, and a wide range of salads, all served in small plates, stacked up around the table, mezzé style.[46] *In the afternoon, my parents used to go to visit friends or relatives, and I loved accompanying them on those visits.*

The synagogue was the center and the heart of our communal life. On Shabbat and during the holiday services, the synagogue was crammed with people, and the children used to play and run around in-between the four palm-trees that stood outside, in the large courtyard at the front of the synagogue. Lebanese Jews who took part in the festivities and attended synagogue services weren't particularly religious—at least not in the full sense of the word and not as far as I can remember. But Shabbat and the high holidays were observed, and respected, especially in public. For example, no one in my family or circle of friends and neighbors dared smoke in public during Shabbat.

---

[45] Caek or Ka'ek is a traditional Lebanese "street-bread," usually crunchy, sprinkled with sesame, and eaten with Zaatar (thyme). Sold mainly by peddling vendors roaming the neighborhoods, its commercial concept is not unlike the "ice-cream van" in the USA, with its target customers mainly children playing in the streets outside their homes.

[46] *Mezzé* is the Eastern Mediterranean, and namely Lebanese, version of the Spanish tapas—a large selection of small dishes of various foods, usually served as appetizers, and to accompany alcoholic beverages.

In my family, as was the case also with a number of other Jewish families in the Wadi Boujmil neighborhood, we often went out to the street on Shabbat morning to fetch the local Kurdish woman whose job it was to light the fire for us and prepare our morning coffee. It was often the same Kurdish woman; she sat and waited in a specific place in the neighborhood, and her task was to help the local Jews with the chores that they could not engage themselves during Shabbat.

During the course of the week, men were busy with their work and women were in the main stay-at-home mothers, caring for the household, cleaning, cooking etc. The children, with their clean and ironed uniforms (girls had also white and large collars and big white headband "ruban") went to school for a long day, interrupted by an hour-long lunch break at noon during which they came home. At the Alliance school we learned French, Arabic and Hebrew, but the language of instruction for the main subjects was French.

My memories of teachers that I had at the Alliance school include Madame Preciado the headmistress, Madame David who taught us Hebrew, and Mlle Renée Levy, our then young French teacher. Many years after leaving Lebanon, I met by pure chance (and reconnected with) Renée. We subsequently became colleagues, with both of us teaching Arabic. I also remember Mme Shani, who was a French teacher and who lived in the house opposite ours. She was my brother's teacher, but I think that she liked me, and I used to visit her at her home from time to time. I remember sitting with her in their living-room, reading books while her husband read a newspaper. Mme Shani taught me a lot of things, and she was my model of European charm and dignity and class.

From the Alliance school I remember recess time in the schoolyard where we used to sit in groups sharing our sandwiches and also occasionally a big lemon (yes, a lemon) that we peeled and salted and divided between us. I liked very much this cooperative friendly atmosphere that characterized our childhood life in Beirut as well as in Zahlé. In the afternoon, we did our homework, usually in groups, with a friend or two, then we ran through the streets in the neighborhood for hours on end. I remember myself in the street with my friends, jumping rope, or playing hopscotch, or running and singing and shouting.

I faintly remember a curious series of events or disturbances that occurred in 1957 or 1958, when there were American soldiers patrolling the streets of Beirut. One afternoon, I was playing with my friends in the street, near the seashore, not far from a schoolmate's house. A group of soldiers were walking along the shore and they stood and looked at us. Then one of them gave us a dollar bill. We were so happy with our dollar bill, and we ran to the bank to change it into Lebanese currency.[47]

I have another fond memory connected with Americans, this time a missionary family with a boy my age named Johnny. I remember their big house with their beautiful living-room where the mother used to play hide-and-seek with Johnny and me. I also remember their kitchen with a box of chocolate-chip cookies on top of the refrigerator. The parents used to organize Sunday gatherings in their big home for the neighborhood's Jewish children. During those gatherings they told us gripping stories about Jesus and distributed candy and small cards with pictures of Jesus on them. Occasionally, the kids who were able to collect the largest number of "Jesus cards" got a special present. I remember that I was once one of those lucky winners, and I received a big chocolate egg as a reward.

In retrospect, I now wonder how community leaders and the Rabbi did not protest or complain about this family's proselytism, trying to seduce and bribe small Jewish children into Christianity. Yet I do remember quite distinctly that this American family was well-liked and respected in our milieu. I was fond of their young child; my older brother was a close friend of theirs, and my family knew them socially, visited with them often, and received them regularly in our home. We remained in touch for many years after they returned to the United States.

---

[47] This story has many corollaries, in many other neighborhoods of Beirut, and in many reference works on that period of Lebanese history. It marks the landing of 10,000 US Marines on the Lebanese coast south of Beirut, signaling the end of the 1958 Lebanese Civil War which had pitted Arab nationalists against Lebanese nationalists (see earlier references in Yitzhak Levanon's narrative). Many Marines from that time period do recall their surreal encounters with a Lebanon supposedly in the throes of civil war. Instead of a war-torn battlefield, disembarking US Marines noted being met by Lebanese children with flowers and Coca-Cola bottles. Returning the "favor," the Marines themselves often distributed American candy or chewing gum (and in this particular case of Zahava's, dollar bills) to passersby. This might have been the 1950s iteration of America's "winning hearts and minds." But the 1958 Lebanon war was nevertheless a serious political event, considered by many scholars the "dry run" of the more devastating 1975 conflagration, which that was to tear into Lebanon for more than 15 years and lead to its utter collapse and the ending of "Christian" prerogatives in it. The fact that Zahava breezes through the War as "disturbances" is reflective of her very young age in 1958, and arguably the "cocooned" or sheltered existence of the Lebanese Jewish community that ambassador Levanon spoke of earlier. Yet, there is no denying Lebanese Jewry's entrapment at the time. See earlier footnotes for more detail on the harassment, intimidation, and outright physical violence that Lebanese Jews were subjected to during that time period.

Besides my Beiruti Jewish friends, I had a Christian Lebanese friend named Liliane. She lived in a rich part of town, outside the Jewish neighborhood. I don't exactly remember the circumstances under which her and I met, but it could very well have been at my Christian elementary school, the Saint Vincent de Paul. I don't remember Liliane ever visiting our house, but I do remember visiting her often, going on road-trips with her family in their family car, and also accompanying her to her ballet classes and watching her dance lessons, an activity I could only dream of for myself.

I remember once that Liliane's mother was shocked (and I now I think she might have been offended) because I declined eating their food—because I only ate Kosher. She didn't understand that it had nothing to do with the cleanliness of her food, and went on and on trying to convince me that she washes and cleans and shines her dishes and utensils as well as my own mother. The point wasn't cleanliness, of course. But she would not understand, and I don't think I had the ability or the language to explain things to her better than I had.

I have plenty of other little vignettes and fond memories from Beirut, but I would like to also say a few things about our life in Zahlé. Zahlé is a small beautiful town surrounded by mountains, and populated mostly by Christians. I think that with one other family related to us, we were the only Jews in Zahlé during the summer. But on Sundays, Zahlé's "Jewish population" grew considerably, due to visitors flocking to its famous restaurants and cafés from other neighboring resort towns like Aleyy and Bhamdoun. Zahlé's river Berdawni, with the dozens of restaurants lining up its banks, was a prized destination for Lebanese of all stripes during the summer, especially those Beirutis trying to escape the heat of the coastal region. In Zahlé, I particularly remember the horse-drawn black carriage that we often took to go back home from the restaurant on Sundays.

We lived in a small private house in Zahlé. It consisted of a single big room, a kitchen, a bathroom, and a spacious open terrace. In front of our house there was a big mountain and every now and then the neighborhood's children used to get up very early (at five or six o'clock) and hike up the mountain. Every child brought with him his breakfast and we used to share our foods with each other: My sisters and I liked the traditional homemade bread of our Christian friends, and they liked the bread that we brought. Our almost daily trips were not only to the mountain as we used also to get up quite early to go down to the river Berdawni, all alone, without the adults, taking with us fresh vegetables, oil, lemon, salt and pepper, in order to make in situ *the traditional Lebanese salad called "taboulé." Generally*

*speaking we had a lovely time running freely through the streets and along-
side the river, playing, singing, and having fun.*

*Thank you very much for the opportunity that you have given me to go
back in time, to my fond memories of my private Lebanon.*

THE GOOD DOCTOR

*I was born in Beirut. I had a beautiful childhood. I studied at the Alliance
school, after which I moved to the Collège de La Salle (a private Catholic
high school) where I completed my secondary education in Philosophy. After
high school I entered Université Saint-Joseph's Medical School. Soon after
receiving my medical degree in 1964, I moved to the United States where
I stayed for two years before going back to Lebanon in 1966. There, that
same year, I met my beautiful bride, Batia Sasson,[48] got engaged within
three days, and returned to the United States. Four months later, I returned
to Lebanon, where Batia and I got married. We returned to the US soon
thereafter, leaving our parents behind, in Beirut. My father had a successful
medical practice. He died in Lebanon and was buried there.*

---

[48] Batia Sasson is the daughter of Edouard Sasson, the director of MGM Studios mentioned in earlier chapters. Member of one of Lebanon's most prominent Jewish families,
Sasson was shot to death on February 28, 1970, in his Beirut office, as he was preparing
to leave for the USA to celebrate the birth of his grandson and namesake Eddy, Batia's
and Moïse's second born. Sasson's assassination took place during a very surreal period
in Lebanese political history. At that time, attacks were increasing on Lebanese Jewry—
bombings, destruction of property, kidnappings, harassments, and assassinations—the
Palestine Liberation Organization was given free reign in the country challenging Lebanese
authorities, and the Jews were driven deeper into their communal cocoons. Moreover, as
the attacks grew more frequent and more intense, the PLO's denials of any involvement
grew more brazen and insolent. And as the Lebanese government attempted to assuage
Jewish fears and instate more robust protection measures, the PLO's propaganda machine
remained relentless, denying any involvement in these agitations, condemning the attacks,
and accusing "Zionist agents" of committing them against Lebanese Jewish persons in
order to force their immigration to Israel. Meanwhile, most international and local news
reports confirmed—in the Sasson case—that it was indeed Fatah elements of the PLO that
assassinated Edouard Sasson for refusal to make financial contributions to their guerilla
movement. Batia Sasson revealed that her father was under tremendous pressure to begin
allowing short PLO "propaganda footage" headline all feature presentations at the MGM
movie theaters under Sasson's direction—all at the express and continuous objection of
MGM, New York headquarters, which Sasson relayed repeatedly to PLO representatives in
Beirut.

For some reason that is still unclear to me after all these years, my father had this vision of dying in Israel. Maybe it's because we spent a lot of time there. Even before the 1950s and 1960s, when things began to get more challenging for Lebanese Jews, my dad still thought he would die in Israel. In fact, before the 1948 War and the closing of the border crossings between Lebanon and Israel, my father and I used to travel by car to Haifa, every weekend, where he would see patients at a clinic that he kept there. We would return to Beirut by taxi the following Monday so that my dad could tend to patients in his Beirut practice. When the borders closed, his patients in Haifa begged him to apply for a work permit and remain in Israel. They even asked me to intercede on their behalf and convince him to stay. His answer to me was "Nah, Lebanon is beautiful, it's our country, we're not going anywhere."

My dad had this "hobby" of sorts; he loved buying apartments. Whenever he had some extra money set aside, he would invest it in the purchase of a new apartment somewhere in Lebanon. At one point, benefitting from the rental income that he was reaping from his properties, he decided to build us a nice summer home in the hilltop resort town of Bhamdoun, overlooking Beirut. It was a beautiful place to which he loved to escape and relax on holidays and during the hot summer months. But he was able to enjoy this, his simple little nirvana of tranquility, for barely three years. When he passed away in 1970, Palestinian militants confiscated the property and came to my mother demanding at gunpoint that she sign all of my father's possessions over to them. They offered her a paltry ten thousand dollars compensation for an estate that might have been valued in the millions. The choices she was faced with were death and loss of her husband's legacy on the one hand, or life and still bereft of that legacy. She chose to forgo death, and was forced to leave Lebanon bereft of her Lebanese possessions. She moved to Israel where she stayed with my father's relatives until she died eight years later, in 1978.

Still, I have very good memories of Lebanon. I still dream of Lebanon. I still vividly remember my house, our street, the Wadi Boujmil neighborhood, the temple, the girlfriends, the sweet good simple life.

METRO GOLDWYN MAYER STUDIOS—BEIRUT

Batia was also was born and raised in Beirut. She studied at the *Alliance* school after which she attended the American School for Girls. She did not continue along the Francophone path of other Lebanese Jews of her generation and was accepted in an American institution in the main because her father, Edouard Sasson, was a representative of MGM Middle East, headquartered in Beirut during the 1950s–1970s.

Like many Lebanese of her generation—and indeed like most Lebanese to this very day—Batia's Arabic language skills were sub-par. In fact, she passed the English entrance examinations even though she had no formal training in English, and yet failed the Arabic section—a dilemma, given that Arabic was a requisite for admission. So she could not be possibly admitted into the American junior high school. But an exception was made in her case, given her father's American connections, and she was granted admission provided she got assigned an Arabic tutor. But even then the tutor despaired of Batia, ultimately going to her mother begging to be released from his Arabic instruction duties: "I can't teach your daughter Arabic, Mrs. Sasson" he pleaded. She drove him crazy; she kept telling him "what do I need this language for? I am never going to use it. I am going to get married one day, have children, and change diapers. What am I going to use an Arabic poem, or Arabic grammar for?"

It is worth noting in this regard that Batia's was not an uncommon attitude among Lebanese school children whose languages of instruction remain to this day in the main French and English. Arabic—or what Westerners refer to as "Modern Standard Arabic," or *Fusha*—is a learned, cultic, literary language that is never used as a natural spontaneous speech form. Therefore, studying Arabic in Lebanese schools is not the same as studying to read and write one's natively spoken language. Indeed, studying Arabic in a Lebanese school is more like studying Latin in a French or American school system, which is to say studying a foreign language, indeed a language utterly alien to the pupils' speech habits and cultural rituals. That is why, like Batia, most Lebanese pupils studying Arabic come of age shunning the language and ultimately renouncing it, so onerous and indeed exasperating are the methods associated with its acquisition. The doyen of modern Arabic literature, Taha Husayn (1889–1973) ascribed this dilemma to the Arabic language's inability to express the depths of the modern man's feelings in a modern age. He wrote in 1956 that Arabic is "difficult and grim, and the pupil who goes to school in order to study Arabic acquires only revulsion for his teacher and for the language itself, and employs his time in the pursuit of any other occupations that would divert and soothe his thoughts away from this arduous effort... Pupils hate nothing more than they hate studying Arabic."[49]

Still, noted Batia, "like most everybody will tell you, we all had a great childhood in Lebanon. But given that my father was an affiliate of an American company, and because we were Jewish, we were perhaps more exposed to the danger of anti-Americanism than others." Oddly enough, Batia was also more so exposed to the Muslim side of Lebanese life than other children of her generation who were not Muslim. "Believe it or not," she noted, "most Muslims were kind to us, and protective of us." As a child, Batia danced ballet, and it was Muslim friends of her father's who used to drive her back and forth to and from dance classes. "In hindsight," she noted, "now I know why I always had a Muslim 'escort'; it must have been because we were under some sort of a threat."

Still, in spite of the precautions, Batia's father ended up being murdered in his Beirut office, in late February of 1970. Although no Palestinian organization took responsibility for the murder, it is widely believed that this was the deed of the Palestine Liberation Organization's Syrian Saiqa affiliates.[50] The PLO were at the verge of being expelled from Jordan in early 1970—in what in the summer of that year would become known as Black September. They would subsequently set up shop in Lebanon, turning the country into what in later years would be described as "Fatah-Land"—which is to say a "Palestinian State within Lebanon." In the run-up to those events, tensions were rising in Lebanon, and the Jewish community, along with Jewish businesses, Jewish persons, and Jewish properties, were being subjected to heightened reprisals, vigilante-type attacks, and various acts of violence. It is in this context that the murder of Edouard Sasson may be attributed to Palestinian armed organizations, by way of a series of Palestinian communiqués "denouncing" such acts, "denying" Palestinian involvement, and "warning" Arab leaders against "falling prey to imperialist and Zionist plots aimed at terrorizing Arab citizens of the Jewish faith into immigrating to Palestine, so as the Zionist entity would enlist them

---

[49] Taha Husayn's "Yassiru an-Nahw wa l-kitaaba!" [Simplify Grammar and Writing!], *al-Adab* (Beirut: 1956, no. 11, 2, 3, 6).

[50] *The Spokesman-Review*, "Top Lebanon MGM Man Found Shot" (Beirut: The Associated Press, March 1, 1970), https://news.google.com/newspapers?nid=1314&-dat=19700301&id=1rMyAAAAIBAJ&sjid=YOsDAAAAIBAJ&pg=2119,307840&hl=en.

against their will into the Israeli army in order to make of them defenders of the belligerent, racist, Zionist state." [51]In this vein, and by way of similar bombast and histrionics, the murder of Edouard Sasson was condemned by Fatah, which pointed the finger at "Zionist agents," denouncing the "malicious Israeli reports claiming that Mr. Sasson was killed because he had refused to make financial contributions to the guerrilla movement."[52] "Mr. Sasson was a known opponent of World Zionism," claimed Fatah, and consequently, he "must have been killed [by Zionist agents] to get rid of his opposition."[53]

This version of the story was of course denied by Edouard Sasson's daughter, who noted that the PLO indeed wanted to show Palestinian propaganda snippets in MGM theaters under her father's administration. When Sasson suggested he would seek authorization from the headquarters in Beverly Hills, he was liquidated. Yet, in spite of the intimidation and threats that he was subjected to, and to which his daughter was privy by way of private correspondence between her and her father, Sasson never thought that things would devolve into actual physical violence. Additionally, he had assurances from his American employers that no harm would come to him. "This goes to show," said Batia, "how little understanding the Americans had for the world in which we were living."

She noted that her father had gone early to the office on the morning he was killed. He was giddy about traveling to America that same week. Batia had just given birth to her and her husband's second child, whom they named Eddy, after his grandfather Edouard, and Edouard the elder was looking forward to meeting his new grandson and namesake. He had his airline ticket on his desk and was in the process of writing Batia a note announcing his trip to the USA when he was shot, at close range, "by someone standing next to him" according to the Lebanese police report.[54] There were no signs of forced entry into Sasson's office, and nothing was reported missing from his personal effects according to

---

[51] *Le Monde*, "Al-Fath dénonce l'attentat contre l'école Israélite à Beyrouth" (Paris: January 21, 1970).

[52] Fatah was the armed Palestinian organization headed by Yassir Arafat (the Arabic acronym of the Movement for the Liberation of Palestine) which would become the founding wing of the Palestine Liberation Organization, also presided over by Arafat as Chairman.

[53] *International Herald Tribune*, Paris, March 2, 1970.

[54] *International Herald Tribune*, Paris, March 2, 1970.

those same reports; yet, the Lebanese police, by then beholden to (or bullied by) PLO agitators tightening their grip on Lebanese life, took great care underscoring "there was no evidence to suggest a political motive for the shooting."[55]

Needless to say, after that tragedy, the rest of the Sassons who had remained in Lebanon decided to leave. Even Batia's brother who was studying medicine at the Jesuit University in Beirut decided to call it quits in 1970. He was barely in his third year of medical school then.

Edouard Sassons' assassination might have been the wake-up call for most of the Lebanese Jews to begin seriously considering leaving; 1967 saw a very large wave of immigration out of Lebanon, but the 1970s were in a way the bigger, and perhaps the final catalyst. After Edouard Sasson's death, less than two years later, in early September 1971, it was Albert Elia's turn, the secretary-general of Lebanon's Jewish Communal Council, who was abducted never to be heard from again.[56] In spite of the standard statements issuing from Palestinian sources denying any Palestinian involvement, the *Jerusalem Post* reported in late September 1971, based on Lebanese police sources, that the Lebanese authorities had identified a "Palestinian terrorist organization" responsible for the abduction of Albert Elia, and "planning to abduct other Jews."[57] Exasperated—and indeed powerless—as the Lebanese authorities might have been in the face of rising Palestinian and Arab nationalist exactions, they were paralyzed by indecision and division. Whereas Lebanese Christians in the government were adamant about putting an end to Palestinian violations of Lebanese sovereignty, Muslim Lebanese, with some exceptions, deemed the "Palestinian cause" sacred, superseding Lebanese sovereignty. An oddity in his time, Sunni Prime Minister Saëb Salam issued a stern statement in those days, reassuring the Palestinians of Lebanon's commitment to their cause, "but only within the strictest limits of what is allowable under Lebanese law."[58] "Lebanon is, after all, a sovereign nation," hammered Salam, "an independent nation of laws and a justice system that have to be respected: Nobody is immune [not even the Palestinians can be immune] to the provisions of the

[55] *International Herald Tribune*, Paris, March 2, 1970.

[56] *Le Monde*, September 9, 1971.

[57] *The Jerusalem Post*, September 27, 1971.

[58] *Le Monde*, January 4, 1972.

Lebanese legal system."[59] Noble a plea—or a threat—as he was making, Salam knew he was blowing in a broken bagpipe. Lebanon by the early 1970s had long since ceded its sovereignty to the PLO, and a so-called Lebanese civil war was in the offing, pitting those Lebanese standing unconditionally besides the PLO (in the main Muslims) against those mainly Christian Lebanese intent on clinging to and protecting what little had remained of Lebanese sovereignty. Salam himself would abscond political life in 1973, and subsequently go into self-imposed exile, in Geneva, after repeated attempts on his life by radical elements (Muslim, Syrian, and Palestinian) resentful of his patriotic "Lebanon first" political stance.

The abuses committed against Lebanon's Jewish community would continue into the "civil war" years—beginning in April 1975. In 1985, four leading members of the Jewish community, among them Batia's uncle Isaac Sasson, as well as Dr. Elie Hallak and Chaim Cohen—an elderly member of the community—and Elie Srour were abducted in West Beirut, never to be seen again. Batia's uncle, Isaac, at the time was the director of the pharmaceutical department of one of Lebanon's largest trading companies, Fattal & fils. He had been warned previously by some friends to move his family to the safer Christian section of Beirut, but like most Jews of his time, he was apolitical, well connected to all of Lebanon's ethno-religious communities, and did not think he would be targeted as a Jew. In spite of the fate visited on his brother fifteen years earlier, Isaac Sasson was still an optimist, still convinced Lebanese Jews could still stake their claims and claim their place in Lebanese society.

"We love Lebanon of course," concluded Batia; "we love Beirut, we had a wonderful childhood there. But at the same time Lebanon broke our hearts; it brought tremendous tragedy and sadness and despair into our lives." Unlike other Lebanese communities, Lebanese Jews had to live quietly; they could not make public displays of their religious identity; they could not use Hebrew outside of their schools and homes. Indeed, many of them publically led Christian lives. At Batia's Christian school, she went to church like all the other children in the morning. She was in effect a Christian until Passover came, and then, she'd disappear like all the Jews of her neighborhood into their homes. In one instance, she noted, Muslim friends came to her house inquiring why she

[59] *Le Monde*, January 4, 1972.

hadn't been to school in almost a week; this is when she got fed up and told them "it's Passover," at which point she never saw them or heard from them again.

"But, we *did* have a good life and a good childhood in Lebanon!" stressed Batia."We ought to remember that, even if most of us living abroad still live a certain fantasy about a Lebanon that may no longer exist."

RAS BEIRUT

Raffoul's story is a bit different from those recounted so far. He was eight years old when he, along with his family, left Beirut. So his memories of Lebanon are not as vivid or as detailed as those of others. But Raffoul has kept a cache of fond memories tucked into the folds of his consciousness. He recognizes that many of his recollections may be complemented or colored by stories he'd heard from his parents, but there are certain words, sounds, names, smells, and other daily references in his American homeland that still take him back to the land of his birth and early childhood. A specific date that stands out for Raffoul, or one whose memory may be augmented (or confirmed) by the recollections of his elders, is June 10, 1967. He knows that this was the date of his family's departure from Lebanon. June 10, 1967, marked the end of the Six-Day War. Ironically, it also marked the beginning of the end of Lebanese Jewish life.

Raffoul's family lived in the Watwat neighborhood of Beirut, which was not within the Wadi Boujmil Jewish quarter proper. His father owned a record store, *Philosophe*, which was in the Hamra quarter, very near to the family home. Raffoul's grandfather owned a home appliances store on Rue St-Georges. Those two things Raffoul remembers vividly. Otherwise, his memories of Beirut are very limited. He remembers attending the *Alliance* pre-school; "we'd finish class at one or two o'clock in the afternoon, around the same time my father got out of work, and he would meet us at the school and take us to the *Long Beach* where we would spend the remainder of the day playing in the water." The *Long Beach* during the 1960s and 1970s—before the Lebanese wars—was one of the prime summer destinations for Beiruti beachgoers. Raffoul's father would spend the remainder of his day there with his kids, him playing chess, and the children swimming. They usually ate at a place in the Hamra district called Tarrazi, then went to play some more in the water until their father took them home, and headed back to work. He would stay in the store until 7:30 or 8:00 p.m., come home, have dinner, and that was that.

It was a good life, noted Raffoul. He has no memories of strife or politics or war, or anything of that sort because he was too young for that by the time his family left. All he remembers was that his father had made arrangements for them to get visas and leave for Montreal, on June 10, 1967. Raffoul's father was 27 years old at that time; he had three children, but he left everything behind in Beirut; his store, his property, his memories, his whole life, and arrived in Canada with three hundred dollars in his pocket. Once in Montreal, the Hebrew Immigrant Aid Services (HIAS) helped Raffoul's family get settled. But in 1968 they went back to Lebanon as the grandfather who had stayed behind had taken ill. They ended up staying there for about a year. Raffoul went back to the *Alliance* school in Beirut, and he remembers that he'd begun speaking English at that time, which was a novelty and a point of curiosity in Beirut, and specifically in the francophone environment of the *Alliance*. On account of his English, some of the kids would taunt Raffoul during recess, asking him "*Raffoul, ptehki ingleezee?*" (You speak English Raffoul, don't ya?), and when he said "eh" (yes), they would quip with "*telhas teezee*" ("lick my behind" / with the Lebanese word "teezee" rhyming with "ingleezee"). This might have been a harmless innocent schoolyard taunt, the kind of children's smart-alecky ditties that eight-year-olds might have found funny—even if perhaps crude—but one that Raffoul remembered with some affection.

During that brief trip back to Lebanon, Raffoul and his parents had stayed with family because when they left initially in 1967, his father had authorized some relatives and friends to sell whatever they could sell of their property and belongings. So when they returned in 1968, they had absolutely nothing left to his father's name. His store partners were a Maronite and a Druze to whom he had given his share of the company when he left. They remained close friends with his father for many years to come; they got along very well and even kept the store's original name, *Philosophe*, for as long as it had remained in operation, even as the original Philosophe was no longer the owner.

One thing in particular that Raffoul remembers about 1967 was the air-raid sirens going off in Beirut; "we'd often be at school when that happened," he noted, and one time his parents got stuck (perhaps in traffic) and could not come to pick him up because some of the main thoroughfares in Beirut were blocked. School administrators and teachers kept the children on lockdown in that instance, and Raffoul remembers being the last kid who got fetched by his parents. It was the Arabic class teacher who had stayed with him (the sister of another Lebanese Jewish respondent in this collection of testimonies). Raffoul's mother was worried that she couldn't get to him on time, but finally his cousins came to pick him up, and he remembers that for two days he could not see his parents because of the roadblocks and his folks' inability to get from one part of Beirut to the next (possibly a kind of division mimicking [Christian] East Beirut and [Muslim] West Beirut which became a permanent separation during the 1975 "civil war").

STILL HURTING AFTER ALL THESE YEARS

My mother, who belongs to the Chattah family, was born in Damascus. But my maternal grand-mother is Lebanese originally, from the Maronite town of Deir el-Qamar in the Chouf mountains. Both my father and grandfather were born and raised in Lebanon…

I have a mixed bag of memories and feelings about Lebanon. I grew up and worked in what I often remember to be an increasingly hostile environment in Beirut. My dad owned a shop in the Souks of Beirut. I worked in my father's shop from around 1960–1965. Our store was surrounded by Muslim shopkeepers, in the main Metawli (Shi'ites). They were conservative Muslims to say the least, and I remember them being openly hostile toward us. That's my perspective on our lives as Jews in the marketplace. It may be narrow, limited to a specific space, but those are the memories that stick out to me.

Otherwise Lebanon also spurs within me a host of good memories; beach life, beautiful serene mountain vistas, kind people in general. I spent my school years at the Alliance, and later integrated into the International College (IC) where I completed my secondary education before traveling to France to pursue my studies in Paris.

Today, as I witness the Shi'ite control of Lebanon, I see the country being taken into a direction that, back in my time, I did not think existed, or was possible. The Lebanon of my times, in spite of the tensions that I mentioned in my opening comments, was peaceful, tolerant, devoid of the aggressiveness and antagonisms we see nowadays. With the Shi'ites today overwhelming the Christian minority, I realize that I perhaps have little left to do with this Lebanon, and that leaving Lebanon when I did was perhaps not such a bad idea. I used to have a Lebanon that was peaceful and beautiful; one that I was attached to and infatuated with. Now I feel that this Lebanon was stolen from me, twice: once when I left in 1967, and a second time now, in a Lebanon that no longer conforms to the image of it that I have kept in my memory.

FOUAD

My name is Fouad, I was born in Lebanon, in Beirut, I was a student of the Alliance Israélite Universelle. *I have a twin brother, Ziad, and when we both finished our intermediate education at the* Alliance, *like others our age, we had to apply to secondary school. Typically our choices were either the Lycée Français, or the International College among others. So we both applied and got accepted in both colleges. The problem was that my father could not afford to send us to either of these pricey schools—specially in view of our six-children household. He tried finding a way to obtain schol-arships for us, and succeeded in getting us into the International College, which is the English-speaking "high school" affiliated with the American University of Beirut. This was very unusual, given that most of Lebanon's Jews were Francophones, received a Francophone primary education at the* Alliance *schools,* and ordinarily went to French-*affiliated schools thereafter. "Traitors" to our communal rituals, we ended up in an American insti-tution. We did, however, attend the French Section of the International College, and we remained there until the* "Seconde."[60]

I am very proud to be Lebanese, to have grown up in Lebanon, and I am particularly proud of that particular year (1967, my last year in Lebanon), even though it ended on a sour note. My last day at the IC was on June 6, 1967; that's when the Six-Day War broke out. For some reason, I remem-ber it being 9:00 am; I think we might have been in English Literature class when all of a sudden a throng of AUB students began entering our classrooms—IC was on the main AUB Campus, in Bliss Hall—literally storming the classrooms, forcing students to go out marching with them, to the chants of "Idbah el-Yahood, Idbah el-Yahood" (slaughter the Jews...) I remember there being about eight Jewish kids in our class—it was a class composed of one-third Jews, one-third Armenians, and one-third everything else, probably mainly Muslims, since Christians (besides the Armenians) ordinarily attended Francophone schools, like most Jews.

---

[60] The French "Seconde" corresponds roughly to the American Tenth Grade.

At that point the Armenians and some of the other Christian classmates walked over to us, told us not to panic, got us into walking alongside them, to safety, until we could get on a bus and ride back to Wadi Boujmil. That was my last day at the IC, and the last of my fond memories of that school. I am still emotively attached to it; I am still an alumni of the International College; I still attend annual IC alumni meetings; and I am still very active and involved within that community of old IC students.

Both my children, Nicole and Marco, grew up listening to my stories and remembrances of Lebanon, and so both grew up with a great deal of curiosity, even yearning, for that mysterious "lost world" of their father's. And so, Nicole—Marco as well, but Nicole most relentlessly—had always insisted we paid a visit to Lebanon, as a family; she wanted to see where I grew up, revisit the places of my youth, my roots, and my memories. In that sense, she was unyielding, staying at it, nagging me night and day, "when are we going to Lebanon? when will you take us to Lebanon?" So, I caved in one day, told Nicole to go ahead and plan the trip; that I was not going to plan it myself; and that I will follow her lead whenever she had the itinerary figured out.

The ball was now in Nicole's court. At the time she was working for the United Nations, and as part of a project she was assigned to one day, she was slated to take a trip to Kuwait, Oman, and Lebanon. We all ended up going along with her, and we spent eight wonderful days in Lebanon.

I was very excited to be back. I was very happy to have made that trip with my family. It was a veritable emotional rollercoaster. On the one hand I was delighted to be able to see some of the places I grew up, some of the places that had lived in my memory and of which I had kept vivid images in my mind; on the other hand it was a sad encounter, a heartbreaking sensation to be in the presence of a declining degraded Beirut, a once vibrant cosmopolitan modern city that had regressed so dramatically, lapsing almost into obsolescence.

I remember Beirut from the days of its famous Tramway, which in later years was supplemented by, and later upgraded to an intricate efficient system of bus-service. No such system of mass transport exists in Beirut of today—this being perhaps the most salient symbol of the city's regression and decay, choked as it currently is by endless snarling lines of traffic.

Likewise, during this visit, I was struck by how children of my generation still remembered (as I did), and still valued the multi-culturalism of the Lebanon of old... Of course, our memories often exaggerate and heighten the importance of images from our past; through this lens things *seem brighter, sweeter, often more charming and much bigger. I remember the main street of Wadi Boujmil for instance being a wide avenue; I was shocked to rediscover it as nothing more than a narrow alley. I remember the walk from the Besançon to my grandmother's house being quite a distance; today, no more than two building separate the two stops. Still, there was something magical about the Beirut of my memories that was wistfully absent from the realities of today.*

I was eager to go back to the Alliance *school, to see what it had become, to see whether anything of it had remained in any shape or form. But once there, on that very same spot where the school once stood, I was struck by the beautiful building rising in its place; a lovely delightful modern structure, but nothing like the* Alliance*. I accosted a man who seemed like the grounds-keeper and asked him whether a school once stood where this building was. He was delighted, almost ebullient to tell me, that "yes! it was the Jewish School," saying so with a sparkle in his voice and a yearning in his eye. It was very moving to hear and see him say that. He put his arm over my shoulder as if we were old acquaintances and proudly added "we are rebuilding the Synagogue; walk over with me, let me show you." And we walked over, with his hand still on my shoulder, and he gave me a tour of the Magen Avraham, then still under renovation.*

This incident gave concrete confirmation of the general sense of nostalgia that I felt most "older" Lebanese had for a past that seems to have slipped away from them; a Lebanese past of diversity and multiculturalism and sophistication and purity that still lived in their memories. I felt there was even a sense of anguish and bitterness over a paradise lost; a sense that the loss of a certain affluence and prosperity and emotional and spiritual wealth of times past might have been due to the absence of one of the key pieces of the Lebanese mosaic—the Jewish community. This, of course, is all lost on the younger generations that haven't the faintest recollection or awareness that such a community had once existed or been part and parcel of the larger Lebanese family.

I ended up going to the Jewish cemetery, which was on the Beirut "green line" that separated the warring parties during the Lebanese civil war. It stood on a hill, and at that time was locked and inaccessible by foot; inaccessible, at least from the street where we stood. Finally, somebody came over to us, a young man wearing an "icon" of a Qoran on a chain hanging from his neck. He asked if I needed help. I told him "yes," that my grandparents were buried here, and that I was visiting from the United States and was wondering if I could visit the cemetery. Again, as in an earlier "reunion" with another Lebanese "stranger," this man put his arm on my shoulder, told me how impressed he was that I had made a trip all the way from the United States to see my grandparents, and walked me over to a better vantage point from where I could cast a closer gaze onto the cemetery. Again, I was greeted with another very profoundly moving gesture that made me realize something I knew all along; that the real Lebanese are a fantastic people, benevolent and affectionate toward one another regardless of their backgrounds, proud of their past, wistful and nostalgic for it. This made me realize why I have such fond and proud memories of Lebanon. Sadly, little remains of the Wadi Boujmil neighborhood of old and its old residences; besides the Besançon and Ahliyyé schools, and an old building where my grandmother once lived—a building that developers haven't yet figured out what to do with—little else remains. Even the imposing Alliance structure, which had at one time given its name to the street where it once stood, has now donned a new name, and another street, at some distance from the original Alliance now bears the "Alliance" name.

I often hear that there are some one hundred of more Jews left in Lebanon. Unfortunately I did not reach out to any of them during this trip, and I regret that very much. I am curious to know what had become of my old childhood friends, Jews and others, and I hope to have the opportunity to reconnect with them during a future trip to Lebanon.

Otherwise, we went all over Lebanon, visited many places, had absolutely no trouble whatsoever. Even when we went to Baalbeck, most of which is Hezbollah territory, there were no issues at all. I can't say that I would go back to Baalbeck. I am glad we visited though; it's one of those places that I've longed to revisit. It is now nicely checked off of my bucket list; but I don't think I would ever go back there again.

Going into Lebanon posed a bit of a complication, but I suspect it stemmed more from the inexperience of the immigration officer than anything else. Entering the country with my US Passport, which clearly indicated Lebanon as my place of birth, border police insisted I showed him my Lebanese Identity Card—which is standard with all Lebanese who enter the country on a foreign passport. When I told the border policeman that I didn't have a Lebanese national Identity Card, he insisted I "should have had it." He kept scrutinizing my passport, looking at the screen in front him, going back to the passport, poring over its pages, over and over again. He didn't know what to make of me perhaps. He clearly had knowledge (or perhaps a suspicion) that I was Jewish; I suspect the data base on his computer provided him that information; but he didn't know what to do with it. I don't think he had the training to deal with a situation such as this. After an extended encounter, a long awkward moment of silence, him sweating and wiping his brow, he stamped my passport and I walked into Lebanon.

I spoke Lebanese to everyone. I had no hesitation speaking in Lebanese to anyone. Some people I suspect recognized that I was Jewish, perhaps due to my distinctly Jewish-Beiruti accent, but that did not pose any problems whatsoever.

The best part of Lebanon perhaps, the place that brought me back to my fondest memories, was the IC campus inside AUB; an island of tranquility in the midst of the city's bustle; a veritable oasis all to itself; arguably the only place in Beirut that seems to have been frozen in time, that seems to have undergone no discernable transformation.

This was in November, and it seemed so strange to me that all the public beaches in Beirut were closed, even though "beach season" in Lebanon is ordinarily over by mid to late October. But I kept telling myself that there is no way that I could be in Lebanon and not swim in its waters. But I did remember that the IC campus had its own "private beach." So I said "okay" to myself, "I'll go for a swim at the IC." But it seemed that that beach was closed as well. But thanks to my intrepid son Marco, and much to the dismay of my wife, Justine, once on the IC campus, like the ze'raan (the irreverent hoodlums) of Beirut, I climbed over the fence, went on the beach, and I swam in that Beiruti water.

I should mention that when the War of 1967 broke out, there were curfews all over Beirut, and everybody's movements were somewhat restricted. Schools and most businesses were closed. We were all huddled at home. I remember one Saturday afternoon my father came home unusually late from Synagogue. We had zero plans. We had never thought of leaving Lebanon. None of us in the family had even a passport. But on that evening, my father walked into the house, much later than had been his habit, wearing a long face, he gathered all of us—except my older brother who was away, studying in Paris—and he declared, in his usual resolute demeanor, "I have decided; we are leaving; we will go to Paris; we will figure out from there where to go next." We were all in shock; we thought my dad had gone mad. But there was no going back on his decision.

It took us only the time of getting our passports ready. And we left. Quietly. Not even our neighbors knew we were leaving. Not even our Jewish neighbors. My dad was afraid that we would be stopped. To my sense there was no reason for the extraordinary precautionary measures that he had gone to, but to his sense we had to be cautious. Better safe than sorry. July 9, 1967 we were on an outbound plane never to come back. We left everything behind: our home, our belongings, our memories, our lives, our clothes; there was no time for us to sort any of these things out.

We ended up in Canada eventually, after a brief stopover in Paris. Why not Israel? The decision was largely functional. Canada, specifically Montreal, was a francophone country. But we also had friends and relative in Montreal. So, Montreal, at least for some of us children, had been in the works. Like most young Lebanese of all generations, we thought that Lebanon's professional and educational horizons were limited, and traveling abroad for educational or professional reasons was always a possibility. My elder brother had already left in 1965 to pursue higher education at the Sorbonne. Leaving Lebanon, we would be only answering to an age old Lebanese tradition; following in my brother's footsteps, but also walking in the footsteps of other Lebanese who had done for centuries what we were doing now.

Once we arrived in Paris, the Hebrew Immigrants Aid Services (HIAS) began making arrangements for us to travel to Israel. My father was ada-mant about not going to Israel. It might have been a selfish decision. He was the father of three boys. Isaac, our eldest brother was twenty-one years old. I, and my twin Ziad were sixteen. The three of us were therefore prime candi-dates for the Israeli army. Otherwise, Israel would have been ideal for my father. He had two sisters and a brother there already. He spoke both Arabic and Hebrew. But he was also farsighted. His lodestar was not his own com-fort, but his children's future. He had ambitions for his children. Israel did not offer the future and the ambition that he had in mind. I remember the exact words he told the HIAS agent at the time: "A bomb is a bomb, sir. I shall not go to Israel." He did not wish us to be implicated in someone else's war. My sister Salwa interjected during that discussion with the HIAS rep-resentative, insisting upon being sent to Canada rather than Israel. She had already had a job lined up in Montreal, through the efforts of a Lebanese friend of hers already there, and she told the agent "you are intruding on my life and livelihood; I have a job in Canada; I am going to Canada." The HIAS relented and acquiesced to our demands. I remember my father telling Salwa at the time "inté ekht er-rjéél" in Lebanese ("you are the sister of Men/you have the manly grit.")

We arrived in Canada on Thursday. Friday was Labor Day weekend (observed the first Monday of September). The following Tuesday Salwa began her new job.

It should be noted that the bulk of Lebanese Jews, like us, opted out of going to Israel. Those who did, were ordinarily Syrian Jews, Aleppans to be exact, who had taken refuge in Lebanon after 1948—some even before—who had never acquired Lebanese citizenship, and who were fearful of further expulsions. Like other refugees living a tenuous liminality, they felt that Israel was the only safe harbor left on their horizons. We, on the other hand, were not refugees. We were Lebanese. We were Lebanese nationalists, I would say. Patriots. Certainly, many Syrian Jews, even those living in Lebanon, did end up in New York and elsewhere in North and South America. But the bulk of the Syrians who were leaving Lebanon between 1948 and 1967 opted for Israel, the final destination, they had hoped, of their endless peregrinations.

I Am Lebanese

I am Lebanese. I was born in Beirut. I came of age in Beirut. We lived in the Qantari district, just outside Wadi Boujmil, near Mar-Elias. I remember specifically my years at university in Lebanon. Like most everyone else in our community, I had my early formation at the Alliance Israélite Universelle *school, after which I transferred for secondary education at the Collège Louise Wegmann. It was a wonderful school. It was there that I received my French and Lebanese Baccalauréat degrees. I was studying Arabic literature; I loved it, and I understood it well, but for the life of me, I never became an able writer in Arabic. My Arabic professor, Mme Kababji, I remember her very vividly, she would take me aside during recess and say, "okay, you do understand the story of "Antar and Abla, yes?" "you do know the goings on of their saga!" And I would say "yes," at which point she would retort, "good, now go inside and practice writing, because you are not allowed to receive a disqualifying grade on your Arabic test."*

Needless to say, I was a lost cause in Arabic.[61] *But still, I passed my Lebanese Baccalauréat and its Arabic literature exam. But what I wanted to say is that I am very nostalgic for Lebanon and for my years at university, at the École Normale Supérieure. Those years, from 1963 to 1967, had the greatest impact on my life. There were barely five Jewish girls and a few more Jewish boys in our class; otherwise, the students in the program were essentially*

---

[61] See earlier comments on Batia Sasson's Arabic, which falls within the general parameters of Lebanese students of every generation, through 1950s, 1960s, and beyond, not particularly fond of the idea of becoming Arabic grammarians.

Christians and Muslims. It was an unforgettable bond of friendship that tied all of us together; we were inseparable; we would travel together from Beirut to Zahlé [in the Bekaa Valley,] to have dinner, and drive around carefree, enjoying the countryside, the beach-life, the city-life, the night-life...

That being said, as a Jew, I was not able to freely partake of all of the students' activities. I took a course in geography, for instance, and part of our curriculum, we were required to conduct fieldwork in an area closer to the Syro-Lebanese border. I distinctly remember my professor in this instance telling me, "no, Salwa, you cannot come with us on this trip, because I am unable to guarantee your safety in that part of the world; in Lebanon there isn't much to fear, but in Syria it's another story altogether." And so, I was not able to take part in those aspects of my education. I remember distinctly the day I took my written final exam in Geography; the topic was India; it was June 5, 1967; I was in the exam hall, writing my exam, and radios were blaring all around me, haranguing about Israel, and bombings, and suchlike. As I was leaving the hall, my professor met me as I was stepping out and told me to come with him immediately to take the oral segment of the exam, because no one knows how things will be evolving in a week or so, by the time the initial oral exam was scheduled to take place. It was as if our French professor had a premonition about the events to come; as if he knew there would be an exodus of Lebanese Jews as a result of these events of June 1967.

He quickly gathered up an ad hoc *committee of professors, summoned our class's other Jewish students, and proctored the oral exam right then and there, almost extemporaneously.*

This was also an era during which some Lebanese opened up and showed a side of themselves that we were not aware of previously. Maybe my recollections are being over-exaggerated by my constructive memory, or else I'm being too over-sensitive. But to give you an example, the corner grocer in our neighborhood—the guy whose store we visited regularly, almost every Sunday, to purchase beer, food, labné and suchlike—on one particular Sunday, after the Six-Day War, the guy jeeringly wondered whether we were buying beer to celebrate Israel's victory. Again, maybe I'm being oversensitive, but at the same time, we bought beer from this store almost every Sunday, and there was no reason for the store owner to think we were celebrating Israel on that particular Sunday.

On the other hand, the corner hairdresser, to whom I had mentioned that we may be leaving soon, came to me one day and offered to go with me to the passport office; he was adamant that I not initiate my passport application on my own, without the presence of a non-Jewish Lebanese.

Speaking of passports, I had already travelled a number of times outside of Lebanon, and I already had a passport to my name—which I had renewed twice; once in 1963 and another time in 1965; I think passports in those days were valid for two years only. At any rate, I already had a passport made a few times, and I never remember being subjected to intrusive questioning during the process. 1967, however, things had changed. The passport officer then began a laundry-list of inappropriate questions. The hairdresser accompanying me blew up in his face, yelling at him "how dare you ask such questions of this lady? I am never subjected to this line of questioning when I'm applying for a passport!" A heated altercation between the two ensued. But I recount this story to note that things might have begun changing then, by 1967; being Jewish now began raising a different set of questions of the kind "why do you need a passport?" "where are you going?" "who is traveling with you?" and suchlike... This drove Yazid, the hairdresser, to ask that I sign over to him a power-of-attorney proxy so that he would come pick up the passports for me. Again, the moral of the story is that things had begun changing for us by the summer of 1967. And even though I am proud to be Lebanese; even though I have very fond memories of Lebanon; even though I value my life and time in Lebanon, it is ultimately a mixed-bag of feelings... Something broke in 1967.

I was an active member of the Phalanges Party when I was younger. I learned great skills as a party militant. We attended summer camps, learned first aid, basic survival skills, patriotic marches, anthems, and the like. I took great pride participating in Lebanon's political and socio-cultural life, as just another Lebanese among others, which compounded my love of Lebanon and the pride that I took in being Lebanese. That has not changed; it has not stopped. But as I said earlier, something broke, somewhere deep inside, a Lebanese Jew can no longer feel at home in his country, can no longer feel safe in his country.

Yet, I have remained in touch with some of my Lebanese friends, not all of them Jewish; and incidentally, one of my college mates, with whom I was very close, whom I ran into in Paris recently, who was incidentally not Jewish, has now a Jewish son-in-law (laughter). Again, this is to show you that in spite of it all, there was a certain openness, a certain complicity, a certain diversity and elasticity and fluidity to Lebanon that is perhaps lacking in many other places in the world. There were times where we could be politically transparent. Yet came times where we would still go out, still enjoy each other's company with fellow Lebanese, from all kinds of backgrounds and all kinds political convictions, but where politics and the discussion of "sensitive" questions became sotto voce, *not to say taboo.*

I wish to reiterate that the Lebanese Jews of my generation were Lebanese nationalists. Lebanese patriots proud of their roots and proud of their country. These sentiments might have been the outcome of our Alliance *education. But more importantly, this was also the outcome of our roots in Lebanon. We were active in Lebanese nationalist parties, the Phalanges for instance, and we even got involved in street brawls—present company included—during the civil war of 1958, in the ranks of the Lebanese Kataëb [Phalanges]. But when the war of 1958 ended, and as Lebanon came under the administration of the more "moderate" Fouad Chehab, who tried to assuage Muslims and Arab nationalists—by reigning in the Christian "nationalist" component of Lebanese society—reprisals were for a time exacted against Lebanese Jews who militated on the side of the Phalanges. Many of those Lebanese Jews felt threatened under Chehab, and ended up leaving to Mexico, Argentina, and Brazil. But never to Israel.*

Although my own family never felt threatened to the point of wanting to leave Lebanon, even though I was a militant in the Kataëb, there was still at times unease in my father's heart, and I do remember him telling my mother to always keep a suitcase ready, because we didn't know when the hour of our departure would come knocking. There were times my father was ready to move the family to the Mountains, in the heartland of Christian Lebanon, until we figured out what to do in a Beirut that was becoming increasingly inhospitable. But then things would quiet down, as they did during the Chehab era, life would go back to normal, and "moving" would become an absurd consideration.

But then 1967 came to break the proverbial camel's back; at least it did for our family. This may not have been the case for other Lebanese Jews. For us it was.

No One Can Take That From Me

I was born in Lebanon. I am very proud of this. My family lived on Rue Georges Picot. I was educated at the school of the Alliance, *like most of my friends. But then I graduated to the Lycée Français where I made some very good friends with whom we ended up at Université Saint-Joseph (the French Jesuit university of Beirut) where I earned a law degree. I was very proud to have become a lawyer, but I could not practice law in Lebanon. It was in the main a personal decision; I simply did not want to be a "Jewish lawyer" in a country already blessed with a glut of lawyers.*

At school I had a great variety of friends spanning the Lebanese ethno-religious spectrum; among them were Druzes, Sunnis, Shi'ites, Maronites, etc.... We were a wonderful band of buddies, and whenever one of my friends would introduce me to a new group, they would jokingly say "this is David Bekkay, he is Jewish, but he's okay." I remember this very distinctly. There was always something different about me, even though we were otherwise all alike. I was a "good guy," but I was still the Jewish "David Bekkay."

*Still, I had such good friends that in the early days of the Six-Day War I'd receive phone calls from some of them begging me to come to their homes for shelter, for fear there would be reprisals against me, being Jewish and all: "come stay with us," they would say, "we'd take care of you and your family; we'd protect you..." The war didn't last long—six days, as its name suggests—and I ended up staying at home. But I did not miss the opportunity to call upon those thoughtful friends who'd offered to protect me, and ask if they'd want to "come to **my** house now for [their own] protection" (laughter).*

What I miss about Lebanon are all the girlfriends that I used to have, Jews and non-Jews alike; it made no difference to me; if she was pretty, she was okay to be my girlfriend (laughter).

But all joking aside, one striking memory that I have of Lebanon—and this perhaps applies elsewhere in the Middle East—is whenever you meet new people, once they learn your name, and should the name be "ethno-religiously ambiguous" and not reveal much about your communal identity, the next thing they'd want to ask about you would be your religion. It is so important for people to know what your religion is. I don't know if other Lebanese expats remember this, but it is something that has really stayed with me. For instance, the Lebanese last name Chahine [which is of Persian origin, and means "falcon," fs] can be Jewish, Muslim, or Christian; and in Beirut proper, members of different Lebanese communities had that name in common. Likewise, my name, Bekkay, which means "a native of the Bekaa Valley," is one shared by Muslims, Christians, and Jews. So, needless to say, my name was ambiguous, and new acquaintances were always curious as to my communal identity.

At this point in the conversation, David's American wife teasingly interjects, asking him to "tell us, since the situation was so fabulous with all the girls in Lebanon, why did you leave that fine den of ladies?"

1967 came about. But even before the war, I was beginning to give serious thought to my future. I was twenty-three years old in 1967, and I was beginning to wonder what was next for me in life. So in a sense, 1967 was a catalyst for me personally; I knew I had to leave then; there was no way I could build a future and start a family in Lebanon. My parents were elderly; my mother was ill, she had had a brain tumor, so she was incapacitated and wholly reliant on a special care-taker, 24-hours a day. My father was old, much older than my mom. She was his second wife, because his first wife of twenty years could not bear children, so he had to leave her and marry my mother, as an older man. He must have been forty years old already when I was born.

At any rate, I already had a sister who lived in Mexico; another sister living in Switzerland, and another brother who was studying in Paris. So, in a sense, besides my parents, it was only my sister and I who were still living in Lebanon. So I told my sister, I have to leave this country; I'll leave you here to care for our parents, and in a year or two I will have made a situation for myself and I'll send for the three of you to join me. She agreed to stay back in Lebanon; I was able to arrange for a visa to Canada by way of the Hebrew Immigration Aid Services (HIAS) then active in Beirut. This organization was working on behalf of Jews anywhere in the Middle East wishing to leave—specially given their dire situation in Arab lands. So, it was through HIAS that I was able to obtain an immigrant's visa, almost overnight, to Canada. Next, I purchased a ticket with a stopover in Switzerland, to visit my sister. Once in Switzerland, my sister, whose family had a well-established business, insisted I stayed with them; she promised they would arrange for a job for me, and that in no time we could send for mom and dad and my sister to come join us. It was a tempting idea. I only had $500 in my pocket. But still, I decided to forgo that opportunity and chance it on my own. So I headed to Canada.

I had a friend, Albert Tarrab, who had immigrated to Canada a few years before me, and he had offered to let me stay with him until I was able to fly solo. Two to three weeks after my arrival in Montreal, I landed myself a job in a finance company. Within a year I was able to purchase an airline ticket on British Airways to go back to Lebanon. I was dying to go back. For a year and a half I had dreamt of going back, of seeing that beautiful country once more; its beautiful vistas and building, and its delicious food, and women... (laughter).

But once in Lebanon, I had a great unease reintegrating the culture. Things were no longer as I had kept them fixed in my memory. The streets were dirty; the buildings were decrepit; our neighborhood was falling apart. So, this image that I had of Lebanon, idealized no doubt, was completely shattered upon this encounter, barely a year and a half after my initial departure in 1967. I was happy to spend three days there, and get hell out. But within six months of that visit, I sent for my sister and mother (so that my sister would be released from the responsibility of caring for my infirm mom).

My sister ended up in Israel. She spent two years there, then came to join me in Canada. I likewise brought my other sister, who was living in Mexico, to Canada. Even my brother, who was in Paris, also ended up in Canada. So, in conclusion, I brought all of my family to Canada, and the minute they all got settled, I left them and moved to Boston.

I spent in total five years in Montreal, then I got involved in the banking business in Boston, in 1973. That is primarily why I left Montreal. 1973 was also the year my bride and I got married. So that's my story. I never went back to Lebanon since 1969.

I must add that going to Israel was always an option for me; an alternative to Canada. We always knew that Israel would help us get there, help us get settled, give us housing, and make our transition the smoothest that it can be. But we also heard reports from Lebanese Jews that had gone to Israel that the living conditions were very difficult; a polar opposite of what we were accustomed to in Lebanon. Getting work wasn't easy; duplicating the care-free laissez-faire kind of life that we had in Lebanon was next to impossible. Next to Lebanon's libertine cosmopolitan ways, Israel was austere and grim. To those of us spoiled by the "savoir vivre" of Lebanon, Israel was more hardship than anything else. And so, the possibility of going to North America seemed more attractive in terms of education, careers, and building a future. This was the main impulse against going to Israel. North America offered us the opportunity of "making it" on our own, without having the need of being subsidized by a government. The fact that we were granted visas to Canada almost immediately—as Francophone immigrants—made that option also all the more attractive. This was compounded by the fact that my intention had been to make enough money, in as little time as possible, so as to go back to Lebanon and fetch my mother and sister. Israel would not have offered that opportunity; and going to

Israel meant that—at least for the foreseeable future—I could not go back to Lebanon.

THE CATHOLIC SCHOOL INTERN

Fady Gadeh and I hit it off immediately. The minute our gazes met I was gripped by this odd feeling that I knew this man from somewhere. Even before "hello," our arms had leapt forward, almost intuitively, eager to clasp a handshake. Eyes wide-open, on the verge of saying something (but not), our attention froze in a sort of mental pause—that strange mix of familiarity one feels toward something entirely new; the sense of *déjà vu*, wondering "where have I seen that face before?" I imagine ours having been the searching eyes of those who suddenly recognized one another but couldn't seem to figure out how and where and when they might have met before. To me, these first awkward, fumbled moments being introduced to Fady Gadeh—a split second or two at most—felt like the class reunion of old schoolmates who have just chanced upon each other, many decades after graduation, shaking hands and smiling, their minds racing, embarrassed, in vain trying to recall names they once knew, behind faces they never forgot.

As it turned out, Fady Gadeh, a few years older than I, boarded at the same Mount Lebanon high school where I was a commuter in the early 1980s—the Collège Saint-Joseph Antoura. Affiliated with the Lebanese Lazarist order since the late eighteenth century, Collège Saint-Joseph Antoura is the oldest Francophone Catholic school in the whole Near East. First established in 1651 by the Jesuit Fathers, it was ceded to the local Lebanese Lazarists in 1773, after the Jesuit Suppression. Antoura developed spectacularly—in reputation, curricular, and programmatic terms—throughout the eighteenth and nineteenth centuries becoming the Near East's leading, most prestigious francophone educational institution. Among its most notable alumni figure a veritable "who is who" collection of Lebanese politicians, artists, literati, and academics; Christians, Muslims, Druzes, and Jews alike. Those "celebrity alums" counted among them Presidents (Charles Hélou, Soliman Frangié, and René Moawad)[62]; a Prime Minister (Riad el-Solh)[63]; a Speaker of the

---

[62] All three Maronite Christians.
[63] A Sunni Muslim.

Lebanese Parliament (Sabri Hamadé)[64]; and a number of thinkers, diplomats, politicians, poets, and artists including Romeo Lahoud, Hamid Frangié, Kamal Jumblatt, Elias Abou-Chabké, Checri Ganem, Ghassan Tuéni, and others still. The school was portrayed in the 2015 memoir of a survivor of the Armenian Genocide, *Goodbye, Antoura*. The author, former Antoura "student" Karnig Panian, was "interned" at the school during the Great War, along with a thousand or more young boys. At that time, in 1915, the Ottomans had wrested the property from the Lazarists, turning it into an orphanage—a "Turkification center" really—for captured Armenian children whose parents had perished at the hands of the Ottomans.[65]

But there were happier times at Antoura and kinder depictions of the place. Snippets of Fady's personal story attest to that.

One of Fady's heroes during his life at Antoura was Father Naoum Atallah. One of the college's pillars and a man of impeccable reputation and integrity and decency, Atallah was the school director in Fady's days. His tenure guided the school into a period of unparalleled success, playing a decisive role in its modernization, reorganization, and increased recognition as standard bearer of Catholic education in the Near East. In 1976, Fr. Atallah was awarded the Medal of the National Order of the Cedar, Lebanon's highest civilian and military decoration, in recognition of the cultural and scholastic services that he rendered to Lebanon and Saint-Joseph Antoura. His legacy, and the gratitude and respect that he commanded—even among those who never knew him—is palpable in the way he is mentioned and remembered by those who knew him. Fady was one of those whose lives were touched by Atallah's work. And so, he does understand well why and how such a man would be awarded the Lebanese Republic's highest honor: Fr. Atallah was a compassionate, warm, kind soul, noted Fady, much admired by students, parents, teachers, and administrators alike.

Although I never met Atallah myself—he had long since retired by the time I came to Antoura in 1979—his reputation outlasted his tenure, and students and teachers whom I interacted with during my days at the school seemed to never tire of mentioning him or comparing (wistfully)

---

[64] A Shi'ite Muslim.

[65] See Karnig Panian, *Goodbye, Antoura: A Memoir of the Armenian Genocide* (Stanford, CA: Stanford University Press, 2015).

the newer generation of priests and administrators to "the one" who could be neither imitated nor duplicated.

"He was truly one of a kind," noted Fady when I told him that I'd never met Fr. Atallah, that I had only heard (good things, second-hand) about him, and that my director at Antoura was a different priest from a different era, albeit *also* with the last name Atallah. Betraying a bit of pity (for this poor plebian who never got to meet "the man"), Fady insisted I had truly missed "a once in a lifetime human being," adding, not without a hint of pride, that Atallah had charged him—the school's only known Jewish student—with decorating Antoura's annual Christmas tree. "It was my yearly assignment, my time to shine, and I wouldn't miss it for anything." Fady also noted—this time with a touch of nostalgia—how Fr. Atallah used to tiptoe into his dormitory room early every morning, just before dawn, to try to wake him up for the *Shacharit*—the Jewish morning prayer: "Fady, wake up, son," Atallah used to plead; "*Fady, saar el-wa'et habibi, 'uum, yalla, 'uum ya ibné, 'uum w hott ej-jildé*" ("it's time, son, come on, wake up, get up, and go strap on the skin/leather belt [*tefillin*]").[66]

There is here, in the use of the Lebanese term "jildé" (for a piece of "hide" or "skin") in reference to the prayer *tefillin*, an endearing mix of authenticity and sincerity and guilelessness. Never mind that waking Fady up for the Jewish *Shacharit* was the deed of a priest here, not a rabbi, instructing a Jewish boy, at a Catholic school, in the practice of Jewish tradition and exhorting him to get up and "put on the *tefillin*" (*hott ej-jildé*), when the priest's expected duty might have been "converting" Fady rather than enjoining him to fulfill his Jewish religious obligations.

Needless to say, with sleep still in his eyes, Fady would try to stall, push Atallah away, and plead with him to let him snooze a few minutes more. But Atallah was as relentless as he was gentle, and Fady would be up and running by five in the morning, whether he wanted to or not.

This story is important to tell in the context of Fady's testimony because it speaks to and further illustrates the diversity and complexity of both Lebanese Jewry and Lebanon itself. In that sense, it is a story that is as representative as it may be unique.

---

[66] There is a particularly endearing aspect to the language in which this old priest was awakening his Jewish student for the morning Jewish prayer, as well as his untainted reference to the "tefillin" as a "skin".

And so begins Fady Gadeh's journey!

In 1967 I was manning a store belonging to my family in Souk Sursock. I remember at one time there being a multitude of Jewish businesses in that part of the Beirut commercial district. But many of them had been closed or abandoned by the time the war started, most of their owners having already left the country, many never to return again. So in a sense, we were probably one of the outliers, one of the very few remaining Jewish-owned businesses in 1967 and beyond, and in that sense an oddity and a curiosity. The stores abutting us were in the main Muslim-owned, their attendants on the whole very friendly to us.

The war started in early June, and I remember our store closing for upwards of a week during that time, seven days at least. The war itself lasted for six days, but we closed the store for seven days, just to be on the safe side. On the day I went back to downtown Beirut to "re-open for business," I saw a large poster of Jamal Abdel-Nasser plastered on the store's roll-up shutters. A major dilemma! Not because of the poster itself, but because of the way it was plastered on the metal shutters, which meant that I could not open my storefront without seriously damaging Nasser. I did not want that on my conscience; not to mention the consequences of such optics: Imagine the image of a Jewish storeowner, in the midst of angry Muslims who'd just lost a war to the Jews, taking down the poster of their national hero. I did not want to be that statistic. Add to all this the fact that all the businesses around me were already open, their owners loitering at the front of their stores as if they'd been waiting for me, inspecting me from a distance, wondering impishly "what is Fady going to do now."

I must have been nineteen years old at the time. The son of the storeowners directly across from us was a young man my age, a good friend of mine; he and I and a couple of other friends had at one time owned a bachelor pad in Beirut, where we'd often get together and entertain among friends. And so, Khaled was the first person I went to, to inquire about who had glued that poster on the store-shutters. "I did it," said Khaled rather curtly, defiantly, and "what are you going to do about it, filthy Jew?" At that point, the only choice I had was either lose my temper and get a serious beating, or diffuse the situation and stay alive and open for business. So I decided to opt for the latter, but not without first making a point. So, I told Khaled that I hadn't the slightest problem with the poster itself, but that I still thought that whoever placed it where they did—gluing it on the exterior metal shutters—was an idiot beyond belief. "You're calling me an idiot?" inquired a now angrier Khaled, on the verge of throwing a first punch. "Yes," I replied, promptly adding "all you had to do was ask me to roll the shutters up, and you could have attached all the Nasser posters you wanted on the glass windows, inside my store, preventing any of them from ever being damaged." Khaled's anger dissipated immediately. He called my bluff, puffed out his chest as if he'd just won the war, and promptly proceeded to remove the poster from the exterior shutters, carefully pasting it on one of the windows inside the store, proudly facing it out to the street. What had been an attempt at harassing me—forcing me to display the picture of he who wanted to "drive the Jews into the sea"[67]—turned out to be a victory to my Muslim friends, but more importantly a boon to our family business. In fact, I cannot recall a day our business did as well in sales as the day Nasser's poster began greeting our Muslim clientele; the lines were literally out the door; Nasser was the darling of Arab nationalists in those days, promising to bring back glory and victory and honor to the Arab peoples, and I learned on that "day after" the Six-Day War that trotting him out on a commercial storefront was a brilliant business idea—and it wasn't even my idea. Angry Khaled turned out to be a genius mercantilist without even knowing.

Another memorable story from the 1967 era involves another friend of mine, another Muslim, who worked in a store also in the same area as ours. There was an overabundance of demonstrations in the streets of Beirut in those days and weeks following the Six-Day War. Overwhelmingly—not to say exclusively—those were Muslim demonstrations, as I cannot honestly say that the Christians in Lebanon were particularly grief-stricken with the Arab defeat of 1967. So, I would suspect that the demonstrations were in the main Muslim. At any rate, during one of those parades, there was a particularly loud procession coming out of Georges Picot Street[68] and heading in the direction of my family home on an adjacent avenue. Standing on my balcony, I watched as the spectacle filed by, amused by the marchers' sometimes colorfully creative slogans. The one slogan that stuck out to me on that day was the rhythmically alluring, rhyming "Baddna n'uula 'all makshuuf, yahuudi ma baddna nshuuf" [Let's come out and say it out-loud, we want all the Jews kicked out.] *More so than the shock or consequence of the slogan itself, to me it was the messenger that stunned me most; the*

[67] "Driv[ing] the Jews into the sea" is one of the most famous quotes attributed to Nasser, promising Arabs to win a decisive victory against Zionism, and put an end to the Jewish state.

[68] Georges Picot Street was a major Beirut thoroughfare bordering the Jewish quarter of Wadi Boujmil.

loudmouth spewing his chant into the bullhorn, whipping the crowds into a frenzy, galvanizing them into repeating after him, in unison, "Baddna n'uula 'all makshuuf, yahuudi ma baddna nshuuf." I recognized that chief-cantor, Nabil, one of my best friends and one-third of our inseparable Muslim, Jewish, and Christian trinity—Nabil, myself, and Elie Baddour. So, I recognized Nabil's face behind the voice, and Nabil himself knew exactly where he was as he led the procession. That's why he halted his march under my balcony at one point, looked up in my direction, smiled as if happy to see me, then spurted into his bullhorn, "Fady, 3 o'clock, Hamra Street, don't forget!" then continued on with his chant, "Baddna n'uula 'all makshuuf, yahuudi ma baddna nshuuf..."

Stunned as I might have been, I still went to meet Nabil as previously scheduled, if only to inquire about his wellbeing, to see what had gone wrong with him, and how and when he had switched to "the dark side" spewing out anti-Jewish screeds. Nabil's explanation was that the demonstrators had recruited him on account of his distinctive baritone, plying him with a twenty-dollar bill. "Why not," he said, "I took the money! Wouldn't you? Now, let's go have a drink on them!"[69]

This was my Lebanon, the Lebanon that I remember. Charming and surreal! Great life, great people, great joie de vivre and mockery of tradition and orthodoxy, and sometimes even great problems! But with the enigmas and complexities of Lebanon came a great deal of creativity and flexibility and resourcefulness, and ultimately a great ability to navigate problems! In that sense I am perhaps a genuine specimen of what it truly means to be Lebanese; polyglot, multi-cultural, go-between mediator, able to channel and navigate multiple traditions. Just as I was the product of a Christian-Lazarist education, so I also had highly placed Muslim and Christian friends. I knew, for instance, Bachir Gemayel personally[70]; I spent much of

---

[70] Bachir Gemayel was one of the sons of Kataëb Party founder Pierre Gemayel, an ally of the Israelis during the Lebanese war of 1975, and president-elect of the Lebanese Republic (elected on August 23, 1982). He was assassinated on September 14, 1982, a week before he was to take office.

[69] This elasticity of the Lebanese—some may call it lack of scruples, others may deem it mercantile opportunism—was brought home to me by an anecdote recounted by Ya'ir Ravid, a former Israeli intelligence officer who spent most of his life in Lebanon, and who was intimately acquainted with Lebanese culture, the Lebanese language, and Lebanese ethos. "You ask a Lebanese kid what's the total of 1 + 1" said Ya'ir, "and the answer he will give you is 'that depends'." In other words, the answer the Lebanese will give you is dependent on what you looking to hear.

my summers in Bickfayya, the Gemayels' ancestral home, and I still remember those days in Lebanon as if I'm still living them now. I left Lebanon forty years ago, but Lebanon never left me. I still see Lebanon in my mind's eye, I still speak Lebanon's languages the way I left with them, in all their musicality, in all their cadences, in all their folklore and colorful idioms and inflections.[71]

THE ATTORNEY'S DAUGHTER; THE DAY RAYMOND EDDÉ SAVES THE DAY?

Dany's father was born in Damascus, in 1912, a scion of a long line of Damascene Jewish notables, many of whom became leaders of the Damascus Jewish Communal Council, and one in particular, Joseph Liniado, a representative in the Syrian Chamber of Deputies in 1932 under French Mandate.[72]

The family home in today's Syrian capital, the famous "Stambouli-Liniado House" in Damascus—albeit no longer owned by the family—is an exquisite specimen of nineteenth-century Ottoman architecture, and one of the best-kept reminders of the heyday of Damascene Jewish life. With the downfall of the Ottoman Empire in 1918, the rise of "Arabist" ideas in what was to become Syria in 1920, and a consequent surge in anti-Jewish feelings, the main branch of the Stambouli and Liniado families took refuge in Beirut after a brief stay in Alexandria-Egypt. By 1920, at the age of eight, Dany's father, Desiré Isaac Liniado, had settled in Beirut, where his father Tewfic Yehye Liniado would establish a small bank. Desiré Liniado would quickly take to Lebanese life, completing his studies ca. 1930 at the Jesuit *Grand College* of Beirut—what is today the *Collège Notre-Dame de Jamhour*—after which he would pursue a law degree in Paris.

As a young Beirut attorney, Desiré became a good friend of other children of his trade, having trained in Émile Éddé's law offices in Beirut—home to a veritable "Who is Who" of the city's legal minds of

---

[71] I can attest to the fact that Fady spoke both Lebanese and French languages imbued in the aromas of his native Beirut, like someone who might have, mere minutes ago, left Lebanon.

[72] See, for instance, *Al-Aalam al-Isra'iili*, "An Israelite Representative in the [Syrian] Chamber of Deputies" (Beirut: March 21, 1931), 3.

the early twentieth century. Among his close associates were important figures of the Maronite establishment: young attorneys like Bechara El Khoury (1890–1964), the first President of post-independence Lebanon, who would facilitate the Liniados' naturalization as Lebanese citizens, but also Camille Chamoun (1900–1987), Lebanon's second post-independence President, and Émile Éddé's son Raymond Éddé (1913–2000), a perennial presidential aspirant and unsuccessful candidate.

Our house in Beirut was right across from Camille Chamoun's,[73] *and my father was a good friend of his son, Dany,*[74] *among other prominent Lebanese politicians. He was also a good friend of Antoine Naufal [owner of Lebanon's most prestigious library and publishing house.] I suspect that is part of the reason why he was kidnapped and tortured by the PLO; on account of his connections and perceived sympathies and alliances with prominent Lebanese Christian political figures. He'd been also a close friend of Raymond Éddé's [son of a former Lebanese president mentioned earlier in this volume, a great advocate of Lebanese Jewry, and leader of the Maronite National Bloc party.] Father was naturally a proponent of the National Bloc's vision of Lebanon, and often times, when members of the Jewish community argued among themselves over local partisan politics, the main two parties being the National Bloc or the Kataëb, my father always acted as the "voice of reason," separating the "warring parties," and appealing for common ground. But still, his National Bloc sympathies were palpable.*

He traveled quite often to Paris, and at times he brought back with him suitcases brimming with books that Antoine Naufal will have requested—in the main publications restricted under Lebanon's censorship of certain literary and artistic works. So, yes, like many other Lebanese, our home was a cultural and intellectual mecca, and my father might have owned works of literature deemed subversive at a certain time in Lebanese history. But my father wrote a lot also; mainly his memoirs, and stories culled from our family history, but he was widely published in the Lebanese francophone press, most prominently in the venerable La Revue du Liban, *and the* Commerce

---

[73] Camille Chamoun (1900–1987) was the President of the Lebanese Republic from 1952 to 1958. His policy was openly pro-Western, opposed to Arab nationalist designs, and intent on keeping Lebanon outside the orbit of the Arab–Israeli conflict.

[74] The younger son of Camille Chamoun, Dany Chamoun was a prominent politician and commander of the Maronite Tigers militia during the Lebanese war of 1975–89. A committed opponent of the Syrian occupation of Lebanon, he was assassinated with his family on October 21, 1990, allegedly by Syrian agents.

du Levant.[75] *I can still picture him cooped up in his room, in our Beirut apartment, typing away feverishly, by night and by day.*

I am an only child. My mother died during childbirth, and I was brought up essentially by a single parent. My father never remarried, dedicating his entire life to my upbringing. Everywhere he went, I tagged along! That is why I have distinct memories—and photographs as evidence—of the people my father knew, the places we visited, and the things we did my father and I. Those activities included frequent visits and family gatherings with the Chamouns, the Éddés, the Naufals, and a panoply of Lebanon's foreign diplomatic corps, which were part and parcel of my childhood and my younger years' remembrances. My father gave me every thing he had; his love, his time, his knowledge, his curiosity for knowledge, and his passion for argumentation and clever debate.

I distinctly remember visits by members of Jehovah's Witnesses to our home. This was very common in Lebanon of the 1960s and 1970s. They often entered our home buoyant and energetic, ready to convert the world; they left hours later in tears, their faith shaken. Father valued educated debate, and loved argumentation, regardless of the topic. He was a man of high erudition and varied interests. He suffered a lot in his life; he lost his wife at a young age (and never remarried), he lost his mother to cancer a few years later, he watched his father's business be driven into the ground... So, he had a lot to be cynical and skeptical about; much to make him lose faith. Yet, despite his skepticism, he made sure I received a good "Jewish upbringing," some kind of "spirituality" that I could hold on to and seek out for solace in times of need. I remember one day, during Bible Study period at the Alliance school, the teacher was explaining the story of Creation. I interrupted him with a simple question I had been curious about: "What was God doing before he decided to do the Creation thing?" I asked. Offended by a child's perceived impudence, the teacher expelled me from the classroom and referred me to a "disciplinary council" in the schoolmaster's office. I refused to engage at any level with the teachers sitting in judgment over me,

---

[75] Founded in 1928, *La Revue du Liban* is Lebanon's oldest and longest running French-language weekly magazine. Likewise the *Commerce du Levant* is Lebanon's (and indeed the entire Near East's) oldest, preeminent, continuously published commercial weekly (recently monthly) magazine. Currently published under the aegis of the Société de presse et d'édition libanaise, the journal was founded in 1929 by a Lebanese Jew, Toufic Mizrahi (1898–1974).

and asked to see my father before saying another word.[76] *When my father arrived at the school, the director asked him, "Desiré, what are you teaching your daughter at home?" "Why? What did she do to you?" inquired my father rather impishly. "She asked the Bible Study teacher what God was busy doing before Creation." "So?" inquired my father; "where is the harm in that? Isn't this what I pay you the big money for? Wasn't anyone able to answer a curious child's simple question?" He was a true avant-gardist, Desiré, an elegant, thoughtful, enlightened man of the world, truly ahead of his times...*

When the 1975 Lebanon war started, my father had insisted I left the country for safety, to stay with family in Milano. He remained behind to tend to his own ninety-five year old father, eventually moving him to safer quarters in East Beirut—our Ain el-Mreysé home in West Beirut at the time was pretty much under Palestinian occupation. Still, and against the advice of his East Beirut friends, my father opted to return to the West Beirut home during a lull in the bombardments; he needed to fetch some of his father's personal effects. While there, he was captured by PLO elements who had by then taken possession of the apartment.[77] *Raymond Éddé's personal chauffeur had driven father there. As he sensed that there was something amiss when Desiré did not return to the car at the designated time, he alerted Éddé and his people. But by the time Éddé was able to secure his release, Desiré had already gone through a devastating four hours of intense physical and psychological torture, during which he was subjected to a cruel regime of Russian Roulette and various forms of beatings. Although he made it safely to East Beirut, he never recovered. At sixty-three years of age at the time of his capture, Desiré was in the prime of his mental and intellectual capacities. He was returned to us a few hours later an empty shell of his previous self. He died in exile three years later; the cause of death was a cerebral embolism, most probably brought about as a consequence of the physical and mental trauma of his 1975 ordeal; the senseless death, from a*

[76] Clearly, Desiré Liniado had taught his daughter well; how could the child of an attorney be expected to speak to any potential accuser without the presence of counsel?

[77] This had been a common practice during the Lebanese war of 1975. The prevalent attitude of Palestinian "squatters" had been the following: "The Jews took our homes in Palestine, we take Jewish homes in Lebanon." But there was also the prevailing notion at the time among "Left wing progressives," the Palestinians included—who had created a "state within the state"—that Lebanon would be their "substitute homeland." Of course, the unexpected obstacle to that ambition was the Lebanese Christians, who fought Palestinian hegemony and disrupted their plan.

broken heart, of a kind, gentle man, whose life's work had been that of an intermediary and mender of hearts, bringing people together. It was Éddé who secured my father's release from captivity, and it was Éddé who also set him on another path to captivity: "You must leave, Desiré," he had told my father; "this country no longer wants you."

I suspect those words were very painful for Éddé to utter. But unlike the traditional wily, deceitful Lebanese politician, Éddé was a man of principle and vision and decency. It is hardly a surprise Desiré and he got along. By 1976, it had already become clear to him that "this country" indeed "no longer want[ed]" Desiré Liniado, but also many others from among Lebanon's children; Lebanon was living in the midst of the "age of the scoundrel" in those times. In the end, Éddé's premonitory advice was wise and visionary, and indeed, Éddé practiced what he preached; by December 22, 1976, after three unsuccessful attempts on his life, like the friend whose life he saved by compelling him into exile, Éddé too was compelled into leaving the only land that he knew and loved, never to return again. He died in Paris twenty-four years later, most probably, like Desiré, also from a broken heart.

But that had been the fate of many other Lebanese Jews, who were made to leave behind the only life that they knew, abscond home and hearth and possessions and family and friends, with barely the clothes on their backs. Like my own father, my father-in-law was also among those exiles. He had worked for decades raising a family, building a home, growing a business. He ended up leaving in 1975, shutting a door behind him on all the memories he had accumulated up to that time, carrying all that he could of his worldly possessions crammed in a single suitcase, tied in a simple twine.

It had perhaps been this brittle twine that had held Lebanese Jewish life together. But it was also an age-old twine. It may still be this same frail ancient twine that still draws the exiled Lebanese Jew to Lebanon, in spite of the painful past.

The Pilot

What I found most striking about Isick Kamhin was his high level of erudition and fluency in matters Lebanese, the fact that he was incredibly knowledgeable in Lebanese Jewish life, how he was still connected to Lebanon, Lebanese politics, and news of Lebanon despite the length and breadth of his distance from his native land. Isick still holds the same Lebanese passport that he left with in 1968; he still clings to the same Lebanese national identity card; he still holds fast to the same Lebanese "individual civil registry record," which is not only the proof of his Lebanese citizenship, but indeed evidence of a long multi-generational Lebanese lineage. In fact, despite holding other passports (French and American), Isick has renewed his Lebanese passport multiple times over the past forty years. He did so one last time as recently as five years ago when he had finally depleted the number of times "renewals" were allowed without having to change the actual passport—this, even though Isick had left Lebanon at the age of sixteen, straight out of high school. Like most Lebanese children of his generation who came of age in the late 1960s, the reasons for his "exile" were more economic than anything else—in pursuit of higher education (and better economic opportunities) in the *other* promised land of the Lebanese, France.

Unlike many Lebanese Jews who did end up in France, Isick never Gallicized his name. Thus, his visits back to Lebanon were too few and far between—not to say non-extant—compared to those Lebanese Jewish holders of French passports, with French names, who traveled often back and forth. In his case, given his father's involvement in the tempestuous political culture of Lebanon, and indeed, his membership in a leadership position within the Kataëb Party, it was "safer" for Isick to make his visits to Lebanon as rare as possible. His last one was in 1974. Again, the concerns being *not* his Jewishness, but a mix of his father's politics and the unease of his being a US Passport holder.

Recalling Salwa's story from earlier in this chapter, almost bragging about her membership in the Kataëb Party, Isick's father during the 1950s and 1960s was the Director of the Party's Minet el-Hosn Sector of the Beirut District—a big deal in the context of Lebanese partisan politics. Indeed, Isick's *Brit Milah* in early 1953 was attended by none other than Pierre Gemayel, leader of the Kataëb party until his death in 1984. What follows are Isick's remembrances of what he was able to share with me from remnants of his past Lebanese life.

Based on family legend, the Kamhin trace back their origins to Toledo-Spain. On or around 1492, my ancestors are believed to have left Spain for what was then Turkey, the Ottoman Empire, eventually settling in what is today Lebanon but what may in general terms be deemed the Holy Land for Christians, the Promised Land for Jews. Although we can trace our roots to Lebanon back to the late eighteenth century, I often wonder if we haven't in fact been there for much longer than that. Sarepta for instance, in what is today "southern Sidon" [or Sarafand,] is a very ancient site of "biblical" Jewish presence. The Oholiav Shrine for instance, in today's "Soujoud," is believed to be the burial site of a biblical character referred to in Exodus as a carpenter, a helper of Betzalel the builder of the Tabernacle.[78] So, there may after all be relevance to your claim that Jewish history and Jewish presence in Lebanon are Biblical, and that the Jews are perhaps the "first Lebanese."

In my youth, my family and I often visited this shrine in the South. We would drive down to Sidon from Beirut, and from there ride along goat trails on donkeys to reach the hilltop site. There were no roads yet leading up to it during the 1950s and early 1960s. My remembrances of Lebanon are those of an extraordinary time in my life. Others may have a different experience to relate, but mine cannot be described as anything less than extraordinary. I would say that, to the exception of the Jews of Morocco who also did not suffer exactions like their coreligionists elsewhere, the life of the Jews of Lebanon was indeed a privileged one within the challenging life contexts of the Jews of Arab lands. The only restrictions that we suffered—whether self-imposed or institutional—included military service from which we were exempt, and some traveling within Lebanon proper. As far as I can remember, travel was somewhat "restricted" when it came to "going East," in the direction of Syria; Anjar was as far East as we could go. Now, I am unsure whether or not those were "parental restrictions" given Syria's hostility vis-à-vis the Jews in my day, or whether this was within the parameters of Lebanese governmental ordinances. But I do remember distinctly that we could not go to Syria by car—the Lebanese border police would turn us back once we reached the Lebanese-Syrian frontier—and we could not travel to Tyre (in Southern Lebanon) without a special permit. I am a bit fuzzy on the regional political circumstances that might have been behind such limitations, and I am unsure whether this applied to all Lebanese citizens across the board at that time, but this was at least my own family's experience.

This might have possibly been during the brief 1958 Lebanese Civil War. I do remember my family leaving Beirut at that time and taking refuge in the Mount-Lebanon village of Beit-Chabab—literally down the hill from Pierre Gemayel's ancestral village of Bickfayya. Indeed, most of the Jews who had left Wadi Boujmil as a result of the fighting in 1958, did settle for a

---

[78] During Ottoman times, Soujoud was an important pilgrimage destination for Jews of the Vilayet of Beirut, which included modern-day Lebanon stretching north to Latakia in Syria, and South to Akko in Israel.

while in short-term rentals in Beit-Chabab. We could have very well taken refuge in my grand-parents ancestral village—my grandmother was from Ain-Zhalta and my grandfather from Deir el-Kamar, both in the *Chouf mountains—but it might have been more dangerous for us there than in the Metn district of Mount-Lebanon.*

But overall, in times of peace, we never suffered any forms of discrimination or any kinds of exactions; our lives were very similar to the lives of other Lebanese from other communities; there were the well-to-do among us just as there were the less well-off, as had been the case in any other Lebanese community; socially, culturally, politically, linguistically, there wasn't much that differentiated us from other Lebanese. Even in times of increased uncertainty—1958 and 1967 for instance—the Lebanese government went to great lengths to guarantee the safety and security of the Jewish quarters, Jewish homes, and Jewish businesses. I do remember the Lebanese Army in both 1958 and 1967 turning the "social hall" of the Magen Avraham synagogue into the Headquarters of the LAF units protecting Wadi Boujmil. I must say that they provided impeccable, highly professional and proficient protection, forbidding anyone who was not a resident entering the parameters that they had set around the quarter. That would remain the case long after the end of the Six-Day War in 1967, and I would say the LAF remained in the area well into late Fall 1967. So, I must say, there wasn't a single day where I felt unsafe (as a Jew) in Lebanon.

Of course, there were demonstrations in the aftermath 1967, popularizing such colorful hate jingles as "l-Yahood klaabna w filistiin blaadna" ["the Jews are our dogs, and Palestine is our home" chanted in rhyming Lebanese meter,] *but besides that, I cannot honestly say that my life in Lebanon was anything less than extraordinary. Yes, there were nuisances; we couldn't go by car to Syria, or to Jordan, but so what? There were worst things we could have suffered. Even at the Alliance school we were not "only Jews" cocooned among ourselves; indeed, there were many Muslim and Christian students and faculty members among us (the students in the main were children of our Christian and Muslim teachers), and there were never any problems of prejudice or discrimination and the like...*

For my part, like other Beiruti Jews, I received my primary and elementary education at the Alliance school, then matriculated in the Maronite Collège de la Sagesse high school in Beirut. That was the case with many of my peers who ended up doing their secondary and advanced studies in traditionally Maronites institutions. There were a number of us—five or six—Jewish kids at Sagesse, and early on we'd assumed that we would have a "free period" twice a week, during Catechism, where we could go strolling around Beirut while the Christian boys drudged through their Bibles. But no such luck, I guess. Our priest insisted we all still attended. "You don't have to learn anything," he told us, "but you still have to be in class during Catechism." So I decided to use the time to my advantage, badger the priests perhaps with sassy questions. One day I goaded one of my Maronite classmates to ask the instructor-priest "why are we taught the forbidden 'fruit of knowledge' was an apple when it could have been a grape?"[79] *In Jewish tradition, we are taught the forbidden fruit is a grape. So my friend took the bait, asked the question, and left the priest dumbfounded, unable to produce an answer. Another time I egged him on to ask the priest why he wasn't married given God's commandment in Genesis 1:28 to "be fruitful and multiply?" "What happens to the Christian population," I chimed in, "if all Christians were priests and nuns?" The instructor was visibly uncomfortable, unable to come up with an adequate answer, but in the end, he exempted me from attending Catechism. It was all in good fun, with no malice intended, and it ultimately got us what we wanted; two times a week where we could skip class. Not a shabby deal at all.*

Truly, there was nothing bad or evil that could ever be said about this incredible little country called Lebanon. To this day, it is still a mystery to me why in 1967, almost en masse *and as if on cue, the majority of Lebanon's Jews opted to leave. I don't understand why 1967 was the turning point, and not, say, 1958 for instance, which was a much more serious affair; a serious war with serious violence that resulted in serious losses of life and property. Still, it's a fact that the Jews left Lebanon on or around 1967; they were followed by the Maronites (who left for all intents and purposes also* en masse*); those were subsequently followed by enlightened secularized Muslims who also left in large numbers, and the country is now left to the wolves. In a way, we the Lebanese ought to consider ourselves lucky that the power-sharing system has not yet been changed in Lebanon to reflect current realities. With the country emptied of its Christian, Jewish, and secular Muslim element, and with radical fundamentalist Shi'ites as the majority at the helms, it is remarkable that it is still the norm for a Maronite to be President, a Sunni to be Prime Minister, and a Shi'ite to be Speaker of the House. I think we should count our blessings and consider ourselves lucky, because, if Lebanon were to adopt a universal electoral system, bereft of the*

[79] In Latin, the word for "fruit" is "Poma," which in its French iteration reads "pomme" which means "apple." And since Catechism in Lebanese schools is ordinarily taught in French, the ground was ripe to confuse the Latin "poma" (fruit) for "pomme" (apple).

"voting by district" system currently in place,[80] *the country would be turned into a Shi'ite republic on the image of Iran.*

I blame this on our kind, gentle 1960s president, Charles Helou (1913–2001), whom at the time we called "Charlotte," and who allowed for the Palestinians to be given free reign in Lebanon. This disrupted the balance of power in Lebanon, and things began going downhill from there on out. Palestinian violations of Lebanese sovereignty during Helou's administration were blatant, and truly unacceptable and unbecoming of any "sovereign state" worth its salt. I was privy to those Palestinian abuses—and frankly their scorning—of Lebanese authority. Even in the heart of Beirut, and long before the 1970s when the PLO were expelled from Jordan, they would brazenly parade through the streets of the city, fully armed, brandishing their automatic weapons in their swanky military vehicles, as if they owned the place, as if they were Lebanon's regular armed forces. It was disheartening to see at best; it was revolting at worst.

I left Lebanon in 1968. I can't say that my departure was due to Palestinian abuses. It was mainly in pursuit of higher education, in France. But my parents, who left in 1974 to Mexico, did so because the security situation in the country had become so degraded, so unbearable to the point that many Lebanese were by then beginning to predict a looming confrontation. The straw that broke the camel's back for my father was what he interpreted as a failed attempt on his life in 1974. He was in the kitchen one morning, tending to his coffee, when a bullet shattered the kitchen window hitting a butane line and setting the house on fire. It was later determined, by the trajectory of the bullet, that it had been a sharp-shooter's unsuccessful attempt on his life—at that time, part of a PLO terror campaign targeting Lebanese Jewry. The next day my parents began preparations to leave for Mexico.[81]

---

[80]This is reminiscent of the American "Electoral College" system in presidential elections.

[81]Although none of Isick's immediate family members ended up in Israel after leaving Lebanon, he knows many Lebanese Jewish families who did settle there, among them the family of Alain Abadie who is mentioned at the outset of this chapter. Indeed, Isick's mother is related to the Abadies, and beyond Alain's Lebanese fame as entertainer and gifted musician, Isick knows him well, and he noted what an "extraordinary sacrifice" it was for Lebanese—Beirutis in particular—to end up in Israel. It is indeed a form of "hardship" for a Lebanese Jew to be living in Israel. Despite the cultural affinities, the geographic closeness, the nearness to the Mediterranean, Lebanon is irreplaceable to Lebanese Jews living in Israel, and perhaps their nearness to Lebanon—their ability to see it and know of its presence without being able to "touch" it—makes the distance so much greater and the yearning so much crueler.

Again, the appropriate *leitmotif* here is, sadly, Amin Maalouf's *Les désorientés*, where he notes—by way of both introduction and conclusion—that ultimately all the children of Adam and Eve, all of us humans in all of our iterations and peregrinations, are lost souls, the offspring in perdition of the same mother and father, trying to trace our early footsteps back to the familial home.

Like Maalouf's protagonists, Lebanese Jews—and Lebanese expatriates in general—readily, candidly, eagerly came forward with "their version" of history, *their* story as it were. They did so by way of a pilgrimage, to shrines of their past, dormant but living vestiges of themselves. Their stories retold—sometimes told for the first time—were above all a quest seeking to delay an inexorable slide into oblivion, an attempt at slowing down the course of time. This quest might have been a rediscovery of sorts, a probe into the reasons why they might have drifted away from the land of their birth; it is certainly a rediscovery of why they still never separated themselves from it. The joy and alacrity with which they all shared their "childhood memories" were evidently an act of rediscovery—a serene, appeasing, salutary certainty that, in the midst of the stormy waters of a life strewn about the fringes of continents and times, there remained for Lebanese Jews a few little islands of Levantine tenderness to return to; peaceful comforting memories kissed by a Lebanese past from which they never got detached.

CHAPTER 6

Through the Eyes of Others: History's Reckoning

... je portai à mes lèvres une cuillerée de thé où j'avais laissé s'amollir un morceau de madeleine. Mais à l'instant même où la gorgée mêlée de miettes du gâteau toucha mon palais, je tressaillis, attentif à ce qui se passait d'extraordinaire en moi. Un plaisir délicieux m'avait envahi, isolé, sans la notion de sa cause.

Marcel Proust (1871–1922)

It may not be inappropriate to preface this final section, "history's reckoning," with a personal reflection; an author's testimony of sorts, and my own childhood's remembrances and observations on Lebanon, Lebanese Jewry, and Jewish life in Lebanon as I remember them.

I grew up in a Christian, overwhelmingly Maronite neighborhood of East Beirut. Our home was a small apartment perched on the top floor of an old building; a flat ringed round by windows, with almost no walls, surrounded by a spacious sunny terrace considerably larger than the dwelling itself, overlooking the Mediterranean, drowned in fragrant citrus orchards splayed in the sunny salt-sprayed wave-driven breeze rising from the West. Contrasting this, my childhood's Mediterranean vista, Mount Lebanon stood near, to my back, soaring in the East, august, white, dignified, casting its hoary snowy shadow on the coastal playgrounds at my feet. As a child, I needed only race down our apartment building's four flights of stairs, cross the street below, hop over the now disbanded coastal railway that had once connected northern Lebanon to northern Israel, and there I was, on the beach, wading

© The Author(s) 2019
F. Salameh, *Lebanon's Jewish Community*,
https://doi.org/10.1007/978-3-319-99667-7_6

through the tall sugarcane bogs and into the warmth of an ancient Mediterranean embrace.

Often times on Sunday mornings, at dawn, I watched my father from my bedroom window cross that very same street, *my* causeway to the sea, heading in the direction of my beach to meet fishermen coming ashore, laying their nets open on the sand, their catch of the day still fidgety, alive, still glittering silver-bright under the remaining glimmers of moonlight, still fragrant with aromas of the sea, flailing, gasping for air, or water, in their final throes fending off a looming kitchen sink, an eager scaling tool, a hungry dinner plate. It was often so quiet on those Sunday mornings that I could still make out the faint sounds of my father's voice in the distance making some small talk, negotiating some price. I could still hear the soft thuds of saltwater ripples lapping at the creaking fishing boats, the sounds of fish flapping against the wooden hulls, beating against each other, thrashing about, staying alive. Sunday lunch was often those fish, this bread of the Mediterranean, the bounty of this old lake of history and of dreams, hemmed in by three continents that had been my backyard and playground and home, my escape and my fantasy, my future, and the beckon of my exiles to come. I've traveled the world since Lebanon, sailed thousands of miles away from my mountain sanctuary and beyond my balcony on the Mediterranean. I've lived in many other beautiful places swayed in melodies conjugating mountains and seashores. I've fallen to the snares of America and Europe, savored the language of France and cuddled passionately with her culture. I even married one of France's daughters, surrendering my offspring to the traditions and melodies of those Gauls who had always captivated my imagination, my affections. Yet I still have to find a place remotely approximating the enchanting imageries of that Lebanon of my younger years.

It was *there*, in that Lebanon of my memories, in the same quaint coastal neighborhood of my childhood, that I began flirting with questions of identity—*my* identity—trying to figure out who I was, where I was, what Maronites were, who Muslims were, who was "something else" entirely, and what it meant to be Jewish, Christian, and "other" in Lebanon's jumble of identities, that homeland of "old stones [...] and varied vertigoes."[1]

---

[1] Franck Salameh, *The Other Middle East: An Anthology of Modern Levantine Literature* (New Haven and London: Yale University Press, 2017), 165–66.

In our Maronite neighborhood—and I dare say in our Maronite building and on or near our Maronite streets—we had Armenian and Jewish neighbors, Kurdish and Circassian vendors, French, British, and American expatriates, and Muslim, and "other" schoolmates and family friends of every stripe. As an eight year old in 1970, I began constructing a faint notion of who those non-Maronite "others among us" were. I began distinguishing that vital ingredient of Lebanese social and cultural life, the pieces of that distinctly Lebanese mosaic of identities, precisely because I knew that my family was Maronite and that others were not. I was proud of that, of the fact that we were Maronite. I became conscious at that very young age that only Maronites could become presidents in Lebanon, and I relished that revelation, that certitude that I was "saved," "chosen," "distinct"; it gave me a great sense of security and place, a sense of confidence in the knowledge that, unlike the "luckless" others, I could one day become president.

Yet my childhood dream was that, as a grown-up, I would become a traffic policeman, *not* a president. Presidents were old. Traffic cops were stylish, had guns, jazzy uniforms, and rode noisy Harley-Davidsons. You see, Lebanon's traffic control grids and national systems of motorways were built by Italian contractors. To this day, a highway in colloquial Lebanese is still referred to as *autostrade*, plural of *autostrada*, which is Italian for "motorway." Consequently, all of Lebanon's traffic officers of the 1960s were trained, uniformed, and equipped to mimic the Italian *Polizia Stradale*. From their polished Harleys, to their shiny leather boots, to their fancy elbow gloves, and down to the flashing lights that they wore across their chests and the elevated platforms on which they stood and gestured affectedly, Lebanese traffic cops were glamorous and appealing in ways a president could never be in the eyes of an eight-year-old boy. To me, this was an open and shut case of glamour trumping gravitas! It was settled, then. I would be a traffic cop on a Harley when I grew up, not a balding gray-haired president in a palace. Yet it was still nice to know that I could always fall back on the presidency of the Lebanese republic should my dream job plans fail to pan out.

At school, I had a classmate who was from Zghorta, a village in northern Mount Lebanon and from which hailed Soliman Frangié (1910–1991), the recently elected president of Lebanon in those days. It must have been the fall of 1970. That classmate never missed an opportunity hectoring the rest of us at school that he was a *Zghortéwé* (a native of Zghorta), a relative of the president, and therefore infallible, invulnerable, *the* "most chosen" among the chosen. We were all in awe of this boy and his proud "pedigree," and at barely eight years of age, I wanted to be him. In fact, there was nothing I would not have done back then to become a *Zghortéwé*, like my friend, and I resented the fact that his origins were not my own. I was envious of him, and I wanted his swagger, his conceit, his invincibility, his place. I wanted to be a *Zghortéwé*, a relative of the president, a member of that guild of the privileged few—even as I never doubted my own ancestral privilege, my birthright as a Maronite.

In time, my mother must have sensed my dilemma. "Moms have a sixth sense, you know?" she often teased me, "don't you imagine that we don't know what's going on in those cute little heads of yours. We do! So there is no sense keeping things from me, or keeping your feelings pent up." Sixth sense or not, my mother must have noticed that the question of this bumptious *Zghortéwé* schoolmate was consuming me. To be fair, I must have been incessantly talking about him at home. In fact, some fifty years later, I still remember this boy's name, Bassel, a fairly uncommon name at my elementary school at the time, and perhaps for that reason a name still etched in my memory. And come to think of it today, Bassel was probably not a *Zghortéwé* at all; only a plebeian like the rest of us, but a wily plebeian blessed with some magic formula; a mix of charisma and thuggery; a brilliant precocious eight-year-old who knew exactly how to bully and hector and manipulate the impressionable among us. So, one day, to put me out of my misery, mother revealed "a little known family secret," confessing that my maternal grandfather, Joseph, was in fact originally from Zghorta and that I too could take pride in, and like Bassel, boast my *Zghortéwé* lineage—minus the bombast and petulance of the "upstart."

There was great comfort for me knowing that my family issued from a proud mountain backbone, a venerable rural sanctuary, from Zghorta no less, a mere stone's throw away from the Biblical "Cedars of the Lord."[2] You see, in Lebanon, there is always attachment and profound sentiments of "belonging" to some mountain sanctuary, even among those dyed-in-the-wool Beirutis and other coastal townspeople who only lived in the shadow of Mount Lebanon, who evinced the mannerisms of townspeople, who spoke with funny "sissy" (Beiruti) accents often

---

[2] "Cedars of the Lord" is the colloquial term used in Lebanon in reference to the Biblical "cedars of Lebanon."

inflected with hints of French.[3] Even among Lebanese who might have spent the entirety of their lives in urban centers along the littoral, there was always yearning and affection and a sense of belonging to some ancestral village on Mount Lebanon. It may be said that if Lebanon's lungs and windows to the world were along the Mediterranean sea-coast, its spinal cord and the dwelling of its soul had lain on Mount Lebanon. "The mountain is to Lebanon what the desert is to Arabia," wrote Philip Hitti; it is the mountain that etches onto the Lebanese their characteristic ruggedness, authenticity, and sometimes their intransigence; characteristics discernible even in the worldly urbanites among them.[4] Mountaineers at heart, even among city dwellers, the Lebanese have through the ages thwarted invasions and fended off conquests and suppressions by foreign interlopers, all in part due to the tradition and spirit of autonomy and independence afforded them by their mountain sanctuary.[5]

And so, there is both dichotomy and complicity between village and city in Lebanon, between mountain and coastal towns. Most Lebanese spend most of their lives torn, scattered between mountain and sea, village and coastal towns, spending nine winter months in some coastal city, and three summer months sheltered from the pitiless Mediterranean heat in some ancestral village on Mount Lebanon. Even those families not fortunate enough to own an ancestral summer home of their own in their family's ancestral village, do find recourse in summer rentals for that distinctly Lebanese "rite of passage." Trucks with home furnishing spilling over, trekking along the coastal and mountain highways, from and to Beirut, were a familiar sight in the Lebanon of my childhood during the months of May and September. Those were the annual national sacraments of summer and winter, marking the transhumance of peoples, their belongings, and their lives, between the country's lowlands and its adjacent mountains, announcing the beginning and end of the summer season; hallowed annual rituals, anticipated and relished by children and parents alike—bidding farewell to the old school year, and three months later yearning in anticipation for the new school year to come.

---

[3] Arabs and Arab nationalists have traditionally mocked the Lebanese dialect and its inflections—which are not deemed sufficiently guttural by Arabic standards—as "sissy-like" and not sufficiently "virile."

[4] Hitti, *A Short History of Lebanon*, 5.

[5] Hitti, *A Short History of Lebanon*, 6.

In this context, my mother establishing a familial filiation to the Lebanese highlands—to Zghorta no less—was great comfort for me, and a source of added pride, even though I had never been to Zghorta, and even though our "ancestral" summer home was in Bickfayya. Yet something told me the newfound Zghorta "connection" was a loving mother's white lie; a fairytale; and my own mother's "sixth sense" mending an offspring's bruised "first sense," the sense of pride cherished and honored by any Near Eastern male worth his kind. But I bought the mythology she fed me, and I remained quiet about it, discreet, thoughtful, dignified as she had cautioned. This gave me an added sense of pride and place; a new kind of poise and composure and reserved wisdom; and a new spring in my young step, whereby I was now prouder of my "noble lineage," yet needed not be boastful about it. Still, deep down inside myself I knew that my family was Beiruti, and in that sense, and for some in certain quarters in Mount Lebanon, we were perforce shifting, cosmopolitan, fluid, multi-cultural "pansies," perhaps even lacking the "authenticity" of rootedness, of hailing from the mountains, of being a *Zghortéwé*.[6]

Yet I was still proud of my Beiruti fluidity—that is, so long as I had the quiet certitude of its entrenchment in some mountainous bedrock. I was proud of the bustle of Beirut, that "peninsula of noise" that was my home, that cacophony of peoples and languages and religions and races. To me, there was a different, spirited kind of authenticity to Beirut's diversity; a merchant city teeming with fleets of cultures and seaports and colorful horizons. It was in Beirut, in its dizzying rainbows of peoples and variegated shades of colors that I came to discover a uniquely Lebanese kind of Jewry.

The Jewish neighbors who lived downstairs from us were Sabri and Hnayné Sakkal. I still remember Hnayné very well. Sabri had been dead for a while, I think, by the time I came of age and became conscious of her presence. The Sakkals' apartment was often dark, its windows always

---

[6]Ultimately, my mother's "white lie," meant to boost my eight-year-olds confidence, might have not been a lie at all. Indeed as I came to discover years after my mother's passing, the patronym Achy, which was my grandfather Joseph's last name, figures prominently among the main families of the village of Zghorta. So, even though Beirutis to the marrow, as it turns out my mother's family could trace their lineage to Zghorta no less than Bassel's. In fact, I cannot say with any level of certainty that Bassel's family name, as I remember it, was particularly *Zghortéwé*, or figured among one-hundred traditional families of Zghorta.

shuttered, and Hnayné came home only occasionally, every two months or so, to "aerate" the place. I remember the musty smell of her apartment. I remember being scared to death every time I walked by it during her absence, running like hell up (or down) the stairs going past it. I can't recall what it was exactly that frightened me, but the feeling must have been the combination of being close at hand to an empty house, a "dead man's house," the mystery of the "Jewish neighbor," and the fact that the place seemed semi-abandoned, eerie, unlit, empty. Even seeing some dim lights on occasion filtering from under the front door scared the living lights out of me and sent me racing home; to my young mind, this could have been Sabri's ghost roaming the place at night. But Hnayné, the very few times that I saw her, was the farthest thing from the spook I imagined prowling her home. She was always gentle, soft-spoken, kind, sparkling like a human, not a ghost. She was an "ecumenical Jew" one might say; a woman whom, were I not told that she was Jewish, I might have gone on believing she was another "one of us," a widowed childless Maronite lady from the neighborhood who occasionally came to our place for cookies, cigarettes, and coffee.

The most endearing memory that I have kept of Hnayné dates back to the times I had been cramming for my *Baccalauréat* (official Lebanese high-school exit) examinations, during the summer of 1981. She had come up to our apartment one day with a basket of fruits and nuts— energy foods she'd called them, to help me stay awake and alert, and pull all-nighters reviewing for my exams. During that same time period, I also remember my mother telling me that Hnayné had begun a Novena prayer to the Virgin Mary on my behalf; a traditional Catholic devotional ritual consisting of prayers dedicated to a saint, repeated for nine consecutive days, imploring favors and graces for oneself, or on behalf of others. The "favor" that Hnayné had been asking of the Virgin Mary was for me to pass my *Baccalauréat* exams. I had become a somewhat cocky eighteen-year-old by that time and could not have cared less about Novenas or praying for success. But for some reason I was profoundly moved by Hnayné's gesture; a Jewish woman, in a Lebanese Christian neighborhood, imploring the Virgin Mary, on behalf of a teenaged Maronite neighbor. One doesn't try to understand Lebanon because Lebanon, even to the old hand, is truly a riddle, wrapped in a mystery, inside an enigma. But perhaps Hnayné may offer different kinds of insights into that complexity. Lebanon is unlike any other country in the Middle East—and indeed unlike any other place anywhere for that matter. Likewise, Lebanese Jews, like other Lebanese, are unlike any other Jewish community anywhere in the world.

Perhaps what shall follow, the testimony of non-Jewish Lebanese might bring confirmation to the above personal reflections.

In the summer of 2017, I had a good conversation with academic and current director of Tufts University's Center for Eastern Mediterranean Studies, Nadim Shehadi. The topic of our discussion was Lebanese Jews and their place in Lebanon and the world today. Shehadi noted that there may be many more Jews in contemporary Lebanon today than any of the censuses and the community's records could ever reveal. This is indeed a question which many Lebanese Jews still living in Lebanon today still return to, and still interrogate. In fact, many of the testimonies that follow, all by non-Jewish Lebanese, seem to assert that there is indeed a sizeable Lebanese Jewish population, counting in the thousands, even if local censuses reveal more anemic figures. In sum, most Lebanese Jews living in Lebanon today do not lead an outwardly Jewish life, most marrying into Christian—in the main Maronite—families, and melding their distinctness into that of their traditional allies in modern Lebanon.

To wit, one of the leading young historians of Lebanon, Carol Hakim, author of *The Origins of the Lebanese National Idea*, is a Lebanese Jew. Yet, noted Shehadi, she is part of a cohort of Lebanese Jewry he qualified as "*Yasaranjiyyé*"—which is to say "Left Wingers," expressed in a playful, taunting expression; a Lebanese idiomatic take on the English "Champagne Socialists." Yet, that is the way Lebanese Jews might have opted for survival in a Lebanon riven by conflicts of identity and membership in communal and sectarian groups. By opting for the high-browed life of *Yasaranjiyyé*, Lebanese Jews may still live as "Crypto-Jews," yet above the lines of sectarian identities, and uninvolved in—and indeed contemptuous of—Lebanon's sectarian divides. In a sense, Lebanon's crypto-Jews today are uninterested in sectarian identities, much less their own Jewishness.

In the case of Carol Hakim, as she could not afford the expenses of traveling to Cyprus for a civil matrimony with her future Maronite husband, they both thumbed their noses at both their communal traditions, converted to Islam, and were married by a Sheikh in Beirut. Opting for a Muslim social/matrimonial identity was in the end less onerous ceremonially speaking, and much cheaper in terms of matrimonial theatrics. Likewise, divorce, should that become an eventuality, would be a much easier process than in either the Maronite or Jewish rites.

Likewise, noted Nadim Shehadi, Dr. Ishac Diwan, a renowned Berkeley educated economist, and heir to a Lebanese Sidonian-Jewish family—arguably one of the oldest Jewish families in Lebanon—is married to Dr. Joelle Abi-Rached, a Maronite medical doctor, ethicist, and historian. Like Hakim, Diwan, at least outwardly, could not care less about his Jewishness and is himself a *Yasaranji* of renown as well.

One wonders then if this detachment from Jewish life in Lebanon of modern times is the outcome of apathy? Dissimulation? Self-preservation? Or truly proof of "high minded" identity narratives unconcerned with communal accretions and primordial parameters of selfhood?

Incidentally, Diwan was instrumental in the renovation of the ancient Sidon Jewish cemetery, one of the last remaining monuments attesting to a millennial Lebanese Jewish history. Yet, when he learned about my "memory project" aimed at preserving, indeed celebrating the Jewish facet of Lebanese history, he wondered "why"—and questioned how he could be relevant, or useful to my endeavor. Indeed, after our initial email interchange, I was left wondering whether he was Jewish; whether I had committed a faux pas making a false assumption about some Jewishness he did not ascribe to.[7] I had hoped to put my doubts to rest when we met in Paris. But even that meeting never materialized, admittedly because I did not push hard enough for it—and most probably because Dr. Diwan's initial reaction, supremely proper and polite and classy as it might have been, can best be described as tepid. Incidentally, Diwan's wife, a physician by training and a recently minted Harvard Ph.D. (2017), was able to support considerable aspects of her doctoral work in the History of Ethics and Philosophy in the Levant in part thanks to a grant from the Edmond J. Safra Center for Ethics; a unit of Harvard University whose main benefactor is the Edmond J. Safra Philanthropic Foundation, an association named after a scion of a major Lebanese Jewish banking dynasty.

But Lebanese Jews who remain connected—not to say attached—to a Lebanese state no longer hospitable to diversity may be justified being cagey, circumspect, aloof. "In order to live happily we ought to live quietly" famously said one of Mario Levi's characters. But Levi's Jewish protagonists were in Turkey, *not* Lebanon, and Lebanon prides itself on

---

[7] It is worth noting that the Diwan patronymic in Lebanon is common among Christians and Muslims, as well as Jews, and in that sense can be deemed ethno-religiously ambiguous in a part of the world where every name may carry with it centuries of history.

being the epitome of liberalism and openness, and diversity, and multiple identities; a home for Jews and others, but certainly not a Muslim theocracy—nor even a Muslim majority country—where non-Muslims, Jews and Christians included, are relegated to a demeaning minoritarian dhimmi status.

Yet the Lebanese "confederation of minorities" alluded to throughout this volume, the "state of minorities" with a dominant confident Christian political class that the French brought into being in 1920 is no more. And so, Lebanon's Jews today may be justified in their aloofness and circumspection. A case in point, Nadim Shehadi relates a seminar organized in 1998 by one of Lebanon's leading leftist thinkers, the historian Fawaz Traboulsi. As conceived by Traboulsi, this event was intended as a commemoration of the "Nakba," which is to say the Arab exodus from British Mandate Palestine on the heels of the establishment of the State of Israel. Traboulsi had four Lebanese Jews lined up for one of the conference's main panels. Those token Jews were slated to speak of their recollections, as non-Zionists, indeed perhaps even as "anti-Zionist" Lebanese Jews witnessing the Arab exodus from British Mandate Palestine and the birth of a Jewish state. So far so good! By all accounts, this is a fairly anodyne intellectual exercise, featuring a wide spectrum of participants, who were expected to contribute something different, new, and useful to understanding and, a robust diversity of perspectives. Ah, but wait! Hezbollah, the Iranian proxy organization ruling Lebanon in classical colonial fashion since the mid-1990s, vehemently objected to the participation of Jews—Lebanese Jews no less—in an academic exercise dedicated to Arabs, and to indulging the Arabs' sense of victimhood and martyrdom and grievance. Not only that, but Hezbollah denied those Lebanese Jewish participants—who had been living abroad—entry into the country of their birth, in effect annulling the possibility of their being even in the audience, as attendees and spectators rather than active participants.

Traboulsi still went ahead with the proceedings, and the panel slated for Lebanese Jews remained on the conference program. But instead of Lebanese Jewish panelists sharing their experiences with—what might have been—a riveted curious audience, Traboulsi took the stage in front of an empty table, engaging a monologue on the sad state of Lebanese politics in 1998, when diversity got trampled, and opposite opinions got muzzled, and where pluralism got slayed on the altar of the one-party politics of Hezbollah's "Resistance"—"resistance" to Israel and to the "normalization" of Israel to be sure, but resistance to good judgment and understanding and Lebanon's raison d'être more importantly. This remains the case until today, at this end of the second decade of the twenty-first century and on the seventieth anniversary of the "Nakba," where Lebanese Jewish memory is not only suppressed, but indeed wiped out, falsified, obliterated. No wonder then that world-renowned and respected Lebanese scholars, public intellectuals, literati, businessmen, artists, and others, who happen to be Jewish, who still maintain very strong ties to Lebanon, who still live in Lebanon, or who still make annual pilgrimage to Lebanon from their places of exile, no wonder they feel compelled to abnegate their Jewishness. And so, perhaps the reactions of those Jews whose testimonies were collected for this volume, and who opted to withhold their consent to publish, perhaps their reaction is understandable. It is to those "mute" Lebanese Jews, whose voices are given sound by "others," that this segment of this chapter of recollections ought to be dedicated.

The first "other" is a youthful Lebanese septuagenarian, a Maronite native of Tartous, Syria, whose father had been a lifelong Francophile and at the time of her birth a petty officer of the French *Armées du Levant* stationed in that Syrian port city. Georgette's testimony about Lebanese Jewry matters in this context, *not* because she knew much about Lebanese Jews, or knowingly ran in the same circles as they, or went to school with them, but indeed because she knew very little about them. A child of her times, Georgette grew up in a diverse cosmopolitan Beirut, where few children her age knew who among her friends was Jewish, or Muslim, or Christian for that matter. "We lived in Achrafiyyé," she noted, "summered in the mountains; but we did not know who was Jewish or who was not, and didn't even think whether or not there were Jews among our friends or neighbors. And those of us who knew Jewish families, knew that they were '*awédim*' decent respectable people, like any other Lebanese in our circles."[8] Life was beautiful in the Beirut and Ashrafiyyé of Georgette's youth during the 1950s and 1960s. "Life was carefree," she noted wistfully, and "Beirut bustled with tourists and life and fragrances and noise; it was an open, reasonable, receptive, unintimidating space for exchange and ideas and freedoms, where Christians,

---

[8] The term "awédim" is the plural form of the Lebanese adjective "édamé," literally "a progeny of Adam," or "son of Adam," to mean "decent," "honest," "honorable," "trustworthy"; a condensation of "humanity" in other words.

Muslims, Druzes, Armenians, and perhaps even Jews mingled and blended and consorted." This is indeed an image that is recalled in many a poetic, journalistic, or historical descriptive of Lebanon and Beirut of the 1950s and 1960s. Recall a Lebanese poet's description from earlier in this volume, a leading Phoenicianist who praised the Lebanon of the Jews where the enigmatic Druzes rubbed shoulders with the Maronite Catholics; where the Melkites bickered with the Armenians; and where all in turn trafficked, feuded, and reconciled with Syriacs, Gregorians, Latins, Jocobites, Sunnits, Shi'ites, and Israelites. This is given further credence in another poetic musing, by another Francophone Lebanese poet, Nadia Tuéni (1935–1983), who in 1968 wrote the following verses of Beirut; "Be she concubine, scholar, or zealot," noted Tuéni,

> Be she a peninsula of noise, of gold and colors, / A pink merchant city like a fleet of ships, adrift, / Scouting the horizons for the warmth of a seaport, / Beirut is a thousand times dead, and a thousand times still living. / [...] Be she pious nun, or be she sorcerer, Be she both, or be she the swivel / To the portal of the sea or the Levant's entryway, / Be she innocent or be she deadly, / Just the mere fact of her being, Phoenician, Arab, or Plebian, / Just the mere fact of her being, this Levantine of varied vertigoes, / [...] Beirut remains in this Orient the very last shrine, / Where mankind can still adorn its kind with a mantle of light.[9]

In the end, "the Jews were Lebanese, like any others" stressed Georgette, no different from any others, and "Judaism remains one of the eighteen or more officially recognized and protected creeds in Lebanon today." Again, she stressed, "people didn't know who was Jewish or who was not, but we knew that Lebanese Jews constituted the most active and vibrant and enterprising merchant class in Lebanon and the city of Beirut." Based on hearsay and family gossip, and perhaps even popular stereotypes, Georgette noted that Lebanese Jews were often compared to Lebanese Armenians; they were a bustling "living people"—she referred to them as "*Sha'b Hayy*" in Lebanese, which may roughly translate into the Hebrew "*Aam [Yisrael] Chai*," which is to say "the people of Israel are alive." Georgette noted that "like the Armenians," the Jews were diligent, hardworking, industrious,

---

[9] Quoted in Franck Salameh, *The Other Middle East: An Anthology of Modern Levantine Literature* (New Haven and London: Yale University Press, 2017), 165–66.

self-sustaining, well-off, and self-sufficient, "and that is probably why they were successful, and had no paupers among them, and no one depending on handouts, from the government or otherwise." Also based on hearsay and popular gossip, Georgette noted that "it was common knowledge" that different businesses in Lebanon were "dominated" by different communal groups; Armenians and Aleppans (probably Jewish Aleppans) were active in the jewelry business, whereas Beiruti Jews were in the main fabric merchants. "But generally speaking," she stressed, "the Lebanese barely knew who was Christian and who was Muslim in Lebanon, so how does one determine who was Jewish and who was not in that same vein?"

Georgette recounted a time during the 1975–1976 Lebanese war, when she had to drive to Beirut to pick up her twin daughters from their school as their school's neighborhood was being subjected to sustained artillery fire. She got to her children safely, drove them back to safety, and brought along with them two of their classmates who happened to be Muslim. Georgette was put in the uneasy situation of having to explain to her daughters why their schoolmates' mother was unable to pick them up on that day: "She is Muslim" quipped Georgette rather reluctantly, "and Muslims are unable to cross into the Christian dominated zones now, in the thick of battle." Georgette further recalled how difficult it was, subsequent to that incident, trying to explain to her 12-year-old daughters what it meant "that they were Christians, and that their schoolmates were Muslim," let alone that Christians could not go into areas where Muslims lived, just like Muslims would not venture into a neighborhood that was Christian. And so you see, she concluded, "we barely knew" or "could hardly explain who was Christian and who was Muslim... This same paradox or disinterest, mundanity, applied to Lebanese Jews."

But this was before the war of 1975 and on the eve of it. Things changed with the coming of the war. People of all communal and religious backgrounds left Lebanon at the onset of 1975, noted Georgette; "hundreds of thousands of people left, among them our own family. Lebanese Jews were no different, I suppose. They had to leave their Beirut quarter, their homes, and their businesses because they were smack in the middle of the war zone. The Wadi Boujmil quarter had lain between Ain Mreisséand Bab Idriss, one of the hottest most dangerous zones during the war. But they are coming back, and the Magen Avraham Synagogue is being rebuilt."

"It is time to make peace," concluded Georgette;

> it is time for the Lebanese of all creeds to be able to go to Israel, visit the holy land, make pilgrimage to Jerusalem, without being branded a traitor to a cause that is not Lebanon's, and hang ups that belong to another culture and another time. Even the Palestinians have made peace with Israel and are negotiating with Israel. Why is it that Lebanon has to be made to remain the outlier, fighting other people's wars. Leave us be. Let us live.

Not only that, she noted, but just like any other Lebanese, whether Christian, Druze, or Muslim, who was expelled from his home and driven into exile, and who was subsequently given restitution and redeemed to his assets and his property, so does the Lebanese government owe Lebanese Jews full restitution and redress and reparation, she stressed. Lebanese Jews are before anything else Lebanese; Lebanese whose lives were ransacked and damaged and shattered and scattered, Lebanese who suffered injury by other Lebanese and their foreign agents, and who are owed restitution, like any other Lebanese group, by the Lebanese as a whole, society and government alike. "I'll take this statement to its most extreme extremity," concluded Georgette, "and submit to you that the Jews are the first Lebanese; before Christians and before Muslims, in Lebanon there were Jews; Jesus himself was a Jew. This is not only a matter of right, or emotion, or empathy; this is a matter of fact."

GEORGES

As a teenager in the early 1950s, Georges spent his summer months working in the mountain resort town of Bhamdoun. At that time, Bhamdoun was a prime summer-tourist destination, many of whom were Beiruti and other coastal Jews who owned summer homes in the region and frequented its posh resorts and restaurants, converging on its hotels and summer rentals as part of the annual Lebanese Summer–Winter "transhumance" mentioned earlier. There, in Bhamdoun, Georges befriended many Jews, frequented Jewish businesses, and came into close contact with a Lebanese community that he remembers as affable, enterprising, and carefree. But that was generally speaking the social and cultural climate of Lebanon of the 1940s and 1950s as a whole; a sort of cultural *laissez-faire* that was Lebanon's mode of being, and that suited all of its varied communal groups. Georges likewise noted that within Lebanon's Christian communities, the Jews might have lived a less anxious life. Many of his classmates at the *Collège des Frères*, a Marist Christian school, were Jews, and it made no difference that they were Jewish.

In today's Lebanon, notes Georges, there remains a relatively speaking large Jewish community many members of which live a life of Christians. "I have a colleague at the hospital where I work," he noted, whose sister (currently living in Paris) is Jewish although the colleague is herself a practicing Maronite Christian. "I suspect there are many Lebanese Jews today living similarly an outwardly Christian life," he said. The town of Beit Mery in Mount Lebanon has a sizeable Jewish community today; "they may not be living an ostentatiously Jewish life," he stressed, "but they are openly Jewish." "In the end, Lebanon is where they belong," he concluded: "Even those Lebanese Jews who are exiled in Paris still yearn to return to Lebanon—imagine that; living in Paris and yearning for Lebanon! As for Israel, let's not go there. I know many Lebanese Jews currently living in Israel, who have been living there for decades, and who are still maladjusted, unable to shake off Lebanon's *joie de vivre* from their memories and engage the austerity and swelter of Israeli life." Unfortunately, he concluded, Lebanon, "the state that should have remained multi-cultural and multi-ethnic and open to the world's divergences," should have made amends and brought Lebanese Jews back to where they belong; "they are Lebanese no different from any others. Sadly, even the Christians who established this state as a refuge for minorities have been made to despair of it, and have also begun what may be deemed a Christian exodus."

The Middle Eastern adage "first the Saturday people then the Sunday people" might have come to pass in Lebanon. With that, the forgotten exodus of those who kept their Sabbath day on Saturday is all but complete, and the extirpation of Lebanon's Christian character is now well underway. The country with the most "hope" in the early twentieth century has been rendered the homeland of most abject "hopelessness." Georges concluded with searing premonitory words reminiscent of another cautionary tale offered by another Lebanese, this time a former Muslim. With the candidness of the neophyte, Mark Issa noted that the destruction of Lebanese Jewry, and the denuding of Lebanon of the blessings of Jewish history and life has opened the door to the spread of Arab nationalist and Islamist fascism in the twentieth century, paving the way to the so-called Lebanese "civil war" of 1975–89. In any society, stressed Issa, liberal and progressive as it might be, the persecution of Jews has always been a harginger of further persecutions to come, against other minority peoples. Anti-Semitism, he concluded, is not only a form of Jew-hatred; it is hatred of freedom, human dignity, and humanity tout court.

CHAPTER 7

On Lebanese Jewish History and Memory: A Conclusion

Le talent de l'historien consiste à faire
un ensemble vrai avec des traits qui ne
sont vrais qu'à demi.

Ernest Renan (1823–1892)

It is sometimes said that trauma survivors, exiles and expatriates among them, are so troubled, some even say "damaged," that they remain mute on their past's painful experiences, suppressing some of their memories, opting not to share them, not even with loved ones. But that is not necessarily always the case; survivors of personal and collective trauma have indeed written about and memorialized their experiences; they might not have done so methodically, consistently, or in droves, but they have done so regardless.

With that in mind, and save the discreet social media chat group here, the random blog or instagram photo-sharing there, and the occasional newspaper article issuing from a diffident Lebanese press often featuring reticent respondents—usually a "token good Jew"—Lebanese Jews seem to have been written out of Lebanese history. They have in any case almost never written publicly about their Lebanese experience, neither past nor present. And although a few (outlier) scholarly books and articles treating the topic of Lebanese Jewry do in fact exist, none may be said to carry the unadulterated unvarnished voices of Lebanese Jews emitted *by* Lebanese Jews—or, for that matter, by *other* Lebanese who knew them, who remembered them, and who proposed

© The Author(s) 2019
F. Salameh, *Lebanon's Jewish Community*,
https://doi.org/10.1007/978-3-319-99667-7_7

to memorialize them. In that sense, there is in fact a wealth of (largely untouched) archives and private collections relative to Lebanese Jewry, and there exists a decent body of scholarly volumes dealing with the topic thoughtfully, scrupulously. But there are almost no works treating Lebanese Jewish memory as such, and none that are readily available to both academic and general audiences, written or narrated by Lebanese Jewish subjects describing their daily lives, their struggles, the Lebanese cultural and social universe that shaped them, and the exile that still forms and informs their experience. Indeed, there exists no Lebanese Jewish "memoir literature" as such, even though there is a sizeable Lebanese Jewish expatriate community that, as snippets of this volume have demonstrated, "still yearns for Lebanon," "still dreams of Lebanon," still questions the circumstances surrounding its exodus, and still valorizes a past Lebanese life. Speaking of his final (forced) move from Beirut to Cyprus in June 1986, and with a touch of sadness sitting upon a smiling resignation, Henri Baghdadi poignantly noted that "it's been thirty-two years since I first came here [to Cyprus,] and I have yet to unpack and get settled in."[1] A day may come when he will get settled in, he admitted, "in Cyprus or elsewhere," but Baghdadi's voice and demeanor did not seem convinced by his own words' bearing.[2]

Modest a contribution as this volume might have been, it has attempted to voice the anguish of Henri Baghdadi and others like him; fill a lacuna of silence and neglect and forgetfulness; initiate a process of conservation codifying elements of both "history" and "memory" of Lebanese Jewry. And although not a "history" exclusively, and not a "memoir" in the traditional sense, this book has striven to bridge both categories of retrospection and knowledge, bringing to the fore snippets of both, uncovering, collecting, examining, and interpreting both. And so, this may not be a "history" as such because it does not tell a story with a beginning and an end; it is likewise not a "memoir" strictly speaking because it does not recount the recollections of a single person or a single event, opting instead to record the voices of many, from the purview of many. So in a sense, this is a hybrid "memoir," "cultural history," "historiography," and "oral biography" bringing together personal stories and other

---

[1] "Les années de guerre civile; interview d'Henri Baghdadi," *Patrimoine et Cultures des Juifs du Liban* (Paris: Yves Turquier, Fondation pour la Mémoire des Juifs du Liban, ND), https://www.pcjl.org/detail.php?id_accueil=282&lang=L0.

[2] "Les années de guerre civile; interview d'Henri Baghdadi."

accounts not ordinarily found in the normative literature, in archives, or in traditional history books. This book, therefore, has aimed to take certain episodes of significance in the lives of Lebanese Jewry, document them, memorialize them, reflect upon them, and try to make some sense of them, drawing some lessons from them, and conveying a message through them—a universal message, it is hoped.

That in essence is what the reader might have drawn from these *fragments of lives arrested*; a series of Lebanese Jewish lives in all their charm, their simplicity, their idiosyncrasy, their fragility, and their complexity, *all* of them suddenly interrupted, brought to a halt, displaced, upended.

In less than a hundred years' time, spanning the birth of modern Lebanon in 1920 and into its transformation into a satellite state by the end of the twentieth century, the Lebanese Jewish community has gone from being the most prosperous and secure of Near Eastern Jewish communities outside of Israel, to becoming a museum curiosity; a brittle specimen of a once proud community, today on the brink of oblivion.

As was revealed in these pages, the early twentieth century was a period of high optimism and intense, even antsy "state-building" in the Middle East. Granted it was also a period of great disappointments for some. But on the whole, in Lebanon, and among Lebanese Christian intellectuals, politicians, entrepreneurs, church leaders, and visionaries, there had been great optimism and hope in a Lebanese future edifying a distinct Lebanese entity and identity; an identity that, as some had envisioned, would find political expression in a modern republic conceived as a "federation of minorities," dominated by Maronites, discrete and dissimilar from the Arab-defined entities taking shape on a post-Ottoman political map still "under construction." And so, it was in the main "Maronite Lebanese nationalism," and its vocal rejection of an inchoate Arab identity taking shape on the debris of a defunct Ottoman Empire, that drew Lebanese Christians to other Lebanese minority groups, among them the Jews, but also the early settlers of the *Yishuv*, laboring to foster personal, commercial, intellectual, cultural, and political ties, hoping to translate what they deemed "natural" and "existential" affinities into a concrete alliance of interests and a commonality of fates.

Things, of course, did not turn out as planned—or hoped. By 1943, the distinctly non-Arab Lebanon of the Maronites had morphed into a "sovereign" republic "with an Arab face," beholden to Arab fears, Arab hopes, and Arab resentments to the detriment of Lebanon's own interests. Over time, vaunted Lebanese state sovereignty capitulated to normative Arab inhibitions—and indeed Arab phobias—vis-à-vis Israel, and by association vis-à-vis "Jewishness" as a whole, ultimately surrendering to the requisite anti-Israel/anti-Jewish rhetoric and its rejectionist antics—by now a banner of the dominant political cultures of the majority of Arab-defined states. Lebanon as a whole paid the price for Lebanon's dithering. Lebanese Jews paid the ultimate price. *Fragments of Lives Arrested* was a modest attempt at giving voice to their silent plight; their forgotten exodus.

BIBLIOGRAPHY

ARCHIVES

Archives de l'Alliance Israélite Universelle (AIUA), Paris, France.

Archives du Ministère des Affaires étrangères (MAE), French Foreign Ministry Archives, Paris-Quai d'Orsay. Correspondence Politique et Commerciales, Serie "E", Levant-1918–1940, Sous-Série: Syrie, Liban, Cilicie.

Charles Corm's Archives and Private Papers, Beirut.

Patrimoine et Cultures des Juifs du Liban.

United Nations Assembly Ad Hoc Committee on the Palestinian Question, New York.

United States Holocaust Memorial Museum, National Institute for Holocaust Documentation, Jacob Rader Marcus Center of the American Jewish Archives, The World Jewish Congress Collection, Series H: Alphabetical Files, 1919–1981, Washington, DC.

PERIODICALS

Al-Aalam al-Isra'iili, Beirut
Al-Adab, Beirut
The Associated Press, New York
Bayroot al-Masa, Beirut
Les Cahiers de l'Est, Beirut
Cahiers de l'Orontes, Beirut
Al-Hasnaa', Beirut
The Huffington Post, New York
International Herald Tribune, Paris

© The Editor(s) (if applicable) and The Author(s) 2019   201
F. Salameh, *Lebanon's Jewish Community*,
https://doi.org/10.1007/978-3-319-99667-7

Israël Informations, Paris
Jerusalem Post, Jerusalem
The Jewish Chronicle, London
Le Jour, Beirut
The Middle East Quarterly
Le Monde, Paris
L'Orient, Beirut
L'Orient le Jour, Beirut
La Revue Phénicienne, Beirut
Le Soir, Beirut
L'Univers Israélite, Paris
World Jewish Affairs, London

PRIMARY SOURCES

Abousouan, Camille. "Présentation." *Les Cahiers de l'Est.* Beirut, July 1945.
Anzarouth, Fred. *Les Juifs du Liban.* Lebanon, ND. http://www.farhi.org/ Documents/JuifsduLiban.htm.
Asmar, Michel. *Les Années Cénacle.* Beirut: Dar al-Nahar, 1997.
Barrès, Maurice. *Une Enquête aux pays du Levant.* Paris: Librairie Plon, 1924.
*Brill Encyclopedia of Jews in the Islamic World.*http://referenceworks. brillonline.com/entries/encyclopedia-of-jews-in-the-islamic-world/ moyal-esther-azhari-SIM_0015860.
Corm, Charles. "L'Ombre s'étend sur la montagne..." *La Revue Phénicienne.* Beirut: Éditions de la Revue Phénicienne, July 1919.
———. "Déclaration de M. Ch. Corm." *Les Principes d'un Humanisme Méditerranéen.* Monaco, November 1935.
Panian, Karnig. *Goodbye, Antoura: A Memoir of the Armenian Genocide.* Stanford, CA: Stanford University Press, 2015.
Reynaud, Charles. "Catholiques et Français, Toujours!" *Le Voyage en Orient; Anthologie des Voyageurs Français dans le Levant au XIXème Siècle.* Paris: Robert Laffont, 1985.
Tabet, Jacques. *La Syrie; historique, ethnographique, religieuse, géographique, économique, politique, et sociale.* Paris: Alphonse Lemerre, 1920.
Vogüe, Vicomte de. "Voyage au Pays du Passé." *Le Voyage en Orient; Anthologie des Voyageurs Français dans le Levant au XIXème Siècle.* Paris: Robert Laffont, 1985.

SECONDARY SOURCES

Chiha, Michel. *Le Liban d'Aujourd'hui (1942)*. Beirut: Éditions du trident, 1961.

———. *Visage et présence du Liban*. Beirut: Le cénacle Libanais, 1984.

Corm, Charles. *La montagne inspirée*. Beirut: Éditions de la revue Phénicienne, 1987.

———. *6000 ans de génie pacifique au service de l'humanité*. Beirut: Éditions de la revue Phénicienne, 1988.

———. *La Terre Assassinée ou les Ciliciennes*. Beirut: Éditions de la Revue Phénicienne, 2014.

Deeb, Marius. *Syria, Iran, and Hezbollah: The Unholly Alliance and Its War on Lebanon*. Stanford, CA: The Hoover Institution Press, 2013.

Duboscq, André. *Syrie, Tripolitaine, Albanie*. Paris: Librairie F. Alcan, 1914.

Gibran, Jean, and Kahlil Gibran. *Kahlil Gibran: His Life and Work*. New York: Interlink, 1998.

Gordon, David. *Lebanon: The Fragmented Nation*. Stanford, CA: The Hoover Institution Press, 1980.

Hitti, Philip. *Lebanon in History: From the Earliest Times to the Present*. London and New York: St. Martin's Press, 1957.

———. *A Short History of Lebanon*. New York: St. Martin's Press, 1965.

———. *Taarikh Lubnan*. Beirut: Dar al-Thaqafa, 1985.

Lawrence, T. E. *Seven Pillars of Wisdom*. New York and London: Anchor Books and Doubleday, 1991.

Levi, Tomer. *Jews of Beirut: The Rise of a Levantine Community, 1860s–1930s*. New York: Peter Lang, 2012.

Maalouf, Amin. *Les Échelles du Levant*. Paris: Éditions Grasset, 1996.

———. *Les Désorientés*. Paris: Éditions Grasset, 2012.

Mansel, Philip. *Levant: Splendor and Catastrophe on the Mediterranean*. London: John Murray Publishers, 2010.

Morand, Paul. *Méditerranée, Mer des Surprises*. Paris: Éditions du Rocher, 1990.

Nantet, Jacques. *Pierre Gemayel*. Paris: Éditions Jean-Claude Lattès, 1986.

Phares, Walid. *Lebanese Christian Nationalism: The Rise and Fall of an Ethnic Resistance*. Boulder and London: Lynne Rienner Publishers, 1995.

Proust, Marcel. *À la recherche du temps perdu*. Paris: Éditions Gallimard, 1987.

Salameh, Franck. *The Other Middle East: An Anthology of Modern Levantine Literature*. New Haven and London: Yale University Press, 2017.

Schulze, Kirsten. *The Jews of Lebanon: Between Coexistence and Conflict*. Brighton: Sussex Academic Press, 2001.

Stillman, Norman. *The Jews of Arab Lands in Modern Times.* Philadelphia and New York: The Jewish Publication Society of American, 1991.

Zamir, Meir. *The Formation of Modern Lebanon.* Ithaca and London: Cornell University Press, 1985.

Zittrain Eisenberg, Laura. *My Enemy's Enemy: Lebanon in the Early Zionist Imagination, 1900–1948.* Detroit: Wayne University Press, 1994.

INDEX

A

Al-Aalam al-Isra'iili, 10, 13, 15, 16, 28, 51, 52, 79–83, 85–98, 111, 112, 169

Abadie, Alain, 113, 178

Abdel Nasser, Jamal, 166. *See also* Nasser, Jamal Abdel

Abi-Chahla, Habib, 51

Abi-Rached, Joelle, 189

Abou-Chabké, Elais, 164

Abousouan, Camille, 17, 39

Acre, 17

al-Adab, 143

el-Ahdab, Kheireddine, 51

Ahiram, King of Tyre, 27. *See also* Hiram

Ain Mreissé, 193

Ajami, Fouad, 5, 57

Akl, Saïd, 108

Aley, 139

Alliance Israélite Universelle, 28, 29, 54, 61, 68, 70, 85, 90, 120, 125, 136, 150, 156

Alliance School Beirut, 54, 61, 67, 98, 120, 132, 137, 140, 141, 148, 150, 176

Alliance School Sidon, 54, 120

Amal Militia, 25

American University of Beirut, 62, 122, 150

Amitiés Libanaises, 40

Anglo-American Commission of Enquiry, 6, 9

Anjar, 175

Ann-Margaret, 53

anti-Jewish press articles, 86

anti-Semitism, 116

anti-Zionism, 6, 53, 190

Antoura, 32, 37, 163–165

Anzarout, Fred, 51

Arab boycott, 88, 119

Arab face (Lebanon), 58, 64, 199

Arab Higher Committee, 6, 7

Arabia, 7, 34, 36, 118, 124, 185

Arab-Israeli conflict, 131

Arab-Israeli wars, 99

Arabists, 38, 41, 56, 59, 62, 68, 96,
    97, 99, 108, 110, 112, 116, 123,
    124, 127, 128, 133, 169
Arabization, 13, 38, 52
Arab League, 6, 47, 118
Arab nationalism, 5, 31, 36, 47, 48,
    57, 59, 64, 67, 72, 89, 93, 96,
    116, 117, 126
Arab Spring, 26
Arab unity, 124
Arab world, 38, 57, 58, 65, 77, 106,
    108
Arafat, Yasser, 69, 131, 144
Archives de l'Alliance Israélite
    Universelle (AIUA), 68–72
Archives du Ministère des Affaires
    Étrangères (MAE), 25, 35, 36,
    79, 86, 87, 92
Arida, Anthony Peter (Maronite
    Patriarch), 25, 28, 41, 42, 49, 50,
    84–86, 89
Armées du Levant, 191
Ashrafiyyé, 191
The Associated Press, 53, 143
Atallah, Fr. Naoum, 164, 165
Attié, Joseph, 71, 127
Attié family, 29
autostrade, 183

B
Baalbeck, 128, 153
Bab Idriss, 193
Bardot, Brigitte, 53
Barrès, Maurice, 26
al-Baydarane, Izzeddin, 61
Bayroot al-Masa, 61, 62, 96
Baz, Georges Nicholas, 10–13
Béart, Emmanuelle, 52
Béart, Guy, 52
Beirut, 4–6, 10, 15, 18, 28, 40, 43,
    49, 53, 61, 67–69, 75, 84–86,

88, 98, 103, 110, 114, 117,
    120–123, 125, 127, 128, 130,
    132, 136–140, 143, 145–152,
    154, 156, 157, 159, 160, 166,
    167, 169, 171, 172, 174–176,
    178, 181, 185, 186, 188,
    191–193, 198
    Community Council, 70, 121, 127
    port, 20, 26, 27, 89, 113, 115
    synagogue, 16, 23, 102, 117, 125, 136
Beirut (Mother of Laws), 18
Beit-Chabab, 175
Beit Mery, 195
Bekaa, 128, 136, 157, 160
Bellamaa, Ra'iif, 61
Ben-Avi, Ithamar, 81
Ben-Gurion, David, 61
Ben-Zvi, Rachel, 40
Bhamdoun, 115, 139, 141, 194
    synagogue, 121
Bialik, Haim Nahman, 40
Bickfayya, 169, 175, 186
Bikur Cholim, 121
Black September, 143
Bnai Brith, 121
Bourj Hammoud, 125
Boustany, Emile, 62–65, 87
Brill Encyclopedia of Jews in the Islamic
    World, 11
British Mandate
    Palestine, 5, 6, 20, 29, 30, 38, 42,
        56, 58, 75, 88, 97, 190
Bsharré, 15

C
Cahiers de l'Est, 17
Cahiers de l'Orontes, 33
Cairo Agreement, 102
Cassin, René, 61
Cedars, 15, 127
    of Solomon, 28, 32, 50, 84

of the Lord, 1, 3, 184
Chagall, Marc, 40
Chamoun, Camille, 58, 67, 170
Chamoun, Dany, 170
Chams, Nessim, 52, 67
Chéhab, Fouad, 67, 127
Chesed Shel Emet, 15
Chiha, Michel, 16, 18, 19, 34, 59, 61, 107
Chouf Mountains, 62, 71, 149, 176
Christians
  community (Lebanon), 25, 36, 48, 54, 60, 160, 195
  -Jewish relations, 48, 92, 188, 195
  -Muslim relations, 24, 29, 31, 46, 54, 58, 72, 102, 123, 124, 157, 176, 193
  Social Democratic Party, 37. *See also* *Kataëb; Phalanges Libanaises*
Cohen, Haim, 146
Cohen, Shula, 103, 133. *See also* Kishik-Cohen, Shula
Collège de la Sagesse (Maronite high-school), 176
Le Commerce du Levant, 53
Community Council (Beirut), 70, 121, 127
Corm, Charles, 18, 27, 38–41, 46, 47, 49, 59, 92, 105, 106
Crémieux, Adolphe, 90, 91
Crusades, 32, 36

D
Damascus, 55, 85, 86, 88, 98, 102, 127, 135, 149, 169
Danon, M., 54
Deeb, Marius, 5, 57
Deir el-Kamar, 178
Deneuve, Chatherine, 53
Deuxième Bureau, 133
Dhimmi status, 48

Diwan, Ishac, 189
Dorléac, Françoise, 53
Druze, 15, 17, 62, 70, 120, 128, 160, 163, 194
  -Maronite relations, 26, 27, 33, 49, 90, 91, 148, 192
Duboscq, André, 36

E
Eddé, Emile, 41, 51, 75, 98, 169
Eddé, Raymond, 169
Egypt, 14, 17, 31, 35, 47, 118
Eisenberg, Laura Zittrain, 25, 40–42
Elia, Albert, 145
Emir Faisal, 81
Epstein, Eliyahu, 39, 40

F
Farayya, 128
Farhi, Joseph, 28, 40, 49, 51, 84
Fatah organization, 69. *See also* Palestine Liberation Organization
Fedayeen, 56, 123
Fitzgerald, F. Scott, 40
France, 5, 11, 19, 20, 28, 31, 32, 36, 40, 41, 54, 57, 74, 85, 87, 90, 91, 93, 98, 113, 115, 117, 130, 149, 174, 178, 182
Frangié, Hamid, 65, 164
Frangié, Soliman, 163, 183
French Mandate, 24, 39, 45, 54, 78, 87, 92, 93, 169

G
Gadeh, Fady, 163, 166
Ganem, Checri, 164
De Gaulle, Charles, 93
Gemayel, Bachir, 168

Gemayel, Pierre, 48, 49, 51, 72, 84,
  124, 133, 168, 174, 175
Gibran, Kahlil, 2–4, 15, 16
Gouraud, General Henri, 54, 78, 79
Grand Liban, 46
Greater Lebanon, 48, 52, 78, 81, 82,
  84, 91, 111
Greater Syria, 14
Greek Orthodox community, 31

H
Hachnasat Orchim, 15
Haifa, 17, 20, 39, 41, 43, 52, 67, 141
Hakim, Carol, 188, 189
Hallak, Elie, 146
Hamra District, 126, 147
Hamra Street, 126, 168
Al-Hasnaa', 10, 11
Helou, Charles, 68, 119, 178
Herzl, Theodor, 111, 112
Hezbollah, 109, 110, 134, 153, 190
Hiram, 23, 41, 102
Hitler, Adolph, 85, 126
Hitti, Philip, 35, 102, 106, 135, 185
Holocaust, 77, 91, 94
Hoyek, Elias Peter (Maronite
  Patriarch), 79
The Huffington Post, 52
Humanism, 18, 26, 42, 48–50, 84, 90
Husayn, Taha, 81, 142, 143
al-Husseini, Hajj Amin, 94

I
International Herald Tribune, 144,
  145
Islam, 7, 16, 21, 25, 48, 55, 106, 188
Israel, 5, 10, 14, 17, 20, 25, 30,
  31, 43, 47, 52, 55, 56, 59–65,
  74, 75, 81, 93, 97, 103, 104,
  107–111, 114–117, 119, 122,
  123, 127, 130, 132, 133, 140,
  141, 155–157, 159, 162, 175,
  178, 181, 190, 192, 194, 195,
  199, 200
Israël Informations, 108, 109, 117
Israelis, 25, 60, 63, 65
Israelites, 27, 38, 49, 51, 52, 65, 86,
  93, 192

J
Jabotinsky, Ze'ev, 81
Jaffa, 17, 20, 115
Jerusalem, 5, 17, 20, 38–42, 108,
  131, 194
The Jerusalem Post, 118–120, 145
The Jewish Chronicle, 117, 124
Jounié, 58, 94, 128
Le Jour, 59, 60, 107
Jumblatt, Kamal, 70, 71, 164

K
Kamhin, Ishak (Isick), 173
Kanaan, Checri, 13, 14
Karamé, Rachid, 123, 124, 131
Kataëb, 38, 125, 126, 134, 159, 170,
  174. *See also Phalanges Libanaises*;
  Christian, Social Democratic Party
Khadduri-Louise Zilcha School, 68
el-Khazen, Farid, 67
El-Khoury, Bechara, 58, 87
Kishik-Cohen, Joseph, 103, 131
Kishik-Cohen, Shula, 103, 132, 133.
  See also Cohen, Shula
Kishik-Cohen, Yitzhak (Ambassador),
  103, 117. *See also* Levanon, Yitzhak

L
Labaki, Kesrouan, 30, 64, 65
Lahoud, Romeo, 164

Lawrence, T.E., 36
Lebanese Army
  Arab–Israeli war, 67
  civil war, 1, 24, 56, 126
  clashes with Palestinians, 110,
    145
  protection of Jewish community,
    38
Lebanese civil war, 131, 138, 146,
  152, 175
Lebanese constitution, 49
Lebanese Jewish community
  anti-Zionism, 6, 190
  biblical times, 102
  education, 69
  emigration, 102, 127
  equal rights, 10, 82
  identity, 55, 160, 174
  loyalty and patriotism, 59
  Zionism, 29, 30
Lebanonism, 49, 105. *See also*
  Lebanonist; Phoenicianism
Lebanonist, 46, 63, 64, 133
Lebanon-Palestine Society, 41
Levanon, Yitzhak (Ambassador), 103,
  114, 117, 131, 138. *See also*
  Kishik-Cohen, Yitzhak
Levant, 16, 17, 19–21, 31, 35–37, 41,
  46, 75, 78, 85, 93, 99, 171, 189,
  192
Levantinism, 19–21, 57, 79, 179
Levi, Mario, 189
Levi, Tomer, 45, 46
Liniado, Dany, 75, 76
Liniado, Desiré Isaac, 169
Liniado, Tewfic Yehye, 169
L'Orient, 30, 38, 62–64, 66, 70, 71
L'Orient le Jour, 109, 110
L'Univers Israélite, 28, 52, 54, 55,
  80

M
Maalouf, Amin, 19, 20, 73, 99, 114,
  179
Maccabis, 15
Magen Abraham Synagogue, 132,
  136, 152, 176, 193
Mann, Eliyahu Salim, 52, 87
Mansel, Philip, 16, 17
Maronite community (Lebanon)
  Arab–Israeli war, 48, 59
  French Mandate, 45, 93
  and Israel, 45
  and the Jews of Lebanon, 26, 30,
    37, 45, 50, 85, 86, 88
  and Palestinians, 49, 107
  Zionism, 30, 39, 41, 85, 86
Mediterraneanism, 7, 16, 37, 39
Mediterranean Sea, 32, 35
Metn district, 176
Metro Goldwyn Mayer (MGM)
  Studios, 53, 141
Minet el-Hosn, 174
mitzvah, 16
Mizrahi, Toufic, 52, 53, 171. *See also*
  La Revue du Liban
Mneimné, Ibrahim, 66
Mobarak, Patriarch Ignatius, 10, 15
Le Monde, 69, 70, 123, 124, 131,
  144–146
Montaigne, Michel de, 101
Morand, Paul, 27, 40
Mount Lebanon, 2, 4, 114, 115, 128,
  163, 181, 183, 184, 186, 195
Moyal, Esther Azhari, 11, 12
Muslim community (Lebanon)
  allegiance to Arabism, 107
  Arab unity, 124
  attitude to Jews (Judaism), 20
  independent Lebanon, 48, 55
  support for Palestinians, 70
  Zionism, 29, 54

N

Naccache, Albert, 38
Najjaadé (Arab nationalist political
    party), 126, 128
Nakba, 75, 190
Nantet, Jacques, 49, 84
Nasser, Jamal Abdel, 14, 127, 130,
    166, 167. *See also* Abdel Nasser,
    Jamal
National Pact (Lebanon), 58, 64
Naufal, Antoine, 170. *See also* Librairie
    Antoine
Nazi Germany, 85, 94
Neaman, Yfrah, 52
Niven, David, 53
Notre Dame de Jamhour (Jesuit high
    school), 142
Novak, Kim, 53
al-Nusuli, Muhyiddin, 126

O

Orloff, Chana, 40
Orozdi-Back department store, 126
Ottoman Empire, 19, 20, 26, 32, 33,
    37, 78, 90, 91, 169, 174, 199
Ottomans, 33, 91, 164
O'Toole, Peter, 53

P

Palestine, 6–9, 17, 25, 29, 30, 38,
    41, 56, 58, 64, 70, 83, 94, 111,
    112, 123, 143, 172, 176. *See also*
    British Mandate, Palestine
Palestine Liberation Organization
    Black September (1970), 143
    Cairo Agreement (1969), 56
    Jews of Lebanon, 68
    Lebanon as main base, 58, 68, 99

relations with Lebanese Christians,
    6, 25, 29, 31, 46, 134, 145,
    170, 187, 199
relations with Lebanese Muslims,
    29, 30, 38, 145. *See also Fatah*
    Organization
Palestinians, 49, 53, 56, 70, 72,
    110, 119, 123, 124, 131, 141,
    143–145, 172, 178, 194
Panian, Karnig, 164
Penso, Elie, 98
Phalanges Libanaises, 38. *See also*
    Kataëb; Christian, Social
    Democratic Party
Phares, Walid, 55
Phoenicianism, 39, 46, 49, 63, 108,
    192. *See also Young Phoenicians*;
    Lebanonism
Phoenicians, 17, 27, 34, 35, 38–41,
    46, 81, 92, 102, 192
Plisnier, Charles, 40
Protocols of the Elders of Zion, 89, 94,
    118
Proust, Marcel, 45, 73, 181
Puaux, Gabriel (French High
    Commissioner), 98

Q

Qabbani, Nizar, 12
Qodishe, 2

R

Règlement Organique, 90, 91
La Revue du Liban, 170. *See also*
    Mizrahi, Toufic
La Revue Phénicienne, 18, 92
Reynaud, Charles, 32
Riachi, Alexandre, 91
Rihani, Amin, 11, 12
Rogers, Ginger, 53

S

Sada Loubnan, 64
Safra banking family, 53
Safra, Edmond, 189
Salam, Saëb, 145
Sandström, Alfred Emil Fredrik, 6
Sanjak, 26
Sardou, Michel, 113
Sasson, Batia, 140, 141, 143, 144, 146, 147
Sasson, Edouard, 53, 140
Sasson, Isaac, 146
Sasson, Raymond, 109, 113
Schulze, Kirsten, 24, 25, 28, 45, 50, 84, 116, 133
Selim Tarrab School, 66, 120
Semiramis restaurant, 126
Sharif, Omar, 53
Shehadi, Nadim, 188–190
Sidon, 17, 52, 54, 67, 175, 189
Slivert, Elie, 61
Sloucshz, Nahum, 40
Sofar, 6
Le Soir, 30, 64, 65
al-Solh, Riad, 6, 133
Solomon, King, 23, 41, 102
Solomon's Temple, 27, 38
Soujoud, 175
Srour, Elie, 146
Stambouli-Liniado House (Damascus), 169
Stillman, Norman, 11, 29, 54
Suq Sursock, 128
Syrian Social Nationalist Party (SSNP), 63

T

Tabet, Jacques, 34
Talmud Torah School, 120
Tanzimat, 37
Tarshish, 58
Tel Aviv, 103, 113–115

Télé-Liban, 113
Traboulsi, Fawaz, 190
Tuéni, Ghassan, 164
Tuéni, Nadia, 192
Tyre, 17, 23, 27, 41, 102, 175

U

Umayyads, 55
Umma, 55
United Nations, 6, 9, 18, 65, 151
United Nations Special Committee on Palestine (UNSCOP), 5, 6, 9
Université Saint-Joseph, 140, 160

V

Valéry, Paul, 40
Vilayet, 8, 26, 175
Vogüe, Vicomte de, 32
Volney, Comte de, 33

W

Wadi Boujmil, 67, 68, 71, 113, 114, 122, 125, 126, 132, 136, 137, 141, 147, 151–153, 156, 175, 193
Wadi l-Yahood, 122
Weizmann, Chaim, 42, 50
World Jewish Affairs, 121, 122
World Jewish Congress, 13, 23, 46, 102

Y

En-Yehuda, Eliezer, 81
Yishuv, 30, 40, 41, 77, 199
Young Phoenicians, 37, 39–41, 46, 59. *See also* Phoenicianism; Lebanonism

Z
Zahlé, 136, 137, 139, 157
Zamir, Meir, 30
Zghorta, 183, 184, 186
Zilkha banking family, 53
Zionism
  Alliance Israélite Universelle, 29
  and Arabism, 40
  Lebanese Christians, 6, 107

Lebanese Jews, 29, 51, 65, 77, 94
Lebanese Muslims, 29, 30

CPSIA information can be obtained
at www.ICGtesting.com
Printed in the USA
LVHW011949081118
596438LV00003B/4/P

9 783319 996660